The Pandemic Perhaps

The Pandemic Perhaps

DRAMATIC EVENTS IN A PUBLIC CULTURE OF DANGER

Carlo Caduff

UNIVERSITY OF CALIFORNIA PRESS

University of California Press, one of the most distinguished university presses in the United States, enriches lives around the world by advancing scholarship in the humanities, social sciences, and natural sciences. Its activities are supported by the UC Press Foundation and by philanthropic contributions from individuals and institutions. For more information, visit www.ucpress.edu.

University of California Press
Oakland, California

Library of Congress Cataloging-in-Publication Data

Caduff, Carlo, author.
    The pandemic perhaps : dramatic events in a public culture of danger / Carlo Caduff.
        pages   cm.
    Includes bibliographical references and index.
    ISBN 978-0-520-28408-1 (cloth : alk. paper)
    ISBN 978-0-520-28409-8 (pbk. : alk. paper)
    1. Influenza—United States—Forecasting.   2. Influenza—Social aspects—United States.   3. Influenza—United States—Prevention.
4. Epidemics—United States—Forecasting.   5. Epidemics—Social aspects—United States.   6. Epidemics—United States—Prevention.
I. Title.
    RA644.I6C33   2015
    614.5'18—dc23

                                                            2015011847

Manufactured in the United States of America

24 23 22 21 20 19 18 17 16 15
10 9 8 7 6 5 4 3 2 1

The paper used in this publication meets the minimum requirements of ANSI/ NISO Z39.48-1992 (R 2002) (*Permanence of Paper*).

per bab e mumma

The category of perhaps is perhaps the best category to refer to what remains to come.

JACQUES DERRIDA

CONTENTS

ILLUSTRATIONS

ACKNOWLEDGMENTS

I would like to extend my sincere gratitude to the scientists, public health professionals, and emergency planners in New York City, as well as those in Atlanta and Geneva, who were willing to spend time with me and share their insights, experiences, and expertise. Special thanks are due to Dr. Peter Palese at the Mount Sinai School of Medicine in New York City for engaging with my work and for allowing me to spend time in his lab and familiarize myself with experimental microbiological research. I was lucky indeed to have such an extraordinary interlocutor who always surprised me with his perspective. In the Palese lab, Drs. Anice Lowen, Samira Mubareka, Qinshan Gao, and Gina Connenello introduced me to the virus and its ever-shifting shape. I am especially thankful to these fabulous researchers for offering their precious time, for guiding me through the complex material culture of experimental research, and for responding patiently to what must have seemed to them a never-ending stream of strange questions about rather obvious things.

In New York City, I would also like to thank Dr. Kristine Gebbie at Columbia University's School of Nursing, Dr. Lewis Goldfrank at Bellevue Hospital Center, and Nicholas Cagliuso at the New York-Presbyterian Healthcare System. Eileen Scanlon and her team at the Nassau County Office of Emergency Preparedness were extremely helpful and supportive and always willing to talk to me about their work and their vision. Thanks are due to Doris Varlese at the Greater New York Hospital Association and to Christopher Williams at the Community Health Care Association of New York State. I would also like to thank all the public health officials in the New York City Department of Health and Mental Hygiene who helped me understand the politics of preparedness and who chose to remain anonymous to protect their identities. I owe special thanks to the late Dr. Edwin Kilbourne for sharing with me his insights about the history of microbiology, as well as to his former colleagues, Drs. Doris Bucher and Barbara Pokorny, at New York Medical College, for conversations about the production of vaccines and Dr. Kilbourne's involvement in the swine flu affair. I also appreciate the support of the late Dr. David Sencer, a former director of the Centers for Disease Control and Prevention (CDC) in Atlanta. Thanks to Dr. Robert Webster for an unexpected encounter and conversation at the University of Hong Kong.

At the CDC in Atlanta, I would like to thank the director of the Influenza Branch, Dr. Nancy Cox, for graciously lending her time and facilitating my research. Thanks are also due to Drs. Terry Tumpey and Taronna Maines for explaining their research, inviting me into their laboratory, and kindly offering me their expertise. Drs. Dan Jernigan, Roger Bernier, Amanda Balish, Caroline Bridges, Nicole Smith, Michael Bell, and Andrew Demma have been great interlocutors at CDC. Many thanks to Drs. Art Reingold and Lara Misegades at UC Berkeley's Public Health School and to Dr. Keiji Fukuda at the World Health Organization in Geneva. Thanks to Dr. Mike Ascher for opening doors in Atlanta. Don Greenstein at the Keystone Center and Dr. Paul E. Jarris and Anna M. De Blois at the Association of State and Territorial Health Officials shared their insights about public engagement and pandemic preparedness with me and invited me to observe their projects. At the Institute of Medical Virology at the University of Zurich, I would like to thank Drs. Silke Stertz and Jovan Pavlovic for stimulating conversations and insights.

At Berkeley, I wish to thank Paul Rabinow for introducing me to the idea of fieldwork in philosophy. His insistence on thinking as a critical and creative practice was inspiring. Cori Hayden has provided intellectual guidance in matters of the anthropology of science, medicine, knowledge, and technology. She has helped me with her ethnographic imagination to shape this project and has offered support at critical junctures. Alexei Yurchak introduced me to speech act theory, allowing me to explore the map of misreading. Thanks to Lawrence Cohen for expanding my understanding of medical anthropology and for providing insights about the semiotics of security: I could not have written chapter 4 in its present form without him. David Winickoff has generously read chapters and has provided invaluable comments on the limits of participatory governance and public engagement. I will never forget the extraordinary intellectual and personal kindness of the late Alan Pred. He showed me that one could be a rigorous and generous scholar at the same time—a felicitous combination of virtues. Thanks are due as well to Stephen Collier and Andy Lakoff for inviting me to a workshop on biosecurity and for engaging my work on the flu more generally. Jeremy Greene offered an insightful last-minute reading of my Introduction, facilitating the final push. Frédéric Keck kindly invited me to Hong Kong and has generously shared his insights with me ever since. I continue to learn from his work.

Many colleagues and friends have been essential for this work, which has been a long time in the making. I would like to thank Gerhard Anders, Nikola Bagic, Aditya Bharadwaj, Roger Begrich, Orkideh Behrouzan, Jean-François Bissonnette, Michael Bresalier, Alberto Cambrosio, Flurin Condrau, Susan Craddock, Veena Das, Roy Dilley, Raad Fadaak, Didier Fassin, Jim Faubion, Lyle Fearnley, Angela Filipe, Des Fitzgerald, Anitra Grisales, Jane Guyer, Clara Han, Niloofar Haeri, Gabriela Hertig, Steve Hinchliffe, Charles Hirschkind, Marc Honigsbaum, Julia Hornberger, Karine Landgren Hugentobler, Rohit Jain, Karen Jent, Evangelos Karagiannis, Janina Kehr, Chris Kelty, Naveeda Khan, Hanna Kienzler, Thomas Kirsch, Nicolas Langlitz, Samuel Lengen, Javier Lezaun, Ilana Löwy, Sam Maclean, Theresa MacPhail, Tara Mahfoud, Joe Masco, Andrea Mühlebach, David Napier, Vinh-Kim Nguyen, Francisco Ortega, Randy Packard, Anand Pandian, Bronwyn Parry, Kris Peterson, Deborah Poole, Natalie Porter, Beth Povinelli, Hugh Raffles, Kaushik Sunder Rajan, Peter Redfield, Tobias Rees, Janet Roitman, Nikolas Rose, Salome Schärer, Thomas Schlich, Ilina Singh, Anthony Stavrianakis, Ann Stoler, Stefanie Strulik, Tatjana Thelen, Miriam Ticktin, Fouzieyha Towghi, Andri Tschudi, Jerome Whitington, Scott Vrecko, Austin Zeiderman, Naomi Zumstein, and Patrick Zylberman for their suggestions, conversations, and comments. These scholars are of course not responsible for what I have written. Thanks are due as well to the anonymous reviewers and the editors of *Cultural Anthropology*, Anne Allison and Charles Piot, for their suggestions on my article that served as a basis for this book. Portions of chapters that appear here have been published as articles in *Annual Review of Anthropology*, *Current Anthropology*, and *BioSocieties*.

I would like to express special appreciation to Shalini Randeria for her incredible support over the years; to Hannah Landecker for her editorial advice; to Jim Faubion for his insights into the prophetic condition; and to Angie Heo, Maria José de Abreu, and Nikolas Kosmatopoulos for inspiration and friendship.

At the University of California Press, I am indebted to Reed Malcolm, who believed in the book to come. Thanks to Stacy Eisenstark and Brian Ostrander, and to Gail Naron Chalew for careful copy-editing. Three anonymous readers from the University of California Press provided detailed and thoughtful suggestions for revisions. I would like to thank them for their insights. I received generous suggestions for revising chapters from audiences at Cornell University, the Graduate Institute in Geneva, the Johns Hopkins University, the London School of Economics, McGill University, the New School University, Rutgers University, University College London, the University of Amsterdam, the University of Cambridge, the University of Exeter, the University of Hong Kong, the University of Konstanz, the University of Lucerne, the University of Oxford, the University of Vienna, and the University of Zurich.

Several institutions provided essential support for this research project. I would like to thank the Rockefeller Archive Center for making available its documents on the history of influenza research. I appreciate the Fonds zur Förderung des akademischen Nachwuchses at the University of Zurich for supporting my first year as a graduate student at Berkeley, where I had the privilege of participating in a vibrant intellectual community. Financial support for the research has mainly come from the Swiss National Science Foundation. Its contribution made the project possible in the first place, and I thus extend my heartfelt thanks to the foundation for its generous contribution.

My thanks also go out to those who kindly waived fees and granted permission to reprint images: Stephen Greenberg of the National Library of Medicine at the National Institutes of Health; Richard Hamburg, deputy director of the Trust for America's Health; and Barbara Niss, director of the Mount Sinai Archives. I am grateful to illustrator Kyle Bean and photographer Sam Hofman for letting me use the sculpture of the bird flu bomb. Last but not least, my thanks go to photographer Inês d'Orey.

A group of friends at Berkeley and elsewhere have made social life and intellectual work enjoyable over the years. Thanks to Maria José de Abreu, Jenny Chio, Marc Dosch, Monica Eppinger, Marc Goodwin, Angie Heo, Nicolas Langlitz, Amelia Moore, Mary Murell, Tobias Rees, Dale Rose, Arpita Roy, and Meg Stalcup. My parents have been there all the time, observing, supporting, and facilitating my adventures. I would like to dedicate this book to *bab e mumma*.

Introduction

THE SHAPE OF THINGS TO COME

ON DECEMBER 7, 2005, at a congressional hearing in Washington, DC, Dr. Michael T. Osterholm predicted that an outbreak of pandemic influenza "will trigger a reaction that will change the world overnight."[1] Osterholm, director of the Center for Infectious Disease Research and Policy at the University of Minnesota, speculated that "foreign trade and travel will be reduced or even ended in an attempt to stop the virus from entering new countries—even though such efforts will probably fail given the infectiousness of influenza and the volume of illegal crossings that occur at most borders."[2] It is very likely, he continued, that "transportation will also be significantly curtailed domestically, as states and communities seek to keep the disease contained."[3]

In an earlier article published in *Foreign Affairs*, Osterholm had addressed the threat of pandemic influenza in more detail. He argued that "up to 50 percent of the affected populations could become ill; as many as five percent could die."[4] The implications would be unsettling: There would be "major shortages . . . of a wide range of commodities, including food, soap, paper, light bulbs, gasoline, parts for repairing military equipment and municipal water pumps, and medicines, including vaccines unrelated to the pandemic. Many industries not critical to survival—electronics, automobile, and clothing, for example—would suffer or even close. Activities that require close human contact—school, seeing movies in theaters, or eating at restaurants—would be avoided, maybe even banned."[5] He predicted that the U.S. government would respond to the pandemic by nationalizing its antiviral drugs and vaccine supplies. Patients who survived an infection and became immune to the virus would be employed as volunteers in hospitals and other health care facilities. "That means that the medical community's strong resistance to using lay volunteers, which is grounded in both liability concerns and professional hubris, would need to be addressed."[6]

Osterholm's public contemplation of pandemic disaster invoked a space of apocalyptic expectation, one that seemed to be infinitely expandable. Confronted with a potentially catastrophic outbreak of disease, the nation would require stronger ties to cope with the consequences and secure its survival. This consideration of the nation's precarious foundations was far from unique. In fact, such visions of profound vulnerability circulated widely in the American public sphere while I was doing fieldwork between 2006 and 2008. A relentless stream of newspaper articles, television programs, and radio reports featured expert accounts of worst-case scenarios, placing the pandemic of influenza at the center of political debate. Drastic renderings that often exaggerated the potential implications of a global pandemic for dramatic effect inundated the public sphere. Fantasies of a powerful state and decisive government action in the face of inevitable collapse proliferated in newspapers and magazines nationwide.

Experts watched with great concern how migratory birds and domestic poultry transmitted the highly pathogenic H5N1 avian influenza virus like a wildfire across the Asian continent. A powerful geography of blame materialized as observers pinned the virus to the primordial world of developing nations.[7] In the global village of modern trade and travel, national borders had become permeable, and an erupting pandemic seemed "no more than a plane ride away."[8] When I met Dr. Robert Webster, a charismatic microbiologist often referred to in the U.S. media as the "pope of influenza," he told me that the H5N1 virus was "the scariest thing" he had ever seen, a "killer strain lurking in the shadows." For Webster, the virus was far from inert: It was on the move; it was on its way to become the cause of a dramatic event.[9] "It's trying it on. It hasn't made it yet," he said. "It may take twenty years for the H5N1 virus to move from the wild bird reservoir and change and develop into a human virus." The clock is ticking. The pandemic will happen. "If you don't have the vaccine ready and it happens, you're responsible," Webster warned. "Today we can't take the attitude that it will not happen. We don't have enough evidence to say that it won't happen. And so you must go ahead and prepare. It's like preparing for an earthquake. It will happen."

Webster examined the virus intensively in the laboratory, focusing on the disease and its multiple forms, which range from a seasonal nuisance to a deadly plague. The microbiologist deciphered the signs of the times carefully and predicted the course of events accordingly. In his frequent media appearances, Webster sketched worst-case scenarios, urging health professionals to prepare immediately for the impending disaster. He also supported pharmaceutical companies in the development of effective treatments to protect the health of populations and the wealth of nations. "When the pandemic comes, which is inevitable, he will appear prophetic," a microbiologist mused about Webster.[10] The pandemic was bound to happen: It was not a matter of contingency, but of necessity; not a question of if, but when. Webster's vision of the future came with a strong millennialist undertone, declaring that an event would happen, but without specifying the month, the hour, or the day when it would take place.[11]

The spread of the H5N1 virus throughout Asia disrupted "existing arrangements among species, peoples, institutions, and nations—remaking biological and political relations along the way."[12] Newspaper reporters refracted acute concerns about social, cultural, political, and technological change through the figure of the virus, provoking fresh anxieties about the porosity of economies, ecologies, and societies.[13] Worried about the consequences of contagion, Americans ordered antiviral drugs online to protect their families. Meanwhile, government officials raised the possibility of using the military to enforce quarantines and restrict the movement of people. Journalists emphasized that the threat was "not irrational;" it was based on truth—a truth that was "scarier than fiction."[14] Dangerous germs were surfacing from ecologically damaged parts of the planet as nature's revenge against the human parasite.[15] The earth was about to launch "an immune response against the human species."[16]

The day of disaster seemed near, and the stakes were enormous. Driven by a dystopian vision of the future and the hope of mitigating an impending calamity, scientists struggling to unravel the meaning of the mysterious microbe suggested that it was just one or two genetic mutations away from acquiring the dreadful ability to spread rapidly. Tracking the virus as it jumped from bird swarms to chicken populations, scientists leaped from local causes to global consequences. The U.S. news media were abuzz with dramatic speculations about an imminent disaster. How much time was left? How much time was left to prepare?

But nothing really happened.

In this book, I take encounters with infectious disease experts as a starting point for an ethnographic exploration of pandemic prophecy in the United States. Turned toward the future, prophets claim to see what others cannot see. It is this ability that prompts people to place their lives into the hands of

FIGURE I. The avian flu death threat. "Though we have the ability to prevent or mitigate a flu pandemic, those in the frontline of the battle against H5N1 are preparing for the worst." "Special Report: Inside the Global Race to Avert a Pandemic." *Time Magazine*, September 26, 2005.

such experts, whose special skills have endowed them with power, prestige, and authority.[17]

Not all pandemic discourse is prophetic, to be sure, but a considerable portion is. Drawing attention to eruptions of prophetic speech, my aim is not to expose prophetic claims in the name of true science, but to examine how speculations about the future suffuse the present with the suspicion that something is happening. What is it that allows prophetic claims, cast in scientific terms, to gain traction in public discourse? Why are some prophets more successful than others in conveying their scientifically inspired visions of a coming plague? What, in other words, makes one vision more rational and coherent, more plausible and compelling, more acceptable and respectable than others?

These questions are very general, and they call for a broad range of answers. Clearly, the factors contributing to the popularity of pandemic prophecy are complex and overdetermined. In the United States, it is essential to take into account the long history of apocalyptic thinking in the nineteenth and twentieth centuries. Visions of mass death and mass survival have featured prominently in the nation's narration, and dark images of impending disaster have been a fixture of American cultural production for many decades.[18] According to anthropologists Kathleen Stewart and Susan Harding, the apocalyptic mode of thinking has come to inform the modern American way of life in many respects.[19] Stewart and Harding underscore that there has been much traffic between religious and secular apocalypticism as a mode of thinking "transfixed by the possibility of imminent catastrophe."[20] As Joseph Masco notes, this apocalyptic sensibility has been incredibly productive, politically as well as economically, for actors and institutions in Cold War and post–Cold War America.[21] A generation of U.S. citizens has grown up in a culture of danger, and they remember vividly always having to be alert and prepared for a nuclear attack. In his account, Masco suggests that America conjured order from disorder, constructing its national community systematically "via contemplation of specific images of mass death while building a defense complex that demands ever more personal sacrifice in the name of security."[22]

Over the past decade, pandemic influenza has been perceived in the United States as a "bomb," a "really huge bomb," launching a new phase of "civil defense." The frequency of pandemic exercises and the relentless rehearsal of pandemic disaster across the country made an eruption of disease almost as terrifying a threat as the explosion of a nuclear weapon. A culture of danger expanded, driven by larger formations of science, medicine, media, and the

FIGURE 2. The bird flu bomb. Sculpture of a nuclear mushroom cloud made from feathers for an article in *Scientific American*. "Is Bird Flu Waiting to Explode?" *Scientific American*, June 2012. Artwork: Kyle Bean. Photography: Sam Hofman.

state.[23] This culture was founded on historically distinctive visions of the future in which apocalyptic images of sudden death made for political panic and mass mobilization.

Even though visions of a catastrophic future figure prominently in public discourse, these accounts are not apocalyptic in the strict sense of the term. They cannot count as genuine examples of the biblical genre because they do not point beyond the catastrophic to the defeat of evil forces, the salvation of the elected few, and the rise of a new world order. These visions lack the utopian moment of redemption that is so essential for apocalyptic thinking.[24] Rather, plague visions prosper today as metaphors of modern nightmares. At the core of pandemic prophecy is a particular prospect: destruction without purification, death without resurrection—in short, dystopia without utopia. This means that pandemic prophecy is only seemingly apocalyptic; as a discursive practice, it invokes standard apocalyptic tropes, but it lacks the hope and desire for another world.

Pandemic prophecy both looks forward to the future and back to the past. In fact, anticipations of the future and recollections of the past can become almost indistinguishable in prophetic discourse. It is a characteristic feature of such discourse that it disrupts our sense of time. Prophecy can address future events in the past tense, as if they had happened, and past events in the future tense, as if they are about to happen.[25] This means that in prophecy "the past can refer to the future and the future to the past."[26] Ian Balfour draws attention to the ambiguous temporality of prophetic discourse, emphasizing the "indeterminacy of historical reference."

The perception of history as both recollection of the past and anticipation of the future is evident in contemporary accounts of the great pandemic of 1918. The disease killed between twenty and fifty million people in less than a year. Numerous historical studies, novels, memoirs, reports, documentaries, and exhibitions have brought the "story of the deadliest pandemic in history" back into view, highlighting the capacity of the virus to cross borders and create havoc.[27] A set of iconic photographs showing U.S. soldiers confined to bed has been reproduced over and over again in newspapers, magazines, and on public websites. Drafting plans in the twenty-first century to protect citizens, experts considered the great pandemic a useful template for preparedness; it became an important point of reference in public debate and took on the burden of exemplifying the catastrophic consequences of contagion. Similar to what "plague" once signified, the pandemic acquired a colloquial meaning that conveyed a sense of serious threat and massive scale.

This solidified the perception of pandemic influenza as a sublime event, in the Kantian sense of the word. The disease was so overwhelming that it was almost impossible to comprehend and represent.

This return to the past has structured thinking about the future, fueling fears about a possible repetition of the devastating event. Scientists, journalists, and officials have invoked the historical reality to make the possibility of a pandemic plausible. The great pandemic of 1918 has thus appeared as a dreadful warning sign from the past: It did happen. It could happen again.

Popular and scholarly accounts typically framed the great pandemic of 1918 as "America's forgotten pandemic," the title of an influential historical study.[28] The disease that killed millions of people in 1918 at the end of a long war was said to have been so horrific that it could not enter the nation's consciousness. The sudden eruption of disease was so overwhelming that it resulted in a "curious loss of national memory."[29] Framed in the form of a forgotten event, historians, officials, and the media suggested that it was important for the nation to remember the pandemic, link the past with the present, and consider the possibility of a future repetition.[30] The trope of the "forgotten pandemic" was compelling; it justified the growing number of accounts about the "deadliest pandemic in history." Ironically, the concern with the forgotten pandemic reduced the recent history of influenza to a single event, obscuring the pandemics of 1957 and 1968, which received scant attention. These and other outbreaks of disease remained buried in the dust of history.

The seemingly innocent notion of "America's forgotten pandemic" constructed the nation as the subject of historical consciousness, promoting it as the proper context in which remembrance should occur. It was the nation that had "forgotten" the catastrophic event, and it was the nation that should "remember" it now. The struggle against amnesia appeared as a powerful practice for a collective attachment to the nation and its tragedies. The frequent invocation of the catastrophic event interrupted the movement of history, allowing the past to break into the present and validate a vision of the future. The forgotten event obtained a prophetic aura, radiating across the boundaries of time and space.[31]

The efficacy of pandemic prophecy clearly depends on many conditions of possibility; it can take many forms, accomplish many functions, and serve many actors and institutions. My aim in the book is to examine where, when, and how the prophetic erupts on the stage of science. It is important to emphasize that the book is neither concerned with patient experience nor with the improvement of national and international infectious disease programs.[32]

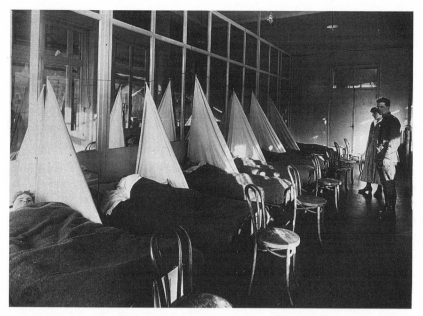

FIGURE 3. The great pandemic. "More Americans died from influenza than died in World War I. As time passed, Americans became less interested in the pandemic and its causes." The Great Pandemic Website of the U.S. Department of Health and Human Services. Courtesy: U.S. National Library of Medicine.

My account highlights not the pandemic itself, but the form that it has taken at a particular moment in history. The book's aim, in other words, is to see like a scientist—and to understand the structure of that seeing we need to explore the practice of scientific prophecy. What the book hopes to offer are insights into the creativity and complexity of that practice.

I write about pandemic prophecy not in the ethnographic present, but in the ethnographic past, a tense that I prefer in response to a temporal orientation that always looks out toward the future, even when it looks back to the past. This means that there is a certain incongruity between the temporality of the analysis and that of the object of analysis.[33] The purpose of this incongruity is to highlight the normative status that a particular orientation has achieved in the context of pandemic influenza.

Equally important is another choice that I made, namely to write the book from an American perspective. In the following chapters, I explore the role of prophetic claims in the making of a global threat. I argue that it is crucial for such an account to avoid the reproduction of universalist assumptions that in fact limit the very possibility of conceiving the global. Thus the book's ambition—to demonstrate how a pandemic imagination is anchored in a configuration of temporal sensibilities and institutional anxieties that is characteristic for a specific historical moment.[34] Rather than assume that we already know what is at stake, the book desires to make us more curious about our ultimate concerns.

The focus on pandemic prophecy extends an important body of scholarly work in the social studies of science that has examined the construction and contestation of facts. At issue here is a category of claims that stretch and perhaps even exceed the domain of the strictly factual. Focusing on the public profile of science, I explore the place of the unknown in today's politics of pandemic preparedness. How is the category of the unknown invoked in scientifically inspired prophetic proclamations about the past, the present, and the future? At stake in this inquiry more generally are the ways in which a prophetic existence is capacitated or incapacitated at the threshold of the known and the unknown. What does it take for the prophet's voice to be recognized as reasonable and accepted as authoritative? Charismatic personality and discursive authorization play significant roles, to be sure. But the efficacy of pandemic prophecy must also be situated in relation to the sensibilities and anxieties to which they respond. What is the architecture of these sensibilities and anxieties?

VISIONS OF VULNERABILITY

A report from the U.S. Institute of Medicine, published in 2005, stated unambiguously, "[M]ost infectious disease experts believe that the world stands on the verge of an influenza pandemic."[35] According to the report, the passage of time was the only condition for the pandemic to occur. Pointing to growing signs of danger, experts presented pandemic influenza as an inevitable event and suggested that it was important to raise the profile of the flu, thereby captivating the public by the bug and making the possibility of a pandemic a priority for the population. The flu was more than just a seasonal nuisance: As a threat to the security and prosperity of the nation, it deserved more respect. It was important to keep up a steady drumbeat to motivate action, mobilize resources, and create more interest in preparedness, nationally and internationally. The result was a call to change, which offered a combination of pessimism—the pandemic was unavoidable—and reluctant optimism: Disaster could be mitigated if the right steps were taken. This combination compromised the modern heroic narrative of the savior scientist. Mitigation was the best that could be achieved.

"I'm not trying to scare people out of their wits, but into them," declared Osterholm, the master of exhortation.[36] Experts emphasized the ability of pandemic prophecy to bolster public health and contribute to national security. Only dire prediction would encourage people to do what was necessary, and so a preference took root for the more extreme over the less extreme. But how much exaggeration was too much exaggeration? What was the right level of concern? A *Financial Times* editorial argued that a "real sense of urgency is needed to prepare health systems for the worst; yet it is essential to avoid public panic and overreaction, which could do more harm than the disease itself."[37] Endemic to pandemic preparedness as a structure of mobilization was a fundamental tension between the need to promote a sense of urgency, on the one hand, and the imperative to avoid panic and overreaction, on the other.[38] Public persuasion was essential for enrollment: The challenge was to strike the right balance between fear and panic, anxiety and alarm, suspicion and paranoia. It was crucial for Americans to continue with their routines of everyday life while at the same time maintaining steady vigilance. An increasing number of technical abbreviations entered the public conversation: H_1N_1, H_2N_2, H_3N_2, H_5N_1, H_7N_7, H_7N_9.[39] Of particular interest was the dangerous ecological intimacy of humans and animals that seemed to make the coast of southern China the "breeding ground" of avian influenza.

According to public health professionals, the United States was not prepared to cope with the consequences of a catastrophic pandemic. The crumbling public health infrastructure, the ease of national and international travel, the fragility of a just-in-time economy, and the precarious condition of a notoriously underfunded and increasingly privatized and fragmented health care system had left the country exposed to the threat of infectious disease. Public health professionals invoked the inevitable future as a point of reference for a critical assessment of the current state of affairs. They underscored the practical consequences of pandemic exhortation, which seemed beneficial: Immediate action would improve public health.

In his 2005 *Foreign Affairs* article, Osterholm pondered what it would mean for the nation to face the sudden spread of a deadly bug. Trade would be reduced, travel restricted, and borders closed; there would be shortages of medical supplies and drugs. Many people would fall seriously ill, and some would even die. "Who would have priority access to the extremely limited antiviral supplies?" Osterholm wondered.[40] "The public," he reasoned, "would consider any adhoc prioritization unfair, creating further dissent and disruption during a pandemic. In addition, there would not even be detailed plans for handling the massive number of dead bodies that would soon outstrip the ability to process them. Clearly, an influenza pandemic that struck today would demand an unprecedented medical and non-medical response."[41] A systematic techno-political mobilization was required to prepare for the inevitable.

"This is a really huge bomb," said Tommy Thompson about the H5N1 virus in 2004, when he announced his resignation as U.S. secretary of health and human services.[42] At the press conference Thompson explained that he was very concerned about the pandemic. He referred to the threat as the "big one" and emphasized that "we're not prepared for it."[43] His successor, Michael O. Leavitt, concurred. In his view, the possibility of a pandemic was indeed "one of the most important public health issues" facing the United States.[44] In an official statement released in November 2005, Secretary Leavitt declared that the threat would make it necessary to create "a constant state of readiness."[45] This would involve everyone. "The right prescription is preparedness," a poster published in 2005 by the Department of Health and Human Services suggested. "Make it your business to help others prepare," another poster proposed. As these public messages revealed, pandemic preparedness was promoted in the United States as a political necessity, a social responsibility, and a patriotic duty. To prepare and survive, and to help others prepare and survive, was supposed to be the concern of every American. Scientists, officials, and the mass media worked hard to make the public "understand the scope of the problems we face as a nation."[46] Preparedness took the shape of a national aspiration, but it also appeared as a unique opportunity to demonstrate the value of good global citizenship in a world of emerging infectious diseases.

Not surprisingly, the business of preparedness became, literally, a business. The U.S. government presented pandemic preparedness as an opportunity for innovation and pharmaceutical product development. Yet some professionals were ambivalent about the project. A few blocks from Ground Zero in New York City, an emergency planner told me in 2007, "Listen, I'm employed by the culture of fear." We were sitting in his Lower Manhattan office, discussing the expansion of emergency preparedness after the terrorist attacks of September 11, 2001. "I make my living from scary things," he confessed. "That's how I make my living. I completely understand that there is a very

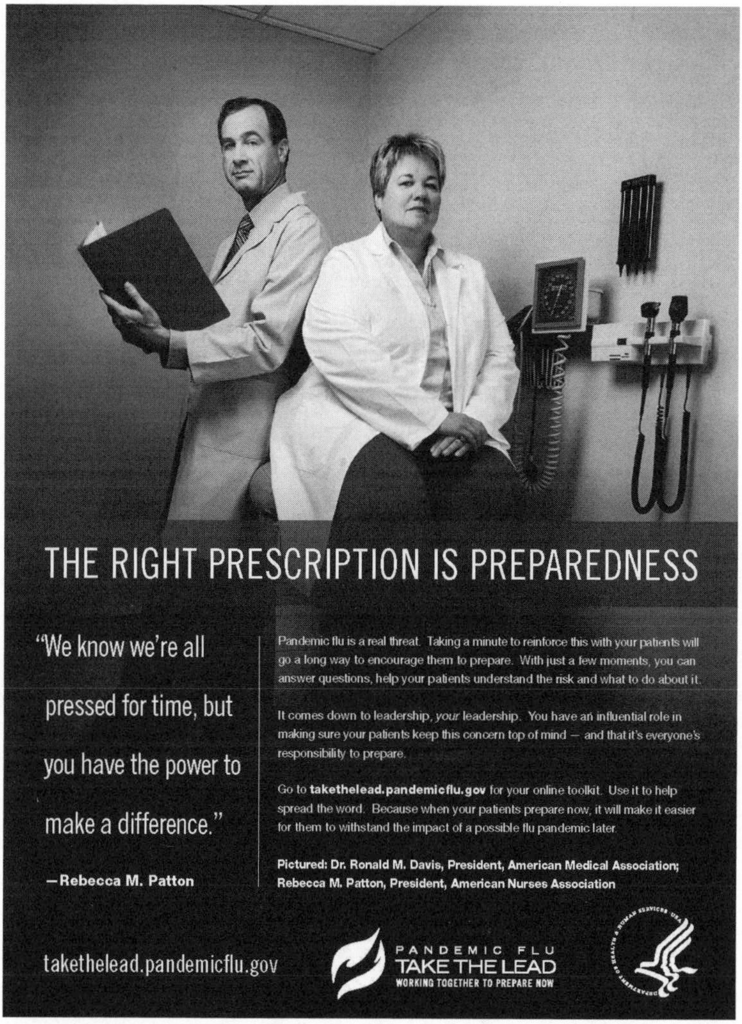
THE RIGHT PRESCRIPTION IS PREPAREDNESS
"We know we're all pressed for time, but you have the power to make a difference."
—Rebecca M. Patton
Pandemic flu is a real threat. Taking a minute to reinforce this with your patients will go a long way to encourage them to prepare. With just a few moments, you can answer questions, help your patients understand the risk and what to do about it.
It comes down to leadership, *your* leadership. You have an influential role in making sure your patients keep this concern top of mind — and that it's everyone's responsibility to prepare.
Go to **takethelead.pandemicflu.gov** for your online toolkit. Use it to help spread the word. Because when your patients prepare now, it will make it easier for them to withstand the impact of a possible flu pandemic later.
Pictured: Dr. Ronald M. Davis, President, American Medical Association; Rebecca M. Patton, President, American Nurses Association
takethelead.pandemicflu.gov
PANDEMIC FLU
TAKE THE LEAD
WORKING TOGETHER TO PREPARE NOW

FIGURE 4. The right prescription is preparedness. "We know we're all pressed for time, but you have the power to make a difference. Pandemic flu is a real threat. Taking a minute to reinforce this with your patients will go a long way to encourage them to prepare." Poster published by the U.S. Department of Health and Human Services.

real focus on a culture of fear. And America is completely wrapped up in it. Everybody gains. And the politicians have nothing to lose from focusing on the threat. It's a business, the business of terror. And I'm part of it."

With the pandemic framed as a catastrophic threat looming on the horizon, preparedness became a matter of survival, and the disease emerged as an opportunity for health entrepreneurs and emergency consultants. Because of the growing emphasis on biological threats, the nation would become ever more prepared for the terrors of the post–Cold War era. "No one in the world today is fully prepared for a pandemic," Secretary Leavitt cautioned, "but we are better prepared today than we were yesterday—and we will be better prepared tomorrow than we are today."[47] Nevertheless, a definition of preparedness was absent,[48] and metrics to measure efficacy were not available.[49] Nicholas Cagliuso, emergency manager in a New York City health care institution, explained to me that there was actually no way of knowing how effective pandemic preparedness was because there were no standards. Would America's involvement in preparedness automatically make the country better prepared, as Secretary Leavitt suggested?

Despite doubts among professionals, emergency preparedness was advanced as a collective project for survival. "The pandemic may be so overwhelming that everyone needs to be prepared," a government official declared. "It's healthy people who are dying," he told me. Osterholm concurred. It was crucial to draft a comprehensive plan for the catastrophic disease, a "detailed operational blueprint for how to get a population through one to three years of a pandemic."[50] It was essential, he continued, for such a plan to involve everyone. "In the private sector, the plan must coordinate the response of the medical community, medical suppliers, food providers, and the transportation system. In the government sector, the plan should take into account officials from public health, law enforcement, and emergency management at the international, federal, state, and local levels."[51] This account of a country on the brink of collapse painted a picture of a totalizing threat with enormous consequences, which required the mobilization of science, medicine, media, and the state. The need to plan for the worst—socially and politically, institutionally and financially, scientifically and technologically—made preparedness a national project.

Notably, the public was addressed in this endeavor not as a passive audience for staged exercises but as an active participant in the project. "What happens to you when the world economy shuts down?" a *Newsweek* article wondered in October 2005, reminding citizens that they were personally responsible for their survival. "People must internalize their preparedness, make it a part of their life," Dan Jernigan, a health official underscored in a conversation with me. Experts and officials recognized the difficulty of spreading the message to the public; they were concerned about the "failure of citizens to understand the importance of their own roles in responding to emergencies."[52] But what exactly were ordinary people supposed to do in the case of a pandemic, in addition to covering their coughs and avoiding contact with sick people? On Oprah, Osterholm counseled citizens to ponder what they would do, where they would go, and how they would work under pandemic conditions. Websites offered lists of essential assets for survival, reminding customers that stores would run out of stock should a pandemic strike. Volunteer organizations such as the Medical Reserve Corps made it possible for people to participate in civil defense programs. Medical blogs posted practical tips for concerned individuals. Books published for survivalists—also known as "preppers"—promised tactics, techniques, and technologies for uncertain times.[53] In September, President Obama called on Americans to observe National Preparedness Month, urging citizens to be disaster aware, make their own preparations, improve self-sufficiency, and enhance national security. The systematic inculcation of the broad-reaching possibility of sudden death "must come from an initiative as bold as the man-on-the-moon agenda that President John F. Kennedy articulated," Osterholm wrote in a 2007 article.[54]

Beginning in 2005, a substantial social, cultural, political, legal, financial, technological, institutional, pedagogical, and bureaucratic effort was undertaken to redefine and reconstruct the nation in the name of pandemic preparedness. Significant resources became available to rebuild the public health infrastructure, but these funds were often diverted from other health and social welfare programs. Despite a substantial influx of money earmarked for preparedness, the nation's overall budget for public health declined.[55] Generous funding was available for the new priority but not for the children's health insurance program, public health professionals pointed out. The state shifted its focus from ordinary to extraordinary and to potentially catastrophic disease events.[56] But the aim was not to prevent a pandemic. On the contrary, it was to reconstruct and redesign the infrastructure to reduce the impact of a pandemic, a pandemic that was considered inevitable. The crucial question, in other words, was not how to avoid the event, but how to respond to it when it occurred. The pandemic was perceived as a catastrophic disease whose prediction could not prevent is occurrence.

In this vision of vulnerability, public health appeared as a contribution to emergency response. It became the prescribed way of adjusting to the fact that fewer ordinary structures such as hospitals and clinics were available for ordinary care and support. The consequences, not the more fundamental causes of the precarious conditions, became the target of preparedness.

In December 2006, a state commission on health care facilities concluded that the costs associated with empty beds were a fundamental driver of the financial crisis in New York's health care system.[57] According to the commission's report, costs were mounting and health care delivery was increasingly becoming "unaffordable" for the state. The system was "broken," it was "on the brink of collapse," and it was in need of "fundamental repairs."[58] Doris Varlese, general counsel of the Greater New York Hospital Association and an expert on the financial implications of emergency preparedness, told me, "The idea behind such proposals is that if you develop a plan for the closure of certain hospitals, the ones that survive will be stronger."

Varlese emphasized that neoliberal plans to close, merge, or shrink hospitals contradicted the idea of having excess capacity in the system in case of a catastrophic outbreak of infectious disease: "There will be less excess capacity, stronger providers, better margins, more financially healthy institutions. And yes, that does contradict the idea of having excess capacity in a system if something would happen." Health care institutions were under enormous pressure to cut costs and consolidate resources. At the same time, they were required to undertake preparedness efforts for a possible pandemic. "Each year we do more and more," remarked Varlese. "But every day we have a nursing shortage."

The call to change was typically not meant to contribute to the improvement of living conditions or the basic needs of public health and medical care. On the contrary, the aim was to reduce "excess capacity" and develop "surge capacity" instead. The purpose was to persuade individuals and institutions to develop emergency measures to secure their survival and respond to the disease. For instance, hospital administrators and emergency managers developed plans to put up tents in parking lots, but no one knew how to staff those tents in the event of an emergency. Meanwhile, the chronic nursing shortage, which challenged operations on a daily basis, continued. Health care institutions did more and more each year, but every day they faced another shortage.

Collapse was increasingly normalized as inevitable destiny in the United States. Time made its presence felt as the mounting pressure to do something, and extreme threats to survival began to shape the reproduction of social, cultural, and political life.[59] There was no way to escape the influence of influenza in the nation under threat. The protean disease had become one of the defining threats of the time, making preparedness a project essential for survival.

FIGURE 5. The national strategy. "Once again, nature has presented us with a daunting challenge: the possibility of an influenza pandemic. While your government will do much to prepare for a pandemic ... individual action is perhaps the most important element of pandemic preparedness and response." National Strategy for Pandemic Influenza, Homeland Security Council, November 2005.

   In 2008, the CDC adapted Homeland Security's terrorism advisory system for pandemic influenza. To communicate the threat to the public, the government agency introduced a color-coded scheme of pandemic phases. For the CDC, even the lack of disease had an important place in the natural order of things. According to the World Health Organization, the obvious place for the lack of disease was in "phase one," the "inter-pandemic phase," which would eventually progress to "phase six," the pandemic proper. The catastrophic event, in other words, was always already in the process of happening, even when nothing was happening. Thus, living in the present meant living in the shadow of the coming plague; that is, living in the gap of time, living in the time that remains. Scientists, officials, and the media perceived the present as a momentary suspension before the next pandemic struck. But how much time before it occurred? How much time was left to prepare? The viral storm "could happen tonight, next year, or even ten years from now," warned Osterholm.[60]

In conversations, public health professionals described to me how they moved from one project to another. Initially, these projects were framed as bioterrorism preparedness, "partly because that's what was going on and that's where the funding was," as one professional put it to me. The U.S. government made billions of dollars available for biosecurity in the aftermath of the anthrax attacks in 2001. "Bioterrorism funding was really hot at the time and so everyone was trying to frame their grant proposals around that." These proposals shifted when pandemic influenza emerged as an important concern. The result of the new priority was a pandemic of projects.[61] As sociologist Melinda Cooper observed, "official documents declared that infectious disease outbreaks and bioterrorism should be treated as identical threats, in the absence of any sure means of distinguishing the two."[62] Flexible notions such as "biological threat" or "biological vulnerability" reflected this confusion, with considerable consequences for the allocation of public health resources: Enormous amounts of funding went to pharmaceutical companies and the biotech industry for projects that had little oversight. Public health professionals worried that the new concern with preparedness might constrain the scope of the public health mission.[63] Of course, public health and national security have always been tightly linked, especially in the United States, but the notions of "biological threat" and "biological vulnerability" enabled an unprecedented conflation between matters of health and those of security.

Searching for security, the state supported biomedical innovation, with the hope that such investment would eventually result in the production of effective treatments against infectious disease. Officials ordered millions of vaccine and drug doses against anthrax, smallpox, and avian influenza for the Strategic National Stockpile, providing pharmaceutical companies with billions of revenue despite uncertainties about the efficacy of treatments such as Tamiflu, Hoffmann-La Roche's notorious antiviral drug for avian influenza.[64] When biological vulnerability became a matter of national security, a new source of profit making appeared in the shadow of the coming plague.

By the end of 2011, the United States had spent more than $60 billion on bioterrorism preparedness. A vision of vulnerability, expanding after the terrorist attacks of September 11, 2001, and the subsequent mailing of anthrax letters, allowed government officials to launch the largest biodefense program in American history. Preparedness had turned into a generic remedy. "We're better prepared for a pandemic because what we're doing for bioterror will also prepare us somewhat for a pandemic attack," explained one expert.[65] For microbiologist Robert Webster, nature was the real bioterrorist: "Regardless of human endeavors, nature's ongoing experiments with H5N1 influenza . . . may be the greatest bioterror threat of all."[66] With this account of nature as the ultimate bioterrorist, the pandemic of preparedness reached its climax of confusion. Insecurity was unlikely to evaporate in the nation under threat, and vigilance became vital in the color-coded scheme of things. We must be on the lookout. We must be ready. "Nature's laboratory never sleeps."[67]

Trainings for public health professionals, emergency planners, doctors, nurses, pharmacists, firefighters, paramedics, and police officers reflected the blurred distinction between the naturally occurring infectious disease and weapons of mass destruction. In 2008, I participated in a pandemic influenza planning and preparedness program that was organized by the Center for Domestic Preparedness of the U.S. Department of Homeland Security. When I arrived at the former army base in Anniston, Alabama, where the training would take place, I met colleagues who told me that the program also included a "Weapons of Mass Destruction Hands-On Training." Mike, our instructor, informed us that the center offered the only program in the world featuring civilian trainings, exercises, and drills in a true toxic environment, using chemical and biological agents.

I was primarily interested in pandemic influenza and was less intrigued by the idea of testing the reliability of my personal protective equipment in a contaminated environment. Therefore the instructor suggested that, instead of participating in the exercise, I should observe my colleagues as they began their day with a medical screening, a blood draw, and a light meal. At 5:40 a.m. in the morning our bus departed to the COBRA facility; participants signed the standard consent form and entered the laboratory where they were exposed to a deadly dose of VX nerve gas.[68] Equipped with full body suits and three layers of latex gloves, the group performed a simulated rescue operation in a large room that was tightly sealed to contain the invisible agent.

Communication was impossible because of the heavy gear that was necessary to protect people from the gas. All the action that occurred was performed in a state of slow motion. A large window made it possible for me to observe the operation from outside the room. At one point, a member of the group walked toward the window to show me the chemical detection paper that indicated the positive test result for the lethal agent.

The growing number of biodefense laboratories conducting research with dangerous organisms blurred the boundaries between defensive and offensive research. It also increased the risk of accidents, abuse, and theft by terrorists. Commentators argued that the new capacities to prevent catastrophic events might create the very conditions for those events to happen.[69]

FAITH AND REASON

The book's argument is situated in recent debates about modernity and temporality. In his *Observations on Modernity*, Niklas Luhmann wonders about the forms in which the future manifests itself.[70] Luhmann's interest, according to Andrew Lakoff, "is not in a prophetic temporality in which an already determined human fate is prefigured in the present, but rather in a distinctively modern time that calculates a future that 'can always turn out otherwise'—a provisional foresight."[71] At the heart of Luhmann's conception of the modern condition as an "ecology of ignorance," however, is a problematic understanding of temporality. Taking for granted modernity's account of itself as a historical project of advancing rationalization, Luhmann believes that "necessity" is increasingly replaced with "contingency." He thus argues that a "prophetic temporality" is gradually substituted with a "provisional foresight." However, on the basis of such an understanding of modernity, a scientifically inspired prophetic enunciation can only appear as a contradiction in terms.

In Luhmann's view, scientists are scientists and not prophets. What scientists embody in their public performances is not a prophetic existence because they have rejected the notion of an inevitable if not predetermined course of events. Yet in scientific discourse, as well as in public debates, scientists are perpetually presented as charismatic prophets with a message for the people. They are generally credited with the power to predict the shape of things to come. Significantly, these predictions are not necessarily based on scientific evidence in the strict sense of the term, but they are nevertheless pronounced in a scientific manner and thus appear to be scientifically inspired. Their tone is both authoritative and imperative. At stake are future events, which are presumed to be "only a question of time." The pandemic is coming. We must prepare. It will happen. It is inevitable. How, then, to account for the scientifically inspired prophetic existence? How to account for the feeling of fate that is emerging today? I suggest that we take prophetic temporality seriously as a social fact. This means that we do not presume a general shift from faith to reason, as Luhmann does; rather, we should follow Hirokazu Miyazaki's lead and explore how prophetic pronouncements calibrate the relation between faith and reason.[72] Faith, in other words, operates at the heart of reason, not at its limits or margins. Faith is an essential part of reason, and reason continues to rely on it. The challenge is to figure out how.

Faith is never without doubt, and the dynamics of faith and doubt are the very driving forces that motivate the production of scientific knowledge. Faith in the inevitable future is an important commitment made by individuals and institutions professionally involved in pandemic preparedness. The entire project would not make much sense without confidence in the coming plague. Such fidelity is a central foundation on which the project of preparedness rests. But faith also entails moments of hesitation, and it is always open to public contestation. In fact, hesitation and contestation are constitutive for the scene of pandemic prophecy. The dynamics of faith and doubt animate the search for truth. It is important to emphasize that the prophet of faith and the prophet of doubt share an important assumption: that there is a truth that must be revealed. "This is how it is . . ."

To better understand the scene of pandemic prophecy, this book draws attention to a number of incidents and episodes. Incidents and episodes are not quite events; instead they are magnetizing moments that are scrutinized systematically by scientists, journalists, and officials. In such moments of intensive discussion and debate, prophets confront the boundaries between the known and the unknown. Enlightened by scientific inspiration, they look into the past, and into the future, and determine the meaning of incidents and episodes that they are witnessing in the present. Are these incidents and episodes warning signs of the coming plague, evidence of imminent disaster? As a consequence of such considerations, the present becomes uncertain, unable to afford a stable ground: "When speech becomes prophetic, it is not the future that is given, it is the present that is taken away," observes Maurice Blanchot.[73]

Incidents and episodes keep the threat fresh for people, a threat that is open to discussion and debate as long as the pandemic fails to happen. As enigmatic riddles with no obvious meaning, incidents and episodes create occasions for the prophet to see and tell. "This is how it is . . ."

As a result of prophetic illumination, incidents and episodes appear as reflections of the coming catastrophe, a catastrophe that would remain invisible without incidents and episodes that are observable. Incidents and episodes make the absent event present; they are embodiments of the evanescent, evidence of the emergent. Incidents and episodes circulate as somber signs, pregnant with prophetic meaning. They come into view as revelations of a daunting future, a future that has already begun, a future that is "closer than you think."[74] Incidents and episodes charge the present with a profound feeling of nervous expectation. The "not quite" of the para-event is the incipient event, the event that is just about to happen, the event that is constantly becoming but never quite there.

Thus, the making of pandemic influenza occurs *in* and *through* the prophetic illumination of incidents and episodes that are not quite events.[75] Actors and institutions invoke the inevitable future as a stable point of reference to determine the meaning of the strange incidents and episodes that are happening in the present. Precisely because these incidents and episodes are not quite events, they can be seen as ciphers of the coming plague, as reminders of the catastrophic disease. Scientists, journalists, and officials are involved in the systematic observation, documentation, and interpretation of these incidents and episodes. Mixing facts with fiction, they flesh out accounts of what might come next. This form of divination makes it possible for people to affirm their faith in the coming plague and cultivate a sense of historical purpose. Yet with an event that never happens, triumph never gets a chance to be achieved.

To understand the creativity and complexity of prophetic temporality, it is important to study the function of the "not quite" for the constitution of the "not yet." The book thus shifts the focus of eventalization, as a concept, from questions of *intelligibility*—"how has a reality become intelligible in a particular way?"—to questions of *infelicity*—"why is a reality not quite what it should be?" My aim is to avoid the reification of intelligibility and emphasize the productivity of infelicity.

The inspiration for such a conception of pandemic prophecy comes from John Austin's account of the performative speech act, the speech act that brings about what it names.[76] Significant for the book, however, is not Austin's concept of the *felicitous* but his concept of the *infelicitous* speech act— the speech act that *fails* to generate what it anticipates. Infelicity is important as an analytic term because it allows scholars to foreground the failure of prophecy to fulfill its promise instantly. The power of prophecy to bring about what it names is suspended at the moment of its utterance because fulfillment is projected into the future. This means that the efficacy of prophecy is always delayed. But the failure of prophecy to immediately generate what it anticipates is not a shortcoming or disadvantage; on the contrary, it is essential for the prophetic condition and the systematic deferral of disease into the future. Infelicity is a form of failure, to be sure, but this failure is not without effect. What the interval enables is continuity: the continuity of expectation.

According to Austin, infelicity does not mean that nothing has been done; in fact, "lots of things will have been done."[77] In prophetic speech, the catastrophic event is kept in abeyance; its occurrence is displaced into the future. Such displacement creates anxiety and apprehension. How much time is left? How much time is left to prepare? The sense of a historical period with uncertain duration fuels repetitive appeals and escalating accusations. What must be done to prevent the worst? Why are we not prepared? Prophetic speech can trigger multiple effects despite, and indeed as a result of, its infelicity.

Prophetic speech is urgent and nomadic.[78] It is rootless, insistent, and relentless. It is never completely anchored in a given context, and the meaning of what it articulates is never fully defined and determined in advance. Prophetic speech is productive because it cannot entirely control its consequences. What it achieves—what it says, what it does, and what it inspires—is not always predicable. The nomadic life of the prophetic word must be traced.

The world that I explore is concerned with dramatic objects—the pandemic virus—and dramatic events, the catastrophic disease. But on closer inspection, the landscape is littered with objects and events that are not quite what they should be. The catastrophic pandemic is on the verge of happening, but it has not arrived yet: Prophetic fulfillment is suspended for the time being. In the prophetic scene, people are constantly confronted with the never-quite-arriving point of the disease, a disease that remains on the horizon as a dark prospect. Emerging in the interval of uncertain duration are discourses and practices that proliferate around incidents and episodes that cannot easily be pinned down, that are not quite as intelligible as they should be, and that never achieve the status of the foreseen event. These incidents and episodes are the result of a more general condition of infelicity, and scholars have set them aside as if they were less important for that reason. However, the failure to find in influenza a figure of fulfillment is essential for the structure of expectation and the sense of being constantly on the cusp of a catastrophe. Eternal deferral makes eternal expectation possible. Failure by no means always leads to the dissolution of belief, but instead to its reinforcement. The pandemic's absence as an event sustains an experience of reality that is in the thrall of a specter.

The result of such spectrality is a perception of the present as a vanishing moment, a transitional phase, a present that is on its way to a predicted future: a future that is already on the horizon, a future that has already begun, even if it has not arrived yet. Almost everything that happens becomes a sign, foreshadowing what has already been foreseen and foretold. To capture how this structure of eventfulness in the absence of events is maintained over time and how it achieves its force and motivates thought, action and passion, it is necessary to avoid an analytic language that is itself couched in dramatic narratives of epochal transformation and, instead, cultivate a sensibility for the strange productivity of infelicity. In the book, I highlight the complex temporality that is characteristic for pandemic prophecy, and I do so with the hope that it will help us better understand how we have come to care about pandemic influenza. Such is the aim of *The Pandemic Perhaps*: to reflect with more nuance on the peculiar presence that pandemic influenza has in a part of the world where disaster is at once close and far away.

In this book, I emphasize the continuity of failure that is so crucial for the constitution of pandemic influenza as a structure of expectation. This emphasis departs in an important way from the constructivist approach, which typically highlights how individuals and institutions succeed in constructing a particular reality.[79] But the efficacy of pandemic prophecy is complex, more complex than we might think at first sight. Thus, I am less interested in conditions that have made a particular reality intelligible. In fact, my argument is that we need to explore the opposite. The focus, accordingly, is not on *intelligibility* but on *infelicity*, and the aim is to examine the failure of prophetic speech to generate what it anticipates. The reality that is not quite what it should be animates people's interest and keeps them invested in what is to come. Such a focus allows us to investigate the construction of biological threats without contributing to the naturalization and normalization of these constructions. It seems that we can only understand power once we study the vulnerability of the constructions that are at the heart of its mechanisms.[80]

While doing fieldwork on pandemic influenza, it increasingly dawned on me that I would not deliver the journalist's fast-moving account of the avian flu death threat. The purpose of my project, after all, was not to chase an emerging disease. I was not tracking a deadly virus in a remote jungle village. I did not, nor did I wish to, find myself on the secret trail of avian flu

FIGURE 6. The monster at our door. "Read this book, and after the inevitable nightmares, take a deep breath. Then start pestering your politicians, demanding they read it and do something, before pandemic influenza claims millions of lives." For Davis, avian influenza is a "viral apocalypse in the making." His book starts with a quote from Ezekiel, the Hebrew prophet. In a vision, the prophet foresees the destruction of Jerusalem. Image: Book cover design from *The Monster at our Door: The Global Threat of Avian Flu* by Mike Davis. Book cover design copyright © 2006 by Henry Holt and Company. Used by permission of Henry Holt and Company, LLC. All rights reserved.

and the coming plague. The eternal struggle between humans and microbes was of no interest to me; neither were heroic disease hunters—the world's brightest scientists. In my work there was no place for the classic figure of the male scientist immersed in a global race to unravel the mysteries of a fatal strain.[81]

These stories were clearly not my story. My project had a different purpose: to observe, describe, and analyze the prophetic scene of pandemic influenza. The book that I envisioned was not waiting for the event to happen; it was not supposed to be a piece of writing that would require a deadly pandemic to prove its point. The story at the heart of the book contained no chilling truth, no tale of inevitable doom, no talk of mystery microbes. My research involved no chicken smugglers, no witch doctors, no fighting cock breeders. There was no viral storm or devil's flu or monster at our door.[82] Such figures make a story riveting, a chronicle gripping, a truth chilling. They generate fear, produce excitement, and create a market for nonfiction bestsellers. They garner attention, galvanize action, and motivate people. They establish the conditions of possibility for the pandemic threat to spread. There was no need for the anthropologist to chase poultry farmers in Hong Kong or Guangdong Province. New York City was the right place to study the influence of influenza.

TALES OF THE FIELD

"If you're a chicken," observed Dr. Peter Palese, chairman of the Microbiology Department at Mount Sinai School of Medicine, "the H5N1 virus is a very bad virus." I met Palese for the first time in New York City in October 2006. Our conversation in his sixteenth-floor office at Mount Sinai eventually resulted in an extended exchange about the pandemic that was looming on the horizon. Insisting that he did not believe that the H5N1 virus was likely to trigger a pandemic, Palese surprised me with his perspective. "I mean, you can never exclude it," he specified, "but I think this is all hyped-up." For Palese, one of the world's leading influenza researchers, the threat was not as imminent as his colleagues were suggesting in their op-ed articles and television appearances. The microbiologist disagreed with the majority of his peers. And yet, the specter had become incredibly productive; it had mutated into a powerful source for the production of knowledge, the affirmation of authority, and the allocation of resources.

"I can tell you, I have a virus in my freezer, which is from 1959," Palese once told me. "It has been equally devastating, it has killed hundreds of thousands of birds in Scotland and it's also an H5N1 virus. It has just not been studied that well. Many colleagues try to suppress that, or don't want to acknowledge that." Palese was upset. What the microbiologist sketched was a different genealogy of the H5N1 virus. His argument did not surprise me. The counter-prophet of American apocalypse was a plain-speaking man—candid, sincere, and naturally disposed to openly speak his mind. For some, his message was controversial, but its purpose was always the same: to communicate his per-spective and expose the prevailing thinking of the time, which he considered to be irresponsible, dishonest, even dangerous. The counter-prophet of Amer-ican apocalypse unveiled the false prophets who, in his view, were deceiving people intentionally. He raised doubts about his rivals to affirm the authen-ticity of his own perspective.

But Palese is not only a microbiologist with a message for the people; he is also a man with an Italian name, an Austrian accent, and an American career. Born in 1944, he grew up in Linz, a city located in the north of Austria, where his parents owned a small pharmacy. Before launching his career as a micro-biologist at Mount Sinai in New York City, where he arrived as an assistant professor in 1971, he followed in the footsteps of his parents by studying chem-istry and pharmaceutical science at the University of Vienna. Palese made his name as a leading scientist when he pioneered the field of reverse genetics for negative-strand RNA viruses (a category that also includes the influenza virus). Reverse genetics is a powerful technology that has become an essen-tial tool in experimental research; it allowed Palese and his colleagues in 2005 to reconstruct the pandemic virus that killed between twenty to fifty million people worldwide in 1918 (a remarkable but controversial project that I dis-cuss in more detail in chapter 4). In 2000, Palese was elected to the National Academy of Sciences for his landmark contributions to the study of influenza viruses. He currently serves on the editorial board for the *Proceedings of the National Academy of Sciences* and is an editor for the *Journal of Virology*. He is a distinguished scientist, has received many honors, and is a prolific author of numerous articles published in the most prestigious journals.

In February 2012, Palese participated in a public debate organized by the New York Academy of Sciences. At issue was an influenza virus that had been manipulated in the laboratory. In the course of the debate, Osterholm became ever more irritated. He accused Palese of denying clear signs of danger and then, sure in his conviction, he declared, "What you're saying is just propaganda." He went on, "You do not represent the mainstream of influenzologists when it comes to this issue." Palese was equally frustrated by Osterholm's accusations. "You can always assume the worst," he replied. "When do we stop being afraid?" The threat may seem unlikely today, but "we can't afford to be wrong," insisted Osterholm. People in the audience nodded. Only a few panelists disagreed with the health professional and his gloomy account of pandemic disaster. In the world of preparedness, there was always a reason to be afraid.

Meeting with Palese in his office was a pleasure, not least because he practiced a form of skeptical reasoning that appealed to me. Palese was right to contest the ubiquitous framing of pandemic influenza as a catastrophic disease. After almost two decades of dramatic pronouncements about an impeding disaster and escalating predictions about hundreds of millions of deaths worldwide, it seemed time to reconsider the language. The worst-case scenario, as well as the fascination with scary things, seemed to increasingly exhaust itself. However, for an anthropological study there was no need to join the competition, expose the false prophets, and speak truth to power. *The Pandemic Perhaps* is not an exercise in the hermeneutics of suspicion.[83] It is not a book of blame; it has no interest in public accusation. My aim, as an anthropologist, is not to situate "good science" on one side and "bad science" on the other. What I wish to examine is not a hidden truth, but the very assumption that there is a truth that needs to be revealed.

The challenge that today's concern with pandemic influenza poses for an anthropological study is not to determine whether the threat is real or not, but to attend to the complex and contradictory ways in which pandemic influenza appears in the prophetic scene. What has made the influenza virus so compelling as an object of scientifically inspired prophetic appropriation? What animates the hermeneutic labor that we are witnessing today? Exploring a configuration of state power, scientific expertise, and pharmaceutical capital, I was increasingly able to appreciate the crucial significance of the strange incidents and episodes that were proliferating in the world that I encountered at the time of my research. I was curious and began to follow these incidents and episodes more closely with the hope that a detailed analysis of them and their trajectories would provide a better understanding of a more general social and political condition.

The threat of infectious disease has arguably become a productive force in the United States (more productive and much less controversial than global climate change, for example), and the analytic task is to identify the possibilities and limits of this force in contemporary American life. Attending to the sense of momentum that a threat like pandemic influenza is able to propel is important if we wish to understand what other threats to human existence are unable to accomplish today.

Palese's perspective was intriguing not because it revealed the "real truth" behind the avian flu death threat. What he said was important because it allowed me to study more carefully how pandemic influenza had become a subject of scientific divination in the United States. How was it possible for pandemic influenza to become a major concern that could stand in for the threat of infectious disease more generally? I foreground this question not to increase skepticism toward science, but to gain a better sense of how faith operates at the heart of reason. The aim of the book is to think with faith and reason and to take both seriously, but not necessarily at face value. Palese's doubt reminds us that there are other ways of bringing faith and reason into balance, that other calibrations are possible. Would these calibrations offer us other possibilities of thinking about infectious disease? Would they allow us to shift from a politics of survival—a politics of minimal existence and minimal care—to an ethics of flourishing, an ethics of living well and faring well? What kinds of social formations and political projects would be possible once we abandoned our trust in the beneficial nature of the worst-case scenario? Given today's concerns with extreme events, what would a politics of ordinary harm look like? What normative horizons of the good are embedded in the everyday?

Having learned immensely from Palese, I am grateful to him, as well as to his postdoctoral fellows and graduate students in the laboratory at Mount Sinai, not only for generously giving their precious time to me and for introducing me to the contingencies, pleasures, and discontents of experimental research but also for helping me understand a virus famed for its structural simplicity and functional complexity. In terms of scientific authority, it would have been difficult to find a more suitable interlocutor than Palese. Working continuously for almost forty years as a microbiologist and influenza researcher in the United States, Palese is on familiar terms with the biology of the virus that I encountered in his laboratory. However, his indubitable scientific authority stands in sharp contrast with his marginal political influence, especially when it comes to the avian flu death threat.

During my fieldwork in New York City, I regularly met with Palese in his office. We discussed recent developments, I learned about contemporary infectious disease research, and I began to study the place of faith and reason in science. Gradually, I also became interested in a number of research projects that Palese and his group of researchers at Mount Sinai were conducting, which were often designed and performed in close cooperation with colleagues at the Centers for Disease Control (CDC) in Atlanta. Palese invited me to spend time in his lab where I was able to learn and familiarize myself with the basic microbiological techniques deployed in the experimental investigation of influenza. My time in the lab also allowed me to work with Palese's postdoctoral fellows and doctoral students, to learn about their current research projects, and to ask them about their sense of what it means to be a scientist today. In addition to my work with Palese, I met with public health officials at the New York City Department of Health and Mental Hygiene, as well as with public health specialists and emergency planners in New York and Long Island. I joined the Medical Reserve Corps and participated in preparedness exercises and public health emergency trainings. I conducted open-ended interviews with influenza experts; local, state, and federal public health officials; physicians; nurses; and preparedness managers in public hospitals and private emergency response organizations. I observed meetings, attended lectures, visited workshops, traveled to conferences, and read newspapers, magazines, and scientific journals. I also assisted public health professionals in their efforts to hold public engagement meetings designed to educate Americans about the pandemic threat. Finally, my fieldwork included trips to the Centers for Disease Control in Atlanta, to the World Health Organization in Geneva, to the Institute of Medical Virology in Zurich, and to the Pasteur Research Centre at the University of Hong Kong; at these institutions I visited labs, attended workshops, enrolled in training courses, and conducted interviews with scientists and public health experts.

A MAP OF THE BOOK

The book's protagonists are microbiologists. Each chapter examines how microbiologists tried to cultivate, replicate, and manipulate the influenza virus in the laboratory so as to contain its spread and control the disease. But what kind of activity is microbiology? What exactly is the relevance of microbiological research for the contemporary understanding of influenza as an infectious disease? And how is it related to the art of scientific divination? At the heart of microbiology, and the germ theory of disease more generally, is a reductionist approach focused on the identification of contagious agents as necessary causes of disease. However, to understand the relation of microbiological research to the art of scientific divination, it is worth following Cori Hayden's advice to resist the tendency of taking reductionism for granted. Hayden underscores that the result of reductionism is not necessarily reductionist.[84] Ever since microbiologists began cultivating, replicating, and manipulating the influenza virus in the test tube, they have struggled to align the virus with the disease. This effort to relate what they differentiate and overcome the gap between the signifier (the pathogenic agent) and the signified (the pathological condition) has not always been successful; on the contrary, microbiological research has become an important source of ambiguity in the understanding of influenza. Ambiguity calls for disambiguation, and disambiguation requires recalibrations in the relation between faith and reason.

In this book, I take microbiological research as a starting point to explore the broader context that is shaping the prophetic appropriation of pandemic influenza. Paradoxically, the production of scientific knowledge about the disease "at once affirms and deprives the world of confidence," in Avital Ronell's words.[85] Microbiologists conduct experiments to confirm claims, but these confirmations are never final; they are always provisional. "Submitted to constant critique and revision, the experimental condition is capable of leaving any conclusion in the dust . . . ; when a result is 'arrived' at, the experimental imagination suspends it in its provisional pose of hypothesis," writes Ronell.[86] The consequence of such suspension is uncertainty. Reality is on the line, speculation awaits confirmation, and truth is forever deferred in a circuit of infinite testing. The suspension of pandemic influenza in the provisional pose is a result of the experimental condition. Tracing the historical trajectory of this condition allows a better understanding of how the provisional provokes prophetic claims.

I begin this book by telling the story of how the influenza virus first entered the laboratory in the twentieth century. Chapter 1 shows how a complex material infrastructure enabled a group of microbiologists from the National Institute for Medical Research in London to isolate a pathogenic agent from a human population and to cultivate it in the laboratory. Successfully infecting ferrets with infectious matter gathered from hospital patients during an epidemic in 1933, the group of scientists was able to reproduce the typical signs of the illness in these animals, determine its probable etiological cause, and authorize influenza's identity as an infectious disease. As a result of this research, the influenza virus became an incredibly productive object of experimental research, turning into "the most amenable of all viruses to detailed laboratory study."[87] The isolation and cultivation of the microbe furnished an important material foundation for the production of scientific knowledge and the accumulation of experimental evidence. Microbiologists developed new projects and devised powerful methods for the characterization of the virus and the diagnosis of the disease. A culture of testing came into being that allowed microbiologists to frame the virus as a determining factor of disease. But this research also resulted in a number of ambiguities that created a demand for disambiguation.

Only a few years after the virus was first isolated, microbiologists developed a protective vaccine against the communicable disease, but they soon realized that the virus was a moving target; chapter 2 examines how they tried to overcome this obstacle and hit the target. In early 1976, hundreds of military personnel suffered from acute respiratory disease in New Jersey. As a laboratory test showed, some of the recruits had been infected with an influenza virus typically found not in humans, but in swine. Microbiologists invoked apocalyptic tropes, envisioned a prophetic structure of foreshadowing and fulfillment, and claimed that a pandemic was imminent. Government officials, concerned about the threat, arranged a press conference and announced an unprecedented immunization campaign. But the outbreak never occurred, and the prophecy remained unfulfilled. Exploring this episode, the chapter shows how microbiologists in stabilizing the influenza virus as an object of scientific inquiry increasingly saw that stability crumble. The microbe turned into an elusive and erratic entity. This elusiveness ushered in a public culture of danger and resulted in dramatic pronouncements about the unpredictable nature of pandemics.

Whereas chapter 1 traces how microbiologists advanced an ontological account of the normal and the pathological, chapter 2 shows how this ontological account resulted in a view of the virus as a moving target. The aim of chapter 3 is to extend these two insights and explore what they mean for the notorious notion of pandemic influenza. Pandemic influenza has become an important category, especially in the context of preparedness. The pandemic, as an event, is the main concern of pandemic prophecy. How is it defined? To what does it refer? What, in fact, is a pandemic? What are prophets foreseeing when they foresee a pandemic? Chapter 3 explores these questions in detail to better understand the nature of pandemic prophecy. According to microbiologists, a pandemic occurs when a virus appears that differs from other viruses. Yet what makes a virus "different"? When is a virus "new"? The chapter scrutinizes immunological notions of identity and difference as microbiologists routinely invoke and enact them in the laboratory. If the influenza virus is ever changing and evolving, if it is constantly making itself different from itself, then how much difference is required for a virus to count as different and therefore "new"? Tracing how immunological notions of identity and difference are specified in the laboratory by means of an important serological test, I show why the matter of defining pandemic influenza cannot be resolved by technical means and rational calculation. Today, the notion of pandemic influenza has come to hinge on a laboratory test, but this test has made it difficult for scientists and officials to agree on what a pandemic is and whether the world is experiencing one or not. Ironically, the very attempt to reduce ambiguity and relate the virus with the disease has made the notion more ambiguous than ever.

In 2005, microbiologists resurrected the influenza virus that caused the great pandemic of 1918. In chapter 4, I explore this controversial research as I continue my study of the prophetic scene. I focus on the scandalous publicity that the project produced and show how security experts articulated concerns about the potential implications of experimental research. At stake in this research was the threat of a self-fulfilling prophecy. Crafting a dangerous virus in the laboratory, microbiologists were accused of bringing about what they envisioned. I argue that iterability—the replicable nature of information—is at the heart of today's concerns with "sensitive information" published in scientific journals. My aim is to explore how concerns over security have sparked a contentious debate over the past decade about experimental research and its mandates, responsibilities, and accountabilities. I examine how biological matter has increasingly become informed matter, arguing that this informational redefinition of biological matter has opened up new opportunities for the understanding of pandemic influenza as a catastrophic disease. It has allowed security experts to highlight biological vulnerability, shape the public perception of scientific research, and turn influenza into a testing ground for security interventions. The threat of a self-fulfilling prophecy has attached microbiologists in unexpected ways to the world, the state, and security.

Chapter 5 moves from terror to error. In 2004, a private company based in the United States delivered scores of testing samples ostensibly containing a pandemic virus to clinical laboratories all over the world. Not surprisingly, the dissemination of dangerous biological matter caused considerable concern among government officials, especially in the United States. News media considered the global distribution of these hazardous samples to be a serious violation of fundamental principles of biosafety. Though the alarm turned out to be false, government officials argued that the incident was valuable. In chapter 5, I suggest that such incidents have become important for practitioners of preparedness in the United States. False alarms can trigger a real response; in so doing, they provide public health professionals with a unique opportunity to test their plans. Yet, strangely enough, this has also meant that pandemics of the present are increasingly perceived as tests for pandemics of the future. The chapter suggests that a circuit has come into being between testing and the real, a circuit so radically installed that it "cancels the difference between the test and 'the real thing.' "[88] What the chapter illuminates is how the practice of constant testing compromises the very possibility of an event's actuality. Ultimately, testing entails a vanishing of the present and a deferral of the event into the future, where it is available for permanent prophetic appropriation.

Scientific facts about pandemic influenza are spreading in the public sphere, where they become objects of intensive discussion and debate. In the United States, experts and officials have encouraged citizens to participate in the prophetic scene. Chapter 6 tracks how government agencies organized public engagement meetings to test a new model of participatory governance, educate ordinary people about the pandemic threat, and create a space for citizen involvement in health policy making. The chapter draws on my work with public health professionals charged with the organization of a public engagement pilot project to help determine how to prioritize the distribution of scarce pandemic vaccine. In these meetings, the failure to provide sufficient vaccine for the entire population in the case of a public health emergency was taken for granted as an inescapable destiny. Framed as a contribution to the democratization of expertise, these meetings reduced the idea of democracy to the narrow question of how to authorize the unequal distribution of a scarce resource. The set of priorities that surfaced during the meetings for the allocation of the scarce resource were focused not on vulnerable populations, but on critical infrastructure protection. People expressed this concern not just because they were worried about a catastrophic pandemic but also in response to Hurricane Katrina, a storm that had just devastated New Orleans and other parts of the Gulf Coast. The chapter shows how the pandemic came into view as a catastrophic event that had just occurred and that could occur again. Suspended between a *no longer* and a *not yet*, another experience of the spectral had become possible in post-Katrina, pre-pandemic America.

In his great account of the prophetic existence, André Neher notes that "there hovers a 'perhaps' over the prophetic perspective."[89] Enlightened by inspiration, the prophet speaks with certainty and conviction, but the foreseen may never come to pass. What are the implications? What are the consequences? The performativity of pandemic prophecy is complex, to be sure. Must the catastrophic event always happen, as it has been foreseen and foretold, or will the prophetic word prevent it from happening? Perhaps the prophet looks forward to a future in which the vision of death and destruction will no longer be necessary. How, then, to determine the true meaning of the prophetic word? "Prophecy is a promise but not necessarily a promise of the fulfillment of its declared content: it does not necessarily mean what it says," writes Ian Balfour.[90] Prophecy is strange speech. It is paradoxical and perhaps fundamentally infelicitous. Perhaps!

This, then, is the perhaps that lingers over the prophetic perspective. Let us now explore its creativity and complexity and trace the nomadic existence of the prophetic word historically and ethnographically.

ONE

A Ferret's Sneeze

THE RISE OF THE GERM THEORY of disease in the second half of the nineteenth century played a crucial role in the history of modern medicine, contributing to a major transformation in the medical understanding of the normal and the pathological. When researchers made invisible colonies of microbial organisms responsible for a number of illnesses, a fundamental change in the medical understanding of disease occurred. Microbiologists, as Georges Canguilhem convincingly argues, conceived of the difference between the normal and the pathological as a difference of *kind* rather than *degree*, in contrast to the common medical understanding. They thus rejected the physiological thesis generally adopted in the nineteenth century that pathological phenomena were largely identical to corresponding normal phenomena "save for quantitative variations."[1] The experimental identification of microbial organisms as causative agents of communicable diseases supported the microbiologists' conception of the normal and the pathological, along with their distinctive view of the sick body. A human body invaded by a thriving colony of invisible germs inevitably constituted a different kind of body. "It is not normal for a healthy subject," Canguilhem laconically remarks, "to have diphtheria bacilli lodged in his throat."[2]

The difference between the normal and the pathological condition was not a quantitative but a qualitative difference, a difference not of degree but of kind, according to microbiologists at the turn of the twentieth century. The experimental investigation of infectious diseases in the laboratories of the late nineteenth and early twentieth centuries was essential to articulating an ontological conception of infectious disease as a specific condition with a specific cause, which in turn contributed significantly to a more general trend in the scientific description of disease. The reification of disease as an entity separate from the patient reduced the question of illness to a matter of infection, symbolized by the suggestive image of invisible germs invading healthy bodies.

This chapter explores the process of disease reification in the case of influenza. Focusing on the first half of the twentieth century, it argues that scientists stabilized the influenza virus as the specific cause of disease only to see that stability crumble over the following decades. The ontological conception of the normal and the pathological disclosed a biological entity that was elusive and erratic.

IN THE REALM OF THE INFINITELY SMALL

Beginning in the 1890s, microbiologists applied existing bacteriological methods to influenza, trying to confirm the assumption that it was an infectious disease caused by a contagious agent. However, attempts to cultivate the pathogenic agent that was presumed to be responsible for influenza were confounded by a peculiar circumstance. The careful examination of nasal mucus gathered from hospital patients in the midst of seasonal flu outbreaks invariably revealed the presence of multiple bugs—a whole range of unexpected bacterial residents—in the depths of the human body.[3] "In a malady in which the secondary invaders give character to a large majority of the severe cases, it is to be expected that many different organisms should be described," wrote Hans Zinsser in a review published in 1922.[4] The growing number of bacterial organisms cultured in liquid media and visualized by means of histological staining transformed the task of identifying the cause of the "sweating sickness," as it was known in popular discourse, into a real challenge. What was the cause of influenza?

At the turn of the twentieth century, many microbiologists concluded that one particular suspect, Pfeiffer's bacillus, was responsible for the seasonal nuisance. However, to the great frustration of the scientists, the experimental exposure of laboratory animals to Pfeiffer's bacillus never quite consistently reproduced the typical signs of the illness: a runny nose, a rising temperature, and a relentless cough. Researchers could not agree on a bacterial agent and began to wonder if influenza might in fact constitute not a bacterial but a viral disease. Perhaps it was not a bacillus but a virus that was causing the notorious condition. Unfortunately, however, researchers then knew little about this biological entity.

Despite relentless attempts, microbiologists were initially unable to cultivate viruses in the laboratory; only bacteria grew well on artificial media. Nevertheless, they assumed that these viruses existed. Strictly speaking, viruses were not completely unknown. "It is true," remarked microbiologist Thomas M. Rivers in 1932, "that the exact nature of these agents is unknown, but to say that the agents themselves are unknown is somewhat of an exaggeration."[5] Rivers reasoned that "in order to know an infectious agent it is not essential to see it."[6] In fact, scientists conceived of the virus as a special group of biological things precisely because they could not be seen. The limits of the bacteriological regime of representation and intervention established a horizon of possibility, in which the figure of the virus gradually emerged as a negative correlate of existing scientific practices. In the early twentieth century the concept of the virus referred to an obscure object defined primarily in negative terms. Bigger than chemical molecules but smaller than bacterial cells, the virus not only escaped the gaze of the most powerful optical microscope available at the time but it also passed the physical barriers of the finest filters. The virus, moreover, also failed to grow on the lifeless media typically used by microbiologists in their laboratories. These mysterious microbes, it turned out, were so minute that conventional methods developed for bacteria could not make them grow. The figure of the virus thus appeared at the periphery of the bacteriological laboratory and its methods of microbe farming.

In a 1931 article, Sir Henry Hallett Dale summarized the three cardinal properties that characterize a virus as "invisibility by ordinary microscopic methods, failure to be retained by a filter fine enough to prevent the passage of all visible bacteria, and failure to propagate itself except in the presence of, and perhaps in the interior of, the cells which it infects."[7] As Dale's brief summary shows, the three distinctive properties defining the virus concept at that time were predicated on the deployment of a number of practices and were formulated exclusively in negative terms. The three properties represented an embarrassing number of technical inabilities: first, the inability to render the virus visible by optical microscopes; second, the inability to retain the virus by porcelain filters; and third, the inability to cultivate the virus in lifeless media. For the microbe farmers, the virus constituted a challenge. Since the virus could not be seen by existing microscopy methods, new ones had to be invented; since it could not be grown by conventional culture techniques, new ones had to be developed; since filtration lacked accuracy, new forms of filtration had to be conceived.[8]

At the turn of the twentieth century, the virus thus emerged as a strange and subtle entity, seeping, in the most literal sense of the word, through a finely woven fabric of technical contraptions designed to capture and culture the smallest biological things that make up the natural world. Paradoxically, the virus came into view as a unique object precisely because it escaped standard efforts conceived to make it concrete. Initially, its prime quality was its profound obscurity. This tiny little entity proliferating ambiguously at the existential polarities of life and death challenged the celebrated power of the modern laboratory and its methods of microbe farming. Microbiologists perceived these limitations as technical problems to be overcome.

This chapter explores how microbiologists brought the disease inside the laboratory and transformed the biological entity that was too small to be seen into an object suitable for experimental research. It follows in the footsteps of recent science and technology studies and highlights the essential role of scientific practices in the stabilization of a historically specific object of concern in the investigation of infectious disease. These scientific practices allowed microbiologists to substantiate the existence of the virus, characterize its structure, and affirm the authority of the laboratory. A distinctive set of knowledge practices made the invisible agent concrete: The virus became detectable, maintainable, manipulable, and transferable. However, what researchers revealed was not the virus itself, but the trace that it left after it had entered susceptible bodies. Exploring the signs and symptoms of experimental infection, microbiologists began to know more about the virus without really seeing it.

The production of scientific knowledge and the accumulation of experimental evidence were important for the social, cultural, and political salience that the virus gained as an object of concern over the following decades. The new concept of influenza as a viral disease increasingly underpinned medical approaches and public health programs in the twentieth century. The concept was also crucial for the constitution of virology as a new specialty of medical research, allowing microbiologists to devise new diagnostic techniques, develop new forms of treatment, and make predictions about pandemics. The challenge for microbiologists was to establish the virus as a legitimate cause of disease, carve out virology as a promising field of medical research, and establish the significance and relevance of the virus for clinical medicine and public health.

As historian Ton van Helvoort pointed out, the ontological understanding of the normal and the pathological "assumed that influenza is caused by a specific agent."[9] Unable to render it visible by means of optical microscopes or to cultivate it on artificial growth media, microbiologists eventually turned their attention from cause to effect. Scientific claims about the existence of invisible microbes as the cause of infectious diseases would become credible once scientists were able to reproduce the effect of a viral infection in the laboratory. If not the virus itself, researchers hoped to see at least the result of its presence, evidenced by the typical signs and symptoms of infection.[10] However, this strategy of tracing the virus through signs and symptoms faced the fundamental difficulty that the cause did not always produce a recognizable effect. How, then, was it possible to identify the virus despite the irregular character of infection? What kind of medical concepts, scientific practices, and experimental forms of life did the microbe farmers need to mobilize for the proper signs and symptoms to appear and authorize the ontological understanding of influenza as a disease triggered by the invasion of an invisible germ?

The first successful isolation of an influenza virus derived from a human population is generally believed to have been achieved in 1933 by Wilson Smith, Christopher Howard Andrewes, and Sir Patrick Playfair Laidlaw at a farm of the National Institute of Medical Research at Mill Hill, a suburb on the outskirts of London.[11] In a celebrated set of experiments that immediately aroused the "greatest interest among medical men," as an article carried by the *New York Times* phrased it at the time, the British scientists were able to accomplish what many had attempted before to no avail; namely, to infect experimental animals in the laboratory with the pathogenic agent suspected to be responsible for epidemics in human populations.[12]

The experimental infection of an animal body in the laboratory constituted, of course, a crucial cornerstone of "Koch's postulates," which define the necessary criteria (isolation—cultivation—inoculation) for a microbe to be accepted as the causative agent of a contagious disease.[13] The procedure that the British scientists followed was relatively simple and straightforward: In the midst of a regular outbreak of seasonal influenza in London in 1933, Smith, Andrewes, and Laidlaw received a battery of vials containing human mucus—derived from nasal and throat washings—gathered by a doctor from hospital patients. First, the scientists filtered the mucus, which they either

FIGURE 7. Can we beat influenza? With the help of an assistant, Christopher Andrewes injects a dose of the influenza virus into the nose of a sedated ferret. Original publication in *Picture Post*, "Can We Beat Influenza?" February 2, 1946. Photo by Kurt Hutton. Copyright: Getty Images.

dropped into the noses or injected into the muscles of several animal species (almost everything from mice to monkeys).[14] All experiments failed, except those conducted with ferrets. By the second day after infection, as the British scientists noticed, the ferrets were remarkably quiet and they also looked ill. By the third day, they were yawning, and they developed a fever that was typical of human infection. "The ferrets are sneezing!" Laidlaw cheerfully exclaimed.[15] The animals, in other words, revealed the characteristic symptoms.

Although the 1933 attempt was primarily designed to isolate the virus by transmitting the microbe from one host to another, the crucial challenge was to render the illness visible as a trace of the viral infection. Many scientists, in fact, had already tried a number of times to transmit the suspected but invisible agent to various animal species in the artificial environment of the laboratory. They all failed, either because the symptoms were not specific enough, or they were vague and variable, or because the animals were not susceptible to the pathogenic agent in the first place. The ferret became a successful laboratory animal for the microbe farmers and their attempt to confirm the virus as the single cause of disease primarily because it produced signs of illness that were strikingly similar to the clinical symptoms of influenza typically observed in the hospital setting. The ferrets were generative not so much because they manifested some kind of sickness, but rather because they manifested the *proper form* of the illness. They produced the characteristic symptoms: The ferrets were not only sneezing but also their temperature was rising and their noses were running. The disease, in other words, assumed a particular form. The pathological effect became effective and provided compelling evidence because it took the right shape in a framework of visibility that was constituted by the clinic and that relied on the set of symptoms observed in humans.[16] The experimental infection of these animals faithfully reproduced the illness, with all its symptomatic characteristics that physicians had witnessed in patients. To understand how the microbe farmers succeeded, we must now look more closely at the peculiar nature of the bodies that the British scientists used in their celebrated experiments.

SIR PATRICK'S FERRETS

In his 1865 *Introduction to the Study of Experimental Medicine,* the French physiologist Claude Bernard argues that the clinic should be considered "only as the entrance to scientific medicine, . . . [the] first field of observation which a physician enters: but the true sanctuary of medical science is a laboratory; only there can he seek explanations of life in the normal and pathological states by means of experimental analysis."[17] In Bernard's view, the physician must rely on the laboratory and the animal body to achieve true medical science. Only there, in the laboratory, will the persistent physician finally be able, with the assistance of an animal model of disease, to account for "what he has observed in his patients."[18]

As Bernard's programmatic account indicates, the emergence of experimental medicine entailed two important shifts: from the clinic to the laboratory and from the human body to the animal body.[19] According to historian Ilana Löwy, the use of animal bodies "was established in the nineteenth century, as an extension and codification of older medical practices."[20] Yet the physiologists' provocative claim that laboratory studies conducted on animal bodies were indispensable to the scientific understanding of human diseases was not completely accepted until the field of microbiology emerged. Indeed, Löwy underscores in her account that it was microbiology itself that finally placed the animal body at the heart of scientific medicine. Investigations conducted by microbiologists, Löwy notes, "vindicated and enlarged earlier proposals to ground diagnosis, therapy and prevention of diseases in laboratory-based research, and firmly linked the fate of sick individuals to that of laboratory animals."[21]

Laboratory animals had already played a crucial role in the scientific research pursued by the microbe farmers Louis Pasteur and Robert Koch and their coworkers in France and Germany. These animals were used not only to isolate bacterial organisms but also to examine their pathological effects with the hope of producing vaccines to fight the battle against germs. Concomitantly, however, this incredibly generative form of knowledge-practice also raised the problem of generalization. What was the medical significance of a scientific fact derived from an experimental test conducted on an animal body? How was it possible to generalize from an artificially generated animal disease to a naturally occurring human condition? Animal experimentation was thus confronted with the difficult problem of aligning the animal's fate with those of humans and, by implication, those of humans with those of animals. How did the microbe farmers achieve this alignment in the case of influenza?

In his essay on scientific experimentation in animal biology, Canguilhem observes that "nothing is as important for a biologist as his choice of material to study."[22] Biologists in general and microbiologists in particular decide to work with specific animal bodies for distinctive reasons. In the case of influenza, the choice was indeed profoundly structured by the need to find an animal species that manifested the symptoms of illness typically observed in the clinic. These symptoms allowed scientists to represent the experimental disease in a clinical frame and thus align the animal with the human pathology.[23] Significantly, the clinical frame of reference that the British scientists mobilized to persuade doctors of the existence of an invisible germ was both enabling and disabling. But before we explore this paradoxical moment in the making of an experimental fact, we must first examine the particular kind of animal life that played such an essential role in the early history of influenza's scientific investigation. It was a particular variety of ferrets that allowed microbe farmers to isolate the virus in the laboratory, establish it as the cause of disease, and describe it in concrete terms.

Smith, Andrewes, and Laidlaw succeeded in their experiments by and large because they worked with the ferret, a domesticated relative of the weasel. As it turned out, this particular species was the "right tool for the job."[24] The ferret represented the right species because it was able to elicit the "right" effect and generate credible evidence. The scientists were able to produce the *same* symptoms in a *different* body and thus align the animal's disease with the human condition and link the laboratory with the clinic. But why was the ferret so well placed to ferret out these compelling facts? Why was it able to produce the proper symptoms? How was the occurrence of asymptomatic infections avoided? To ask the question in a slightly different way: How did the ferret *become* such a valuable testing body for the reproduction of signs that could link the animal's disease with the human condition? What the answers to these questions highlight are the inevitable contingencies that characterize scientific research. These contingencies contributed to the emergence of an ontological understanding of infectious disease as a specific entity with a specific cause that was essential for establishing microbiology's authority as a scientific discipline concerned with the control of epidemics.

In early 1933, Smith incidentally learned about an outbreak of influenza among the staff of the Wellcome Laboratories in London. Apparently, some ferrets housed there for another research project also came down with the flu. This seemed to suggest that transmission between animal and human bodies had occurred. Ironically, as the scientists realized much later on, the ferrets had not actually caught the flu, but dog distemper, an extremely infectious disease affecting the dog populations of the British aristocracy. The disease was known to cause similar symptoms.[25] Misreading these symptoms for influenza, Smith suggested to Andrewes and Laidlaw that they set up a test to explore if ferrets were indeed susceptible to the disease, as appeared to be the case. Significantly, however, the British scientists succeeded not only because they decided to work with ferrets but also, and perhaps primarily, because they were able to work with a particular *variety* of ferrets. Coincidentally, Laidlaw was raising ferrets at the farm of the National Institute for Medical Research for his work on dog distemper. This research had been made possible by a large financial contribution provided by *The Field* magazine, a British sporting weekly.[26] Laidlaw's original interest, however, was not in distemper itself, but in the flu. In fact, he only chose to focus on distemper, a highly contagious disease characterized by fever, nasal discharge, coughing, and loss of appetite, in the hopes that this research would ultimately lead to a better understanding of influenza.[27] Laidlaw thus worked on one disease with another firmly in mind. But despite the similar symptoms, the two diseases were not related at all, as Laidlaw eventually realized. The observation of symptoms was simply not reliable enough for an accurate diagnosis. Nevertheless, the laboratory animal that he had picked for his experimental work on dog distemper unexpectedly turned out to be a perfect model for the flu.

As Laidlaw's colleague Sir Henry Hallett Dale remarked, "An effective method of prophylaxis or treatment would be enthusiastically welcomed by all who bred or kept dogs for sport or companionship."[28] Because of the affective investment of the British not in people suffering from seasonal flu, but in hounds plagued by dog distemper, a group of scientists at the National Institute for Medical Research, headed by Laidlaw, found themselves in a comfortable position to conduct extensive research and to design, manufacture, and maintain a costly technical infrastructure. This, in turn, contributed in no small part to the success of the first experimental transmission of the influenza virus from human to animal bodies. Not surprisingly, the ability to work with uninfected animal bodies, carefully bred and kept in complete isolation, was critical for identifying the unknown cause of a regularly occurring, rapidly spreading, highly infectious disease. Constituting the influenza virus as a unique causative agent, as a concrete biological entity, required—literally—the construction of a living test subject susceptible to the disease and capable of consistently manifesting its clinical form.

ANTISEPTIC ECOLOGIES AND PURIFIED BODIES:
THE ART OF FERRET BREEDING

To constitute themselves as masters of microbe farming and establish their expertise in medical matters, first the scientists had to learn the art of ferret breeding. The rise of the ferret as a productive animal model in influenza research was thus not simply a work of nature. To establish a working experimental system and make the virus visible as a trace, the ferret had to be transformed into a productive body. This transformation highlights the challenges of experimental research, revealing the type of practices that were required for microbiologists to produce compelling facts about a contagious disease. The ferrets Laidlaw had raised since 1926 for his investigation of dog distemper were of a very particular breed.[29] They were immunologically naïve, raised through several generations and under conditions of complete isolation. They were housed in a special building with a floor "constantly covered with a Lysol bath three inches deep," a costly technical feature that Laidlaw proudly noted.[30] Each experimental animal was placed in a cage, which was itself placed in a cubicle. Before entering the isolation facility, a "sanctuary of sterility," workers clothed in rubber boots and rubber coats were carefully cleaned head to toe with Lysol, a common disinfecting solution.[31] Barred from any contact with the outside world, the ferrets found themselves inhabiting a peculiar form of life. They lived in a separate ecological sphere entirely removed from the natural history of infectious disease. It was this rather unusual form of life, generated primarily for experimental purposes, that produced the "right" signs of illness, bypassed the complications of asymptomatic infections, and thus successfully linked the animal with the human disease. As a result, scientific understandings of influenza increasingly came to depend on how this body responded to the virus.

The ferret was neither inexpensive nor particularly easy to handle. In fact, scientists frequently complained that the animals were aggressive and inflicted painful injuries with their sharp teeth. The body of the ferret also came with a large and costly infrastructure to keep animals alive, making it difficult for scientists to produce facts about the virus. Paradoxically, the successful *promotion* of infection required the successful *prevention* of infection. Once the seminal separation of virus and its designated host had been achieved through the strict observation of tedious rules of isolation and containment, the experimental encounter evinced the desired effect. To the great satisfaction of all, Sir Patrick's ferrets were highly susceptible to the influenza virus; they were yawning and sneezing, their temperature was rising, and their noses were running. They had great trouble breathing and they had a "splendid nasal catarrh."[32] As historian Michael Bresalier shows in his detailed account of the British research group, this form of animal testing not only enabled scientists to reproduce the typical signs of illness in the laboratory but it also facilitated the deployment of a clinical mode of measurement—the fever chart—as a

FIGURE 8. A ferret in the cage. Image of a ferret during scientific experiments on the influenza virus. Original publication in *Picture Post*, "Can We Beat Influenza?" February 2, 1946. Photo by Kurt Hutton. Copyright: Getty Images.

visual means of representation.[33] Significantly, this clinical mode of measurement, as Bresalier suggests, rendered the experimental disease legible in a conventional frame that was familiar to doctors.

It is no coincidence that these animal experiments were immediately followed by a series of human experiments—though the latter were not always the result of meticulous planning.[34] Immediately after the successful infection of ferrets with an influenza virus, Smith, Andrewes, and Laidlaw made two consecutive attempts to transmit the invisible agent back from ferrets to humans to establish an even firmer link between the animal and the human disease. However, these experiments failed, most probably because the volunteers had already become immune to the viral strain circulating in London at the time. Just as it was hard to find a susceptible animal body, it was difficult to find a susceptible human body in the context of an explosive epidemic. The invisible virus was everywhere, making accurate scientific research difficult. "Man," Laidlaw observed, "is an exceedingly bad experimental animal and almost useless . . . during an epidemic."[35] However, a consequential incident occurred in early March 1933 while Wilson Smith was inspecting a couple of infected ferrets at the farm. "A ferret with sick, tired eyes and misery in his bones" gazed at the scientist standing over

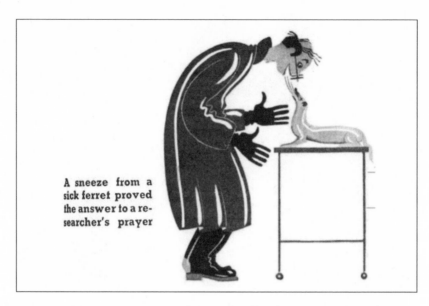

A sneeze from a
sick ferret proved
the answer to a re-
searcher's prayer

FIGURE 9. The answer to a prayer. A ferret accidentally infecting a researcher in the micro-biological laboratory. Drawing by George De Zayas in J. D. Ratcliff, "Cold Comfort," *Collier's Magazine*, February 26, 1938.

him.[36] Unexpectedly, the animal sneezed right in Smith's face; soon thereafter, the microbe farmer came down with the flu.[37]

Unintentionally, the seamless circulation of contagious matter meticulously engineered in the sanctuary of experimental research was suddenly put into reverse, enabling the accidental performance of another test.[38] Despite this awkward moment of medical science temporarily out of control, the researcher dutifully collected the sticky secretions that his body released and requested that his colleagues filter the mucus and drop a few milliliters of the fluid back into the nose of a healthy ferret. A few days later, the animal looked miserable. By accident, the experimental isolation of the influenza virus had come full circle. Now the bodies of the microbe farmers had become victims of their own farming practices, which was perceived as the ultimate confirmation that the virus grown in the laboratory was indeed "human." A ferret's sneeze provided "the tip-off to the biggest question about influenza that remained to be answered," reported an article in a popular magazine.[39] The British scientists termed the strain derived from Wilson Smith "WS"; it was dried, bottled, frozen, and passed on to collaborating laboratories in the United States and Australia. It eventually became one of the classic strains of influenza research, reproduced endlessly in laboratories all over the world. Animating hundreds of experimental studies conducted by generations of scientists, the strain was praised for its unique plasticity; it was exceptionally amenable to laboratory work. It remained remarkably generative, surviving the most drastic technical manipulations to become the triumphant emblem of a scientific discipline on the rise.

HOW THE LABORATORY UNDERMINED THE CLINIC'S DIAGNOSTIC AUTHORITY

In his account of the scientific investigation of plague, Andrew Cunningham shows that the ascendancy of the laboratory fundamentally transformed the identification and representation of infectious disease.[40] At first sight, it might seem as if the microbe farmers simply added a causal model to an existing clinical syndrome, but this addition operated as a true supplement, prompting a reconfiguration of the classification of disease over the following years. The experimental tracing of microorganisms and their conceptualization as causal agents of communicable diseases had a significant impact on the definition of pathological entities; it fundamentally changed the conditions under which a disease is determined. Scientists and journalists have largely overlooked this important transformation in the identity of infectious disease. Popular accounts have presented the rise of the laboratory primarily in terms of ambitious scientists unveiling a hidden nature, discovering the true causes of disease.[41] But these accounts have fundamentally misconceived the tremendous impact of the science, because experimental research did not merely unveil the cause of disease: It changed the very identity of the disease.

In the case of influenza, the identification of the pathogenic agent in the laboratory was initially predicated on a symptomatological concept of the pathological. Although microbe farmers were well aware from other infectious diseases that there are no "true" symptoms of a disease, the influenza virus only became recognizable as a credible cause once a laboratory animal faithfully manifested the "true" symptoms as they were commonly observed in the clinic. Experimental work was conducted under the assumption that "if the initial association between the micro-organism and the disease was a correct one, the inoculated animal would develop the very same disease."[42] But as soon as the "true" symptoms of the disease, as observed in humans, manifested themselves in the ferret body, it increasingly became obvious that no true symptoms actually existed that would unmistakably identify the disease. When Smith, Andrewes, and Laidlaw began to infect mice with the strain that they had just transmitted successfully to ferrets, they discovered that it was possible to make these ubiquitous laboratory animals susceptible to the virus. However, in mice they could detect neither a rising temperature, nor a runny nose, nor a stubborn cough.[43] In fact, almost no reactions, with the exception of weight loss, were recognizable.[44] Were these animals "sick"? And if they were sick, was it the very same disease? Whatever condition the scientists observed in infected mice, it was hardly recognizable as the flu.

The isolation of the virus in the laboratory was bound to subvert the clinical identification of the disease on which the scientific research was predicated. As microbe farmers quickly realized, the *same virus* did not necessarily produce the *same symptoms* in all animal species. Analogies of clinical form, therefore, were not particularly reliable when it came to the determination of a disease in a particular species. As we now know, many animal species are in fact susceptible to the influenza virus, but their bodies are biologically constrained to produce *different* symptoms. Even though chickens are readily susceptible, these animals would not have been a successful model in the laboratories of the early twentieth century because they would have failed to manifest the symptoms typically observed in the clinic. In chickens, influenza presents itself not only as a *respiratory* illness but also and primarily as a *gastrointestinal* condition. In contrast to ferrets, infected chicken neither sneeze, nor do their beaks run. In fact, many die without any visible symptoms. This lack of visible symptoms would make it difficult, if not impossible, to authorize the animal model and link it with the human disease. What scientists once used to call "fowl *plague*" in the early twentieth century only became "avian *influenza*" (and thus the very same disease) once they began to classify infectious diseases on the basis of a *causal* model rather than a clinical *syndrome*.[45] Today's prophetic proclamations about avian influenza as the cause of a human pandemic have thus become possible only due to the ontological understanding of the normal and the pathological that microbiologists established: It is also contingent on the tests that they developed in the laboratory.

When the causal model was added to the clinical syndrome, it slowly began to operate as a supplement, increasingly displacing the diagnostic value of the clinical gaze and prompting a fundamental change in the identity of disease.[46] This model recognized the diagnostic authority of the clinic, only to subvert it. The disease was made different from itself, turning into a new pathological entity defined primarily in the laboratory in terms of causative agents, and not in the clinic in terms of symptoms. Paradoxically, the identification of the cause of the disease fundamentally changed its identity, bringing about a comprehensive process of redefinition and reclassification.

The constraints of clinical form, to use a modified term borrowed from Marilyn Strathern, were thus both enabling and disabling for the microbe farmers.[47] The isolation of the influenza virus in ferrets became possible on the basis of a form of evidence, which rendered impossible the conception that fowl *plague* and avian *influenza* actually represent the very same disease (with different symptoms). The identification of the influenza virus in the laboratory constituted a moment of both recognition and misrecognition. Similar to other cases of infectious disease, the reproduction of the "true" symptoms of influenza in the laboratory enabled scientists to recognize that there are actually no true symptoms.[48] Instead the symptoms depend on the species and their bodies. As long as the isolation of the virus in an animal body and its authorization as a causative agent were predicated on the faithful reproduction of the human syndrome in an animal body, it was predicated on a mistaken model. The scientific claim about the microbial cause of the contagious disease was authorized within the context of a clinical definition of the condition, which the microbiological practice of growing bugs and testing bodies was bound to undermine.

As a disease, influenza has always been notoriously difficult to diagnose. "Clinical findings . . . are not particularly useful for confirming or excluding the diagnosis of influenza," a review published in the Clinician's Corner of the Journal of the American Medical Association recently emphasizes.[49] On the basis of symptoms, a reliable medical judgment is often impossible, except in the context of larger epidemics with multiple cases and similar symptoms. But in the absence of such an epidemic, it has remained difficult for physicians to make an accurate diagnosis. In fact, influenza has entirely disappeared as a diagnostic entity in the clinical context. Physicians are instructed to automatically classify all respiratory diseases as "influenza-like illness." As this notion already indicates, cases of influenza-like illness look like the flu in terms of their symptoms, but they actually might have other causes and might not even be flu. What physicians diagnose today, therefore, is a syndrome. They thus acknowledge that only a test in the laboratory can unmistakably identify the disease and distinguish it from respiratory illnesses that mimic influenza's symptoms.

Over the course of the twentieth century, the microbiological laboratory has thus shattered the clinic's diagnostic authority, introducing a series of powerful tests for the recognition of the pathological condition. Today, it is the laboratory—not the clinic—that is presumed to be the site where influenza is ultimately identified. The lab is perceived as the place where the disease comes into view in its "naked truth," where it shows its "actual nature," where its "real cause" is determined. "You don't really know you have the flu unless you have lab confirmation," an epidemiologist once told me. This shows how the laboratory has become the final arbiter in the world of influenza. Now everything can seem secondary to what laboratory workers say. The practice of growing bugs and testing bodies has allowed microbiologists to create a new concept, laboratory-confirmed influenza, and to talk with much more authority about the disease than physicians in the clinic ever could.[50] Today, the detour through the laboratory has become inevitable not only for patients and physicians but also for journalists and politicians. The very possibility of microbiology as a discipline is contingent on the constitution of its founding object. Microbiology's authority—its ability to produce compelling evidence about the contagious disease and make prophetic predictions about the future course of events—is inextricably bound up with the method of microbe farming, with the ability to characterize viruses, with the ability to grow them under controlled conditions, with the ability to inject them into laboratory animals, and with the ability to modify, manipulate, and reshape them. The masters of microbe farming are able to claim expertise in medical matters because of the microbial natures that they are culturing in their test tubes. These natures have provided microbiologists with a powerful position from which to speak with conviction about a modern dream: the eradication of infectious disease.

"THE GREATEST EXPERIMENT": IN SEARCH OF A VACCINE

Inspired by the work of the British scientists, the International Health Division of the Rockefeller Foundation identified influenza as a major field of research in 1934. Funded by a Rockefeller grant, Thomas Francis Jr. ordered laboratory animals and isolated an influenza virus, confirming the work of his British colleagues. He then embarked on a systematic search for a protective vaccine.[51] In 1936, Paul de Kruif, a former Rockefeller biologist and author of *Microbe Hunters*, boldly told readers of the *Country Gentleman* that American scientists were about to conquer the flu.[52] "Studies were undertaken," Francis wrote around the same time in an internal research report, "to determine whether the artificially cultivated virus could be administered safely to human subjects and whether vaccination would elicit the production of antibodies in the serum of the subjects so treated."[53] These preliminary studies were conducted with research staff at the International Health Division in New York. No adverse reactions or disease symptoms were observed. Francis subsequently consulted Simon Flexner, director at the Rockefeller Institute of Medical Research, to arrange for the enrollment of volunteers in larger immunization studies. A consent form was drafted to allow Rockefeller researchers to introduce into willing participants' bodies "by one or more inoculations or otherwise, the virus of influenza regardless of the manner in which and of the source from which such virus shall have been obtained."[54] The form's main purpose was to release the Institute and the researchers from future liability claims based on potential injuries caused by an invisible virus whose structure and function were almost completely unknown to the scientists. Most volunteers were students at New York University's medical school. Admitted to the hospital of the Rockefeller Institute, participants in the trial were isolated in a special ward before they were immunized with an active virus that had been modified and manipulated in the laboratory.

Over the following years, a considerable number of clinical studies were carried out in the United States. Microbe farmers increasingly perceived seasonal epidemics as proving grounds for experimental vaccines; they were working with the virus while waiting for the next opportunity to vaccinate volunteers. Morris Siegel and Ralph Muckenfuss of the Bureau of Laboratories of the New York City Health Department initiated a series of trials, supported by a financial contribution provided by the Metropolitan Life Insurance Company. These trials were conducted in Letchworth Village, a New York state mental institution. Prison inmates in California were also sprayed with infectious substances that came out of the test tube. The problematic institutional context of these trials and the complete lack of human subject protection allowed scientists and officials to conduct "natural experiments" and keep participants under close surveillance. However, none of the studies, Francis concluded, "gave evidence that the vaccination had any significant effect against the natural disease."[55]

The outbreak of World War II injected a new sense of urgency into the development of an effective vaccine, especially in the United States. During the great pandemic of 1918, the virus had traveled with the U.S. Army across the Atlantic, disrupting military operations, infecting troops, and killing thousands of soldiers. The military's growing concern about a repetition of that pandemic transformed the production of a protective vaccine into a matter of great importance and strategic advantage.[56] A magazine report published in 1941 portrayed influenza as a disease more dangerous for the U.S. military "than bombs."[57] In the same year, the Army's Board for Investigation and Control of Influenza and Other Epidemic Diseases established the Commission on Influenza and charged its members to propose concrete measures against the contagion. Headed by Thomas Francis, the commission included the country's most eminent researchers, including Rockefeller's George K. Hirst. Mobilizing authorities of civilian and military medicine, it "led a crash program to control influenza during the war, and it would remain the focus of American influenza research for twenty years."[58] The military considered influenza a "war disease," made substantial financial resources available for scientific studies, and increasingly shaped the course of experimental research in the United States.

In 1942, eight thousand individuals in two institutions in Michigan were immunized with a vaccine, but there was no epidemic to determine its efficacy. A subsequent, even more extensive trial was carried out the following year. Students at universities across the country were exposed to an inactivated strain. An epidemic of influenza started in November and lasted for several weeks. As Francis reported, "it was the first clear-cut demonstration that subcutaneous vaccination had actually created a significant difference between vaccinated and control groups in the course of a natural epidemic of disease."[59] On the basis of this trial, the Commission on Influenza recommended that the U.S. Army vaccinate all members of the armed forces. A comprehensive vaccination program for military personnel was designed and implemented toward the end of the war, in 1945. The program was based on a combination of civilian and military medicine. Vaccination against influenza worked, and the tide was turning—or so it seemed.

A MOVING TARGET

In February 1947, military doctors at Fort Monmouth, an army training camp in New Jersey, witnessed an epidemic among young recruits. A few months earlier, doctors had noticed a sharp rise in respiratory illness among American troops stationed in Japan and Korea. Although clinically mild, these out-breaks of influenza were nonetheless perceived as exceptional for two reasons. First, the virus responsible for the disease was difficult to identify in the laboratory, and second, the promising vaccine introduced a few years earlier by the U.S. Army turned out to be almost completely ineffective both in the armed services and among the general public, where it was used after 1945.[60] To the considerable consternation of the microbe farmers, the protection, which had been so effective previously, suddenly seemed to fail completely. As it turned out, the virus was difficult to identify because it differed substantially from strains that had circulated earlier. Significantly, these older strains had also been used for the production of the vaccine.[61] Confronted with a striking failure of immunization, microbiologists suggested that a new strain of the virus had caused the 1947 outbreak. Due to the significant shift in the structure, the new strain was eventually designated as a new subtype of the influenza virus and was thus set apart from viruses that had been spreading before 1947. A certain degree of variation among influenza viruses had been noticed before, but never had such a substantial change been observed. It came as no surprise, then, that the 1945 vaccine barely protected the army's immunized troops.

The spectacular success of the vaccine introduced in 1945 was thus short-lived. John Eyler notes that the failure "forced researchers to reconsider the growing evidence of antigenic variation and challenged the model of the virus that had been taken for granted."[62] Researchers initially suggested that antigenic variation was irrelevant for the production of an effective vaccine, but they were wrong. Over the following years, microbe farmers became increasingly concerned with the changing nature of the virus, and they began to study the extent of the variation more systematically. The virus that they had been growing in the laboratory and preserving in the test tube turned out to be a biological thing living in time. Researchers recognized that they could not simply ignore this observation. They wondered whether the change was regular or irregular and whether the variation was finite or infinite. A regular change and a finite variation, they reasoned, would make protection by immunization possible and practical. Yet the more change and the more variation they detected, the less likely they were to produce a successful vaccine and eradicate the disease. The plasticity of the virus, its ability to infect bodies and accommodate changing environments, allowed microbe farmers to transfer the virus to the laboratory, but it also made it difficult for them to develop an effective vaccine. The microbe was a living thing, a moving target that was less stable than it seemed when it was isolated for the first time. As Fred Davenport, Thomas Francis's colleague and successor as director of the Army's Commission on Influenza, noted, the ability of the virus to change "implies that the future of vaccination against influenza should consist of an endless series of crash programs designed to capture, bottle, and distribute each new minor antigenic villain as he mounts the stage."[63] Facing an elusive biological entity, microbe farmers worried that their attempts to control the disease were bound to be too slow and too late: The conquest of the disease was far from close. The vaccine provided a momentary sense of success, but its failure raised new questions about the ontological status of the virus.

BORROWED LIFE

"The man in the street," remarked French microbiologist and Nobel prize winner André Lwoff in a 1957 lecture, "generally considers viruses as the dangerous agents of infectious diseases."[64] Certainly this common understanding of the characteristic nature of viruses is not completely mistaken. But it is not here, in the popular perception of infectious diseases and their presumed causes, where the real danger lies. The real danger, Lwoff proposed in his third Marjory Stephenson Memorial Lecture, actually lies with the scientists. If one systematically studies their publications to better understand the concept of the virus, one gradually reaches, Lwoff observed, "a sort of feeling of the possible existence of some slight theoretical misunderstandings amongst virologists in which it may be dangerous to be involved." At stake, according to the microbiologist, is a crucial, "highly treacherous" notion: the notion of life.[65]

The purpose of Lwoff's lecture was to address the hotly contested nature of viruses. The ontological status of the virus remained a source of heated debate in microbiology. Some microbe farmers, among them several prominent influenza researchers, were convinced that viruses were living organisms, biological entities with basic characteristics of living things.[66] Others, by contrast, felt that viruses should primarily be considered inert chemical molecules. A third group, Lwoff noted, suggested that "statements that viruses are small organisms should be regarded with as much suspicion as statements that they are simply molecules."[67] But if viruses are neither living organisms nor inert molecules, what is their nature? What kind of things are viruses if they are neither living biological entities nor dead chemical substances?

What is the place of these peculiar bodies in the order of nature, and what is their relation to other biological forms of life? "My ambition," declared Lwoff in his lecture, "is to show that the word virus has a meaning." Tackling the problem of the nature of viruses in the hope that there was a definite answer to the question, Lwoff offered an oracular response: "Viruses should be considered as viruses because viruses are viruses."[68]

At the time of Lwoff's lecture, in the late 1950s, a large number of viruses had been isolated in the laboratory. It had increasingly become possible to measure these minute microbial things with a fair degree of accuracy, and some had even been crystallized and rendered visible by means of powerful microscopes.[69] Viruses were chemically purified in the centrifuge and were grown outside the animal body in chicken eggs and tissue cultures. They were dried and stored without significant loss of their pathogenic properties and had thus become available as objects of experimental research over a long period of time. Not surprisingly, the relevant scientific literature expanded exponentially in these decades.

Yet with all the knowledge, an observer remarked in 1938, "it is still not possible to pronounce with certainty on the nature of these agents." What kind of thing are viruses? How can they be defined? "Despite the fact that the solution of this question is not material to the study of most virus problems, it is of such abiding interest that virus workers continue to search for the answer."[70] By the end of the 1950s, as Lwoff's lecture indicates, the microbe farmers were still discussing the question.

The ambiguous place of the virus in the order of nature and the difficulty in deciding whether it is an animate or inanimate entity were due to the fact that the virus manifested some characteristics of living beings. As Edwin Lennette underscored in a 1943 article, "because the infectious agents classified as viruses possess the capacity to multiply or reproduce, because they showed marked specificity under natural conditions for certain hosts and tissues, are able to adapt themselves to new environmental conditions and to undergo variation, it is customary to regard them as living organisms."[71] The fact that viruses can multiply rapidly and adapt systematically to changing circumstances suggests that they are living things. The fact, however, that they can multiply, mutate, and adapt only in the presence of living cells suggests that they are not autonomous organisms. Furthermore, viruses are also unable to perform essential metabolic functions.

Lwoff's enigmatic response—considering viruses as neither living organisms nor small molecules—was inspired by the emerging vision of molecular biology. Viruses, according to Lwoff, are unique. They are "infectious, potentially pathogenic, nucleoproteinic entities possessing only one type of nucleic acid, which are reproduced from their genetic material, are unable to grow and to undergo binary fission, and are devoid of a Lipmann system."[72] The purpose of Lwoff's definition of the modern concept of the virus was to resolve the problem of the nature of viruses by foregrounding the uniqueness of these strange entities in the order of nature.

Ever since microbiologists began investigating viruses in the laboratory as discrete objects that can be known, they have struggled with the peculiar nature of these entities. David Napier notes that microbiologists tend to ascribe notions of agency, mobility, and intentionality to viruses precisely because there is no straightforward answer to the ontological question.[73] The construction and stabilization of a complex material infrastructure for the generation and reproduction of microbial matter made the virus concrete as an object of scientific investigation. This infrastructure not only facilitated the cultivation of microorganisms but also simultaneously provoked the fundamental ontological question: What kind of things are viruses? In this chapter, we have seen how researchers established a complex experimental system, creating a fertile ground for the scientific examination of the influenza virus and the control of infectious disease at the crossroads of civilian and military medicine. Reproducing viruses in an animal species raised specifically for this purpose, microbiologists refined their skills of microbe farming. This virtuosity in the practical art of growing bugs and testing bodies was indispensable for the kind of expertise they claimed. What microbiologists revealed at the threshold of the living and the nonliving turned out to be an organic entity with a potential for life, a creature on the verge of the vital. The nature of this creature made it difficult for microbiologists to reproduce it under artificial conditions. The virus did not grow in the lifeless media of bacteriologists; it could not reproduce on its own and required the active support of a living body. Its life turned out to be contingent on someone else's life.

Galvanizing both the scientific and the popular imagination, the peculiar nature of the virus contributed to the growing fascination with the battle against infectious disease. As a material object, the virus provided a powerful foundation for the production of knowledge and the accumulation of facts. The pathogenic agent reached a threshold of positivity and made it possible for microbiologists to establish a testing ground for new forms of treatment and prevention. Challenging the clinic's diagnostic authority, the laboratory turned into a privileged place and became the final arbiter for the determination of disease, allowing microbiologists to design strategies to control the contagion. It is important to note that the success of these strategies remained precarious ever since the virus was isolated for the first time. The ontological conception of the normal and the pathological and the constitution of the virus as the cause of disease established the dominance of the laboratory over the clinic, but they also prompted further questions about the nature of the microbial creature.

Microbe farmers stabilized the influenza virus as an object of scientific investigation only to see that stability crumbling. What scientists presented as a determining factor turned out to be a moving target that seemed to require a series of crash programs. The reduction of disease to the infectious agent ushered in a series of difficulties, complexities, and ambiguities that have troubled microbiologists ever since the influenza virus was first identified in the laboratory. Microbe farmers envisioned the virus as single decisive factor that would settle conclusively the identity of disease; it is the thing that ultimately determines whether a patient has flu or not. But this thing turned out to be so unstable und unreliable that it threatened to unsettle as much as it settled. The following chapters examine in more detail what it means to make an entity as elusive and erratic as the influenza virus the determining factor of disease. It was not the ontological conception of the normal and the pathological as such that inspired prophetic proclamations in the second half of the twentieth century. What made this mode of speech effective were the ambiguities that microbiologists encountered in the pursuit of their ontological conception. Scientifically inspired prophecy, pronounced by charismatic personalities with institutional authority, arose as an important response to scientifically generated ambiguity. The promise of prophetic appropriation was disambiguation. "This is how it is ..."

In February 1938, *Collier's Magazine*, a popular American weekly featured a report on recent achievements in the microbiological investigation of influenza. "What does all of this mean to you?" the article queried. "Simply this: that research men ... have flu on the run."[74]

TWO

———

On the Run

IN A GUEST EDITORIAL carried by the *New York Times* on February 13, 1976, Dr. Edwin D. Kilbourne observed, "World-wide epidemics, or pandemics, of influenza have marked the end of every decade since the 1940's—at intervals of exactly eleven years—1946, 1957 and 1968. A perhaps simplistic reading of this immediate past," he continued, "tells us that 11 plus 1968 is 1979."[1] According to the scientist's prophetic proclamation, the world was due for another pandemic. Inspired by the stunning regularity that a numerological consideration of the recent past presumably revealed, Kilbourne made a scientifically inspired prophecy of things to come, offering his contemporaries, as befits all true prophets (according to Max Weber), an ethical message for free, namely to "plan without further delay for an imminent natural disaster."[2] Of course, Kilbourne, the founding chairman of Mount Sinai's Microbiology Department, was not a solitary voice preaching in the wilderness; his growing sense of urgency was based on the assumption of pandemic cycles and was shared among his colleagues. Indeed, the prophetic op-ed article gave voice to the general understanding dominant at the time among influenza experts that a global outbreak was likely to occur in the near future. As the late David Sencer, Kilbourne's friend and director of the CDC from 1966 to 1977 told me in an interview, "there was general consensus among the fluologists at the time that a shift in the virus was imminent."[3] The sense of urgency that fluologists shared was expressed by the hyperbolic headline and the ghostly cartoon that ran alongside Kilbourne's article in the *New York Times*. A few months later, after a series of unfortunate incidents, Kilbourne deeply regretted that he had gone public with his ominous foreboding of imminent disaster.

The editorial's dramatic headline, "Flu to the Starboard! Man the Harpoons! Fill 'em with Vaccine! Get the Captain! Hurry!" and the spectacular

FIGURE 10. "Flu to the Starboard! Man the Harpoons! Fill 'em with Vaccine! Get the Captain! Hurry!" Cartoon published alongside Edwin D. Kilbourne's prophetic guest editorial. *New York Times*, February 13, 1976.

illustration suggested a confrontation of biblical proportions; the sensational framing of the coming plague, as Kilbourne complained to me, "presaged later ridicule" on the editorial pages of the *New York Times* when the anxiously anticipated pandemic failed to materialize and "a valid effort in public health was branded a disaster," as he put it. "Better a vaccine without a pandemic than a pandemic without a vaccine," the prophet pointed out in response to later criticism.

Of course, the microbiologist was not responsible for the headline and the selection of the cartoon. But Kilbourne's article contained rhetorical features borrowed from the genre of apocalyptic writing that made it suitable for dramatic elaboration. Among these features are the association of numbers with events, the revelation of historical patterns, the logic of the countdown, and the concern with the end of decades.[4] As a consequence, Kilbourne's scientific prophecy of imminent disaster articulated a millennialist sensibility attuned to the apocalyptic. It made room for a dramatic reading of the guest editorial.

This chapter highlights an important episode in the history of influenza. Focusing on microbiological research in the second half of the twentieth century, it demonstrates how scientific speculations about a virus established a prophetic scene in the United States. This scene was based on stories that were organized around apocalyptic tropes; it expanded considerably over the decades, as we will see in subsequent chapters. In this chapter, I focus on the role of "types" and "cycles" in the making of "crisis," a dramatic form of temporality essential for the prophetic orientation and its preoccupation with the coming plague. As a distinctive structure of temporal experience, crisis has important consequences for the manifestation of the coming plague. It makes an *imminent* event *immanent*; that is, it creates the perception of an event as already in the process of happening even though it is yet to come. A profound sense of instability and insecurity takes root, a feeling that can result in sweeping interventions.[5] "Crisis is seductive in its very conception," writes Peter Redfield.[6] "The term . . . implies a condition of instability or a moment of decisive change. Within crisis, time contracts and one inhabits the present as intimately as possible."[7] Charged with acute meaning, the present achieves a sense of urgency. This condition of instability and moment of decisive change "is the purest environment for a technical expert,"[8] whose task is to watch the world for warning signs. At stake, in a situation of crisis, are matters of life and death.

ROLL UP YOUR SLEEVE, AMERICA!

In January 1976, military doctors faced an explosive epidemic of influenza at an army training center in New Jersey. Subsequent laboratory studies revealed that some of the recruits had been infected with a type of influenza typically found not in humans, but in swine. Experts and officials were alarmed. Faced with an infectious agent that seemed to have crossed the species barrier, they argued that the nation might be on the verge of a devastating pandemic with the potential to kill millions of Americans. The appearance of the virus was troubling and called for decisive action to protect the population. Running for reelection, U.S. President Ford took these concerns seriously and launched an unprecedented immunization campaign in March 1976. The ambitious aim of the national campaign was to protect 200 million Americans against the virus before the end of the year. The U.S. Congress approved the program, pharmaceutical companies manufactured a vaccine, and clinical trials were conducted before flu shots were administered across the country. When a growing number of severe side effects occurred that seemed to be linked to the immunization program, newspaper articles began to raise questions about the vaccine's safety. Journalists wondered whether the cure might be worse than the disease. The program was stopped, and the predicted pandemic never occurred.

It was only after the publication of the guest editorial with its scientifically inspired prophetic message that Kilbourne learned from his former research fellow, Dr. Martin Goldfield, of the sudden spread of the swine flu virus in New Jersey. This episode, deplorable by some accounts, disastrous by others, went down in the nation's history as the swine flu affair. "It gave public health a very bad name in many circles," a public health professional recalled in a discussion with me. Experts and officials were accused of having overconfidence in theories and failing to address uncertainties.[9] Over the following years, funding for public health was cut.

The swine flu affair is an intriguing episode that coincidentally began the very next day after Kilbourne's *New York Times* editorial was published, with the CDC convening an emergency meeting in Atlanta.[10] Among the participants at this meeting on February 14, 1976, were representatives of the U.S. Army, the Food and Drug Administration, the National Institutes of Health, and the State of New Jersey Department of Health. The CDC called the meeting to discuss the isolation of the new virus and assess the current situation. Kilbourne's ominous foreboding, published on Friday, had thus become plausible on Saturday. The projected pandemic seemed on schedule.

A month earlier, on January 5, military instruction had resumed after a holiday break at Fort Dix, a training center for army recruits in New Jersey. According to army doctors, the weather was cold and the reception facility crowded.[11] A few days after the arrival of the new recruits, an epidemic of acute respiratory disease broke out at the base. A rapidly growing number of recruits reported sick. Physicians quickly began to gather specimens from patients and notified the New Jersey Health Department. Most of the patient specimens delivered to the state laboratory contained a contemporary strain of the influenza virus, which had been circulating since 1968. Yet some specimens could not be identified immediately and were thus sent on to the CDC in Atlanta for further investigation. On February 4, a sick recruit left his bed and went on a long run; he collapsed and passed away with acute respiratory disease. On February 10, additional patient samples were delivered to Atlanta. A few days later, laboratory evidence finally confirmed that two different types of the influenza virus were spreading at Fort Dix. One of them was not typically found in humans, but in swine populations of the Midwest.

A meticulous retrospective investigation conducted at the army base revealed that up to 230 recruits seemed to have caught "swine flu." Alarmed by the appearance of the new virus and its spread among military personnel, microbiologists warned that a potentially devastating pandemic was looming on the horizon. Given the general understanding prevailing among scientists at the time—that pandemics tended to occur at regular cycles of approximately ten years—the outbreak at Fort Dix was troubling indeed. These locally isolated cases of infection, scientists reasoned, might well represent an ominous sign of impending disaster, perhaps of the scope of the great pandemic of 1918. However, there seemed to be time enough to respond and intervene, to be faster than the virus, and perhaps even prevent the disease by vaccination. "If we believe in prevention, we have no alternative but to offer and urge the immunization of the population," a member of the government's Advisory Committee on Immunization Practices declared.[12] The catastrophic event that seemed to be happening even though it was yet to come gave officials unusual lead time to prepare for the pandemic and protect the population.

Despite the fact that the swine flu outbreak in New Jersey had caused only one fatality and that the local epidemic had been fully contained by March, experts recommended a national mass vaccination program to protect Americans. They believed that the world had been offered a splendid opportunity to prove the power of preventive medicine and demonstrate the significance of the public health mission. According to Kilbourne, the program was a "gamble with no guarantees," but it would be irresponsible to ignore the possibility of saving thousands of lives.[13] For the first time in the history of humanity, the microbe farmer observed, it might be possible to outwit the virus, prevent a pandemic, and overcome the "last great plague of man." President Ford heeded the advice of his experts and announced a vaccination campaign of unprecedented scope, the National Influenza Immunization Program, on March 24. The ambitious goal of the largest vaccination program in American history was to immunize the entire U.S. population for swine flu before December. The sweeping $135 million program, designed in response to the outbreak at the army base, was announced with the "fervor of a declaration of war," as an article in *Time Magazine* phrased it. The program involved the most extensive field trial of flu shots ever conducted.[14]

Meanwhile, British scientists at the Common Cold Unit at Harvard Hospital in Salisbury had designed a risky test, in which they injected six people with a cultured strain of the New Jersey swine flu virus. In an article published in early July 1976 in *The Lancet*, the British scientists concluded from the experiment that the swine flu virus appeared to be less pathogenic in humans than regular seasonal flu. According to the researchers, it seemed possible that the outbreak at the army base was an isolated incident and that the virus "will not become established in man."[15] Dr. Charles Stuart-Harris of the University of Sheffield concurred in an editorial published in the same issue of *The Lancet*, underscoring that it was highly questionable whether vaccines "should be prepared at the present time for any country, including the United States, until the shape of things to come can be seen more clearly."[16] Scientists in other European countries were equally reluctant, as were public health officials at the World Health Organization (WHO) in Geneva. In a statement released in March, the WHO argued that "it is impossible at this time to predict whether [the swine flu virus] will spread since from previous experience it is known that some strains spread rapidly and others do not."[17] In April, a group of experts gathered in Geneva to discuss the situation; they recommended a "wait and see" policy.[18] These experts thus came to a different conclusion and were much more reluctant to initiate a large-scale vaccination program than their American counterparts.

In the United States, a vaccine was soon produced, but manufacturers encountered technical problems and pressed the U.S. government to grant them unlimited protection from future liability claims. A controversial debate about liability for injuries in mass vaccination programs unfolded.[19] Clinical trials with the new vaccine revealed that children in fact required two flu shots to develop sufficient immunity. Shortly after the start of the immunization campaign in October 1976, which was promoted under the slogan "No flu! Roll up your sleeve, America," a series of reports documented an increase in the number of cases of Guillain-Barré syndrome, a severe neurological disorder. Significantly, the disorder seemed to appear primarily among persons who had just received a flu shot.[20] Confronted with mounting numbers of the syndrome—a total of 535 confirmed cases, including 23 deaths—and no evidence of the pandemic, public health officials suspended the ambitious vaccination program in December 1976. A few months later, the National Influenza Immunization Program was formally ended, and the dreaded pandemic never occurred. In retrospect, Kilbourne wondered, "Now, with no epidemic in immediate prospect, the question arises, have we this time run too far and too fast in our periodic race with influenza, rather than too slow and too late, as is our wont?"[21] Indeed the race with influenza had increasingly become a race against time. In 1976, this race occurred in a situation of crisis and was ruled by speed and urgency. Observing ominous portents of imminent disaster, American experts faced a pressing matter of life and death and recommended a program to immunize the entire population; they took rapid action, leaped over the present, and rushed forward to the conclusion. They succumbed, in Jacques Lacan's terminology, to the "haste function."[22]

The temporary appearance of the virus at the military base had resulted in a local epidemic of respiratory illness; in other words, a minor incident in the natural history of human infection. How, then, was it possible for this incident to become so powerful, encouraging American experts to prevent a pandemic that never occurred? What made it possible for the scientifically inspired prophecy to gain traction and authorize an extensive immunization program to prevent a catastrophic pandemic? What propelled public health professionals to take their chances and propose a "gamble with no guarantees"? To understand what happened, we must explore the virus itself in much more detail. How was it possible for this microbial creature to cause so much concern, create a profound sense of insecurity, and trigger a dramatic intervention? What kind of microbial nature, cultured in the test tube, nurtured the prophetic vision of things to come?

The swine flu virus was isolated for the first time in a laboratory in the early 1930s and had been preserved in the freezer ever since. Notably, the virus had immediately become the subject of a particular interpretation among microbiologists, and it was on the basis of this reading that the virus acquired its extraordinary significance, its dramatic function. Representing a particular type of influenza, the swine flu virus circulated in the world of experts as an important referent with a particular meaning. Microbe farmers linked the virus, originally isolated in Midwestern pig populations, with the deadliest pandemic in human history, the pandemic of 1918. It is crucial to explore in detail the constitution of this link to understand how a speculative framework charged the microbial creature with ominous meaning, created the specter of a possible pandemic, and produced the sense of an important turning point. Such an exploration also allows us to situate the immunization campaign in relation to a perception of history as prophecy. It was a particular understanding of the past that allowed microbiologists to see the present as a critical moment of decisive change and to rush forward to the conclusion.

The battle against the bug became a race against time. In the next section I show how microbe farmers aligned "swine flu" with "human flu."

OF SWINE FLU AND HOG CHOLERA

Swine flu became an acute concern for Midwestern farmers in late 1918, when humans and animals were perishing in the thousands during the great pandemic. In a 1921 edition of *Wallaces Farmer*, a weekly magazine promoting "Good Farming, Clear Thinking, Right Living," Dr. Charles Murray, professor of veterinary medicine at Iowa State College, reminded his readers that pandemic influenza "swept the country in 1918, and thousands died from the accompanying pneumonia. . . . Paralleling this disease of the human race there occurred an epizootic of the swine of the Mississippi valley and parts of the eastern United States."[23] He continued, "The so-called swine 'flu' [has been] one of the most serious causes of loss from disease in swine herds in the last two years."[24] Swine flu was thus recognized as a pathological condition affecting animal populations during the devastating 1918 pandemic.[25] Unfortunately, as Murray underscored in his article, the disease in swine was given the name of "flu," a term "which caused much apprehension among the agricultural people who were led to belief through the similarity of names that the diseases were of the same cause."[26] For the professor of veterinary medicine, however, the two pathological conditions were far from identical. Among farmers, swine flu had become so popular a term that they were drawn "to assign all puzzling cases of disease in swine to the classification of 'flu,' and many a hog has died from cholera or from some other disease because his case has been diagnosed as 'flu,' and he has been treated for that disease." Murray concluded that the "important thing to keep in mind is the necessity of accurate diagnosis. The owner should not be satisfied with his own judgment in the matter of diagnosis, but should consult a competent veterinarian."[27]

But even the most competent veterinarians, alas, could not always be so sure then about what kind of disease they were facing in the field. The virus was still invisible at the time, and an accurate diagnosis remained virtually out of reach. A 1922 issue of the *Journal of the American Veterinary Medical Association* concluded that a broad range of swine diseases exist and that veterinarians often find themselves "very much at sea as to what the trouble really is."[28] It was Dr. J. S. Koen, a hog cholera inspector of the Bureau of Animal Industry in the U.S. Department of Agriculture, who first recognized that the disease was "different from any that he had previously encountered." In fact, Koen was so impressed by the almost simultaneous spread of the disease in humans and nonhumans that he became convinced that the two conditions actually were the same. He thus gave the name of "influenza" to the new disease.[29] The conspicuous coincidence in the prevalence of the two conditions and the striking similarity of symptoms suggested to Koen that he was really observing the very same disease. In 1919 Koen clearly stated, "I believe I have as much to support this diagnosis in pigs as the physicians have to support a similar diagnosis in man. The similarity . . . among people and . . . among pigs was so close, the reports so frequent that an outbreak in the family would be followed immediately by an outbreak among hogs, and vice versa. . . . It looked like 'flu,' and it presented the identical symptoms of the 'flu' and, until proved it was not 'flu,' I shall stand by that diagnosis."[30] Subsequent observations, however, as argued by M. Dorset, C. N. McBryde, and W. B. Niles of the Biochemic Division of the Bureau of Animal Industry in Washington, DC, were unable to substantiate Koen's controversial claim. "[T]he continued and apparently unabated prevalence of 'hog flu,' taken together with the marked decrease in human influenza during the past two or three years, leaves little ground for the belief that there is a relationship between the two diseases," McBryde and his colleagues concluded.[31] As an editorial in a 1923 edition of *Veterinary Medicine* maintained, the term "swine flu" has been applied to a disease "that has been common in swine in sections of the United States since the fall of 1918. The name 'flu' was suggested because of the similarity of the symptoms of this disease and those of influenza in the human. There is, however, no relation between 'flu" in swine and influenza in the human."[32]

A few years later, however, McBryde revised his opinion, inspired by an unfortunate personal experience that exposed him to the influence of influenza. During an investigation of sick swine in a small town in southeastern Iowa, McBryde encountered the contagious agent at a farm. As he laconically remarked, "With fifty to a hundred hogs coughing violently in a dusty barn, the breathing of the contaminated dusty atmosphere by a human being would certainly afford an excellent opportunity for infection."[33] A few days later, McBryde suffered from a loss of appetite. A sudden pain in the back, a dry cough, and a slight fever followed. "This indisposition," McBryde observed, "was so entirely different from the usual run of colds and was so similar in its sudden onset and in some of its symptoms to swine flu, that the writer has been rather inclined to think it must have been a respiratory infection acquired as a result of breathing the dusty atmosphere of the hog barns occupied by swine suffering from acute hog flu."[34] Thus, due to an accidental infection, "hog cholera" eventually became "swine flu."

In the early 1930s, McBryde's conclusion was scientifically validated by a series of experimental investigations conducted by animal pathologist Dr. Richard E. Shope of the Rockefeller Institute for Medical Research in Princeton, New Jersey. Shope, a "born naturalist," as a colleague remarked, was from the Midwest, born in Des Moines, Iowa, in 1901.[35] On completion of medical school, Shope investigated tuberculosis in the laboratories of the Rockefeller Institute at Princeton, working under Paul Lewis. In 1928, Lewis sent Shope to his native Iowa to study a dramatic epidemic of hog cholera. In the field, Shope indeed found sick swine all over the place, suffering, as it turned out, from swine flu. The pathologist immediately autopsied a number of animals and pressed a few small pieces of lung tissue into tubes packed in iced thermos jugs, which he then shipped to the Rockefeller Institute. In the laboratory, Shope managed to infect swine with filtrates of the infectious material isolated in Iowa.[36] As he noted, because of the "highly contagious nature of the disease it has been necessary to exercise extreme precaution in the isolation of individual experimental animals."[37] Significantly, Shope was able to experiment on locally raised animals, which turned out to be more susceptible to the disease because swine flu happened to be much less prevalent on the East Coast than in the Midwest with its huge farms and large swine populations.

Once the swine flu virus was identified in the laboratory, microbe farmers immediately compared it with influenza viruses isolated from humans. Experimental tests conducted by Shope in the United States and by Smith, Andrewes, and Laidlaw in the United Kingdom revealed that these viruses were similar, though not identical.[38] Pigs, moreover, were shown to be readily susceptible to infection with flu viruses derived from humans.[39] On the basis of these results, both Shope and Laidlaw suggested that swine flu might actually have originated in 1918, at the time of the great pandemic that killed millions of people.[40] As Laidlaw remarked in 1935, "It seems to me, indeed, exceedingly probable that the virus of swine influenza is really the virus of the great pandemic of 1918 adapted to the pig and persisting in that species ever since."[41] The pandemic virus that killed between twenty and fifty million people worldwide, Laidlaw speculated, had probably been transmitted from humans to pigs in 1918. Shope concurred, arguing that it was necessary "to consider seriously the theory that swine influenza virus represents a surviving form of the human pandemic virus of 1918, and that it has not had its immunological identity detectably altered by its prolonged sojourn in hogs."[42] As a *New York Sun* article put it in 1939, "Shope is inclined to deduce from serologic evidence that the virus of swine influenza is a surviving variety of the agent primarily responsible for the great human pandemic of 1918."[43]

As these remarks show, the swine flu virus appeared as a "surviving agent," a "living fossil." Significantly, the presumable discovery of a direct descendant of the pandemic virus and its preservation in an animal population created the conditions of possibility for speculating about a return of the virus and a repetition of the disease. The "fossil," after all, was "alive," not in humans but in swine. Thus, there was the theoretical possibility that this type of influenza virus might come back one day and infect humans again. Indeed, prophetic ruminations about a possible return of the virus surfaced regularly in the scientific publications of microbe farmers. For instance, in a 1955 article published in the *Journal of Immunology*, influenza researchers proposed that "a virus similar antigenically to swine influenza may be the first variant to become widely prevalent."[44] The U.S. Army, with its traumatic experience of pandemic disease at the end of World War I, took these concerns very seriously by including swine antigens in the mandatory vaccine that it used between 1955 and 1969 to protect military personnel from a potential pandemic.[45] In 1973, influenza researchers pondered the possibility of a cyclic recurrence of influenza viruses and predicted the "emergence in man of a Swine-like virus about 1985–1991."[46] In their article, the researchers offered a scientifically inspired prophecy of things to come, urging public health professionals to consider seriously "the matter of being prepared to produce Swine virus vaccine rapidly."[47] A few years later, pharmaceutical companies were ready to produce a vaccine, but for a pandemic that never occurred.

IN THE INTERVAL

The possibility was raised today that the virus that caused the greatest world epidemic of influenza in modern history—the pandemic of 1918—may have returned.

New York Times, FEBRUARY 20, 1976

In contrast to other viruses, the swine flu virus was perceived as a particular type of pathogenic agent, one that foreshadowed the event of a coming plague.

Once the virus was detected in the bodies of soldiers at Fort Dix, the outbreak was considered a significant sign, announcing the advent of a future event and the fulfillment of a prophecy. As an article in *Time Magazine* reported in April 1976, "medical experts are concerned that the virus usually seen only in swine, may be similar to the lethal virus that probably caused some 20 million deaths."[48] President Ford's immunization campaign was described as an important step to prevent "a repetition of that disaster."[49]

Concerns about the disease were thus energized not just by the fear of a catastrophic event but also by the prospect of a tragic repetition. A senior government official noted the following in an internal report: "There is evidence there will be a major flu epidemic this coming fall. The indication is that we will see a return of the 1918 flu virus that is the most virulent form of flu. In 1918 a half million people died. The projections are that this virus will kill one million Americans in 1976."[50] An obscure and minor epidemic of respiratory illness at a military training center was systematically linked with a traumatic experience in the nation's history and thus acquired the concrete and dramatic actuality of a critical moment of decisive change. In this critical moment, recollections of the past and anticipations of the future became almost indistinguishable. As we have seen, the microbe farmers who cultured the virus in the laboratory had already predicted the return of the "living fossil." The frightening prospect created a sense of urgency that ultimately resulted in the government's decision to rush forward to the conclusion, anticipate the pandemic, and vaccinate the population.

Frank Kermode, in *The Sense of an Ending*, writes about the interval as a period of time between a beginning and an end. The interval constitutes a distinctive experience of temporality "purged of simple chronicity, of the emptiness of . . . humanly uninteresting successiveness."[51] Kermode argues that there is an existential need for coherence and comprehension, a need to make sense of human life. "To make sense of our lives from where we are, as it were, stranded in the middle, we need fictions of beginnings and fictions of ends, fictions which unite beginning and end and endow the interval between them with meaning."[52] A form of time "conceived of as simply successive becomes charged with past and future: what was *chronos* becomes *kairos*." *Chronos,* Kermode explains, "is 'passing time' or 'waiting time' . . . and *kairos* is the season, a point in time filled with significance, charged with a meaning derived from its relation to the end."[53] *Kairos,* in other words, is a time of crisis, a turning point. It brings the past, the present, and the future into a meaningful relation, offering significance to mere successiveness.

The notion of *kairos*—a special time or season that stands out as different from ordinary or passing time—is insightful not only because it illuminates the temporality of crisis and its distinctive character but also because it shows how this intensive experience of time is able to create opportunities for intervention. *Kairos* is the time when events acquire a prophetic aura, when new possibilities for action arise, when there is a growing sense that actors need to seize the moment and change the course of history. Here, the structure of imagination swerves away from the apocalyptic and turns toward the more properly dramatic.[54] This turn is important for a number of reasons, not least because it leaves room for the figure of the scientist to take on the role as heroic agent in the cosmic drama.

As historian James Colgrove observes, in the 1960s and 1970s "the elusive dream of utterly eliminating one or more infectious diseases came closer to being a reality than ever before, and a spirit of 'eradicationism' took center stage in vaccination policy."[55] Smallpox and diphtheria had disappeared almost completely in the United States, and the number of cases of polio declined dramatically. In 1966, the federal government expanded its financial support and launched a national immunization campaign to control measles, a program that gradually reduced cases of infection. Faith in the power of vaccination was at its apex, even though social conditions and continuing limitations of the health care system periodically resulted in the resurgence of infectious diseases, especially among the marginal and the poor.[56] An optimistic technocratic vision of epidemic control prevailed among scientists at the time. Heroic accounts of final conquest proliferated. For example, in 1961 a *Science* article boldly declared, "[W]e can look forward with confidence to a considerable degree of freedom from infectious diseases at a time not too far in the future."[57] In 1969, the U.S. Surgeon General suggested that it "is time to close the book on infectious diseases and declare the war against pestilence won." In 1974, the *New York Times* mused that "the day when, in reality, nobody gets the flu could be at hand."[58] As these confident pronouncements show, the tide was turning and victory in the battle against germs was thought to be close. Scientists, journalists, and government officials believed that the spectacular promise of preventive medicine was about to be fulfilled.

But the reality of epidemic control was much more complex. As Kilbourne and his colleagues observed in a 1974 publication, "utilization of influenza vaccines by the medical profession and acceptance of immunization by the public have been so poor that the epidemic course of the disease, even in technologically advanced societies, remains essentially uninfluenced by human intervention."[59] Despite immunization, the virus continued to circulate. The vaccine's "underutilization" was attributed to the "misunderstood" nature of the disease, the periodic changes in the virus, and regular problems with vaccine supply and demand in a system largely controlled by unpredictable market forces. Kilbourne accordingly suggested that "steps must be taken immediately to insure an adequate and predictable supply of vaccine." Additionally, the medical profession "must be educated in the value and importance of immunization against influenza."[60] It was a serious disease, not just the usual cold.

When the swine flu virus appeared at the military training center, scientists suggested that it was a unique opportunity to "educate" the medical profession about the pandemic threat and the importance of immunization. They argued that it might have become possible, for the first time in history, to effectively change the course of the disease and contain a pandemic. "Man has never been able to intervene effectively to prevent the morbidity and mortality accompanying the emergence of a major influenza variant, but that opportunity may soon come," scientists declared.[61] When the swine flu virus emerged it came into view as a test site for strategies of control; it provided an occasion to vaccinate Americans against influenza and perhaps even overcome the "last great plague of man." In contrast to the eradication of smallpox, polio, and measles, "[n]o comparable effort against flu has ever been made before," a journalist emphasized in March 1976.[62] The campaign would finally raise the profile of the flu and place it alongside other major infectious diseases, for which national immunization programs already existed. Kilbourne, the leading microbe farmer and vaccine innovator, was keen "to make the country see the virtues of preventive medicine."[63] Even though he expected a mild pandemic, initiating a vaccination campaign seemed an important opportunity to strike a blow for preventive medicine and demonstrate the power of a coordinated public health intervention. In his prophetic op-ed article published in February 1976, Kilbourne reminded his readers that "whenever pandemic influenza next appears, we must improve upon our well-intentioned but uncoordinated individual efforts of the past that have resulted in ambiguous advice to the public and inadequate production and maldistribution of vaccine."[64] The pandemic threat required a timely, vigorous, and coherent response. "The real question," Kilbourne declared, "is why the hell didn't we do something like this before when we had early indicators? Society and government did too little, too late during those pandemics."[65] Now was the time to do more and to do it faster. Now was the time to act with speed and urgency. Now was the time to take advantage of scientific research, protect the population, and hit the moving target.

Pandemics had occurred before, in 1957 and 1968, but there had never been enough time to produce a vaccine and immunize the population in advance. Suddenly there seemed to be time to implement a systematic and comprehensive intervention. As microbiologists maintained, the "unprecedented effort to immunize a large majority of the population against influenza will at the very least provide an opportunity to learn how well the voluntary efforts of the medical profession and citizenry can meet the challenge of pandemic influenza, given the availability of an effective vaccine. It can also lead the way to better acceptance and usage of the present vaccines in interpandemic years."[66] The mass vaccination campaign was thus perceived as an important contribution to public health advocacy; moreover, it was a unique opportunity to test the feasibility of a large-scale intervention. Kilbourne felt that "never in the past had we properly addressed a major epidemic with adequate immunization."[67] Scientists saw swine flu as a chance to advance the "state of enlightenment of the community and its practitioners of medicine concerning the nature of influenza and its prevention."[68] The severity of disease, the availability of technology, and having the lead time required for effective immunization seemed to justify the program.

Figurative interpretations charged the virus and the vaccine with meaning and significance. In 1976, two figures were important. One was dreadful: the "living fossil" threatening to reappear and cause a catastrophic pandemic. The other figure, by contrast, was more optimistic: It was that of a powerful vaccine presumed to protect the population against the return of the deadly germ. The two figures transformed the present into a dramatic moment of fulfillment, both of the prophecies that microbe farmers had pronounced over decades about a virus and its eventual return, and of the promises of public health campaigns to control disease, protect populations, and prevent pandemics.

DOUBTING THOMAS

In the United States, the national immunization campaign had only a handful of detractors. Peter Palese was among them. One day in his office at Mount Sinai, I asked him about the swine flu affair. He stood up and removed a thick volume from one of his bookshelves. He began to search for an article that he had published in *Nature* in 1976 with his former colleague, Dr. Jerome Schulman. He promptly found it and presented it to me almost like a piece of evidence in some trial. On the article's last page I noticed that a paragraph had been underlined heavily with pencil in his personal copy. "I was skeptical from the start," he told me while he was thumbing through the article. At the start of the immunization campaign, in October 1976, Palese and Schulman provocatively argued on the basis of their research that the swine flu virus was an "unlikely candidate for the next pandemic."[69] It was an unlikely candidate because the virus was closely related to other swine flu viruses that were present in pig populations. According to the microbe farmers who studied the virus in the test tube, there was no indication that an adaptation back to the human host had occurred. The absence of any evidence of change in the virus seemed to warrant a certain caution. A few months later, at the Gustav Stern Symposium on Perspectives in Virology in New York, Palese once again challenged the prophetic pronouncements of his colleagues with his own prophecy. He maintained that the puzzling appearance of the virus at the military training camp represented, in all likelihood, an isolated incident, a sporadic case of infection. "He never believed it at all," a former lab technician at Mount Sinai, remembered in a conversation with me. "I always called him doubting Thomas. He was very skeptical. He was really . . . , he was very . . . , I don't know why he was so . . ."

For many, the skepticism of the microbe farmer was untimely. In 1976, Palese swam against the stream. His view stood in marked contrast to the majority of experts in the United States and was diametrically opposed to Kilbourne's position. A charismatic physician turned microbiologist, Kilbourne was an influenza researcher with a distinguished track record who had earned prestigious awards for his achievements. He was, as we have seen, a principal advisor to the U.S. president on the national immunization campaign. His work specialized in the development of vaccines for influenza. At the time, Kilbourne was also Palese's department chair at Mount Sinai, and it was the Mount Sinai group that had developed the seed strain that was used by pharmaceutical companies to produce the vaccine. "The race for a swine flu vaccine," a *New York Times* article noted, "began in a Manhattan lab."[70] As the article reported, Kilbourne and his colleagues successfully generated the recombinant high-growth strain that was required to manufacture the vaccine against swine flu.[71] "It was exciting," said Barbara Pokorny, who worked with Kilbourne at the time. "I wasn't scared. I just had to lock the door to the laboratory." What Kilbourne and his team of microbe farmers accomplished was construction of a new strain by recombining the swine flu virus with a rapidly growing, standard laboratory strain. Only strains that grow efficiently in fertilized chicken eggs are suitable for vaccine production. Pokorny explained, "His approach was to make a high-yielding virus. Before that they always used wild-type and wild-type didn't grow that well in eggs. And that made a big difference, because it took less eggs, and that made a very big difference." Since 1971, Kilbourne's laboratory had generated the strain that pharmaceutical companies used to manufacture vaccines, although Kilbourne proudly noted that he never patented his method. "He was a hard worker. He expected perfection. You know, it was all science," said Pokorny.

In contrast to Kilbourne, the prophet of doubt considered the pandemic unlikely and he made his view public. Over the following years, Palese paid a price for the prophecy that he pronounced at a time when the nation was mobilizing to fight the disease that never came. Pokorny remembered the awkward scene: "Kilbourne told me that he thought we weren't even working in the same laboratory. It was like Palese was across Central Park or somewhere else. We got so much publicity in 1976. And then the whole thing fell apart." According to Pokorny, "there was a big falling out. Peter [Palese] gave an interview to the *Daily News*. That's when Kilbourne said: 'What's all this about?' He thought we were not on the same floor. It was totally opposite of what Kilbourne was saying. And I remember Peter came to me and asked whether Kilbourne was upset with the interview. 'Well, if you're asking me, yes, he is.'" For Kilbourne, the disagreement in the department was, in his own words, "disheartening, to say the least."[72]

Palese's status as a doubting Thomas was dependent on the prophecies of certainty that his competitors pronounced. He, too, was eager to develop his career—and he did so successfully, eventually succeeding Kilbourne as chair. Microbiology was a competitive field of cutting-edge science, and microbe farmers were striving for attention and public recognition. They were searching for distinction in a field of power. "In this flu world there has always been this competition," Pokorny emphasized.

Whether intentional or not, Palese's pursuit of difference, the pronounced choice that he made in opposition to another's choice, caused the scientific practice of growing bugs and testing bodies to function differentially; that is, it served as a means of distinction, in Pierre Bourdieu's sense.[73] The microbial natures that microbe farmers tended in their test tubes operated as a biological substance through which relations of power and author-

FIGURE 11. The flu shot spectacle. Edwin D. Kilbourne gets his swine flu shot in 1976. A camera crew filmed the microbe farmer in the Annenberg Lobby at Mount Sinai Medical School in New York City. Courtesy: The Mount Sinai Archives.

ity were articulated, negotiated, and contested. Matters of *cultivation* are always also matters of *distinction*, which means that appreciating the routine methods of microbe farming is essential if we are to understand how statements about the future galvanize the prophetic scene of science. For microbiologists, the immunization campaign was a trial of strength; it offered a rare occasion to find out whether a pandemic could be contained and the disease finally overcome. The campaign was a gamble, a gamble "with no guarantees."

In the aftermath of the immunization campaign, microbe farmers gradually abandoned the notion of regular pandemic cycles and increasingly invoked the concept of emerging viruses instead.[74] The suggestive term indicated that the scientific understanding of the normal and the pathological was shifting. A distinctive cosmology of mutant strains came into being in the early 1980s, and it continues to be important. What this cosmology highlights is the ever-changing, ever-evolving nature of viruses, which has important implications for visions of the future; it means that the conditions for scientific prophecy have changed. The prophetic word now responds to a different temporal sensibility.

At the heart of the concept of emerging viruses is a particular temporality, a temporality that has left behind the numerological hope of regular cycles and predictable patterns. The concept of emergence has significant consequences: It naturalizes the idea of permanent threat, which seems to require the watchfulness of a seer. In a world of permanent threat, the prophetic office thrives.

At the root of the inevitable event are microbes, "living organisms" charged with the protean power to mutate and recombine relentlessly. There is no end to their mutation and recombination, and the future of their evolution is uncertain. In the cosmology of mutant strains, change is the only constant factor. Microbes can trigger epidemics that end quietly or that return with a vengeance. They are constantly reinventing themselves in response to the antiviral treatments that have been developed over decades. The dream of eradicating infectious diseases for good and overcoming the last great plague has gradually evaporated. Microbes are always able to strike back, "and yet we can never be sure when and how it will happen," as Melinda Cooper observes.[75] Microbes challenge the scientific knowledge on which today's most effective treatments are based. They undermine the capacity of scientists to detect patterns and determine probabilities, presenting microbe farmers with pathogenic agents that are still unknown. The mutant strains are constantly evolving and adapting, they are always on the move, and they will always be one step ahead. They change rapidly, spread instantly, and become ever more dangerous. Yet who is most at risk is unknown.

This historically specific cosmology of mutant strains has radicalized the threat and normalized the limits of power and knowledge. "Often, for newly recognized diseases, the causative agent is unknown, making vaccine and drug development essentially impossible," a 1992 report stated.[76] In the cosmology of mutant strains, probability has become indeterminable, understanding unlikely, and treatment unavailable. Microbiologists, therefore, are destined to be ignorant, at least in part, because the virus is always exceeding what they know about it.

The virus is in charge, said Margaret Chan, WHO's director-general in 2009, when she announced that a pandemic was underway: "The virus writes the rules and this one, like all influenza viruses, can change the rules, without rhyme or reason, at any time."[77] In this view, the virus is the new sovereign. It is not inert, but on the contrary writes the rules and can change them at a moment's notice. This means that the virus has intention, but the intention is inscrutable. In a world without rhyme or reason, almost everything is possible. Influenza viruses are always one step ahead, cooking up more and more new strains that do not even have a name.[78] And once they have been given a proper name and a proper place in an expanding genealogy of microbial descent—H_1N_1, H_2N_2, H_3N_3—they mutate and recombine, making themselves different from themselves again. The next new strain and the next new disease are already in the offing.

At the core of the concept of emerging viruses is a particular temporality. Nature is mutable, has advanced, and is already one step ahead. Microbe farmers, by contrast, are behind and always late. They are permanently struggling to keep up with nature's relentless evolution, a form of life that seems to follow neither logic nor purpose. Every year, pharmaceutical companies produce a new vaccine, but the virus continues to change. In a conversation, a CDC official described for me the challenge of matching the vaccine with the virus:

> We have a new vaccine every single year, but the new vaccine is based upon strains that were selected in February based on surveillance data. We are trying to do a really good job to predict which strains are going to be of greatest concern in the upcoming flu season, which is months away. As we improve our surveillance activities, I think we will have a better match between the vaccine and the strains that are circulating. But it's a challenge because you're seeing different strains emerging at different times. So we can say there is an excellent match between the vaccine and the circulating strains this week in this particular community but another community could be having a different experience. So this is what makes flu interesting.

The cosmology of mutant strains has forced microbe farmers to accept a certain kind of temporal incongruity at the heart of their profession, making it impossible to accomplish the daunting task of "achieving simultaneity with the present moment," to borrow Miyazaki's apposite phrase.[79] It comes as no surprise, then, that this temporal incongruity has created a certain anxiety.

The cosmology of mutant strains has encouraged scientists to accept the temporal incongruity as an inescapable reality. In today's understanding of microbial evolution, it is considered a fact. The object will always be ahead of its knowledge. It is impossible to know how a virus might evolve; it might trigger a pandemic, or it might disappear again, scientists argue. In the cosmology of mutant strains, the temporal incongruity has become a banality, inscribed in the nature of reality.

Tracing mutant strains, microbe farmers have increasingly accepted their destiny. However, they have done more than accepted it; they have also created a powerful place for themselves to speak about the future with certainty and conviction, responding to the temporal incongruity with a call to action. The notion of emergence constitutes a limit to reason and a justification for faith.

Over the past decades, microbe farmers have extended their perspective beyond the domain of the calculable, urging people to protect themselves against the inevitable. "If humans are to survive the inevitable 'counter-strike' from microbial life . . . we need to prepare for the unexpected; learn to counter the unknowable, the virtual, the emergent," Cooper observes.[80] We must have faith in the inevitable and prepare ourselves for the emergent through the application of cutting-edge science, medicine, and technology. Accordingly, simulations have been developed to get ready for the inevitable. Andrew Lakoff has shown how American experts designed scenario-based exercises that arrange for the next outbreak of disease in advance. As he points out, the technique of simulating events serves two functions: "first, to generate an affect of urgency among officials in the absence of the event itself; and second, to generate knowledge about vulnerabilities in response capability that could then guide anticipatory intervention."[81] The crucial problem that the scenario-based exercise responds to is the problem of the catastrophic event—"the event whose likelihood cannot be known, and whose consequences cannot be managed."[82] What the technique of simulating events thus enables is to bring the future prospect of a catastrophic pandemic into the present, even though its probability is unknown.

Time and time again, experts highlighted the precarious character of the nation's state of preparedness as revealed by tabletop exercises. Indeed, pandemic emergency drills were conducted with the very aim of identifying the vulnerabilities of systems, infrastructures, and technologies.[83] Originally developed in the context of Cold War civil defense efforts, simulations were enacted in the context of pandemic preparedness to document the limits of modernist modes of power and knowledge. Indeed, every new simulation and every new scenario exposed new shortcomings. In these drills, "everything that can go wrong does go wrong," observes anthropologist Schoch-Spana.[84] The aim of preparedness is to put the system to the test, challenge actors and institutions with events that exceed their capacity to respond, and create a sense of constant crisis and permanent threat. Failure is the norm in a microbial world without rhyme or reason, reflecting once more the temporal disjuncture of a natural evolution that is always ahead and a form of understanding that is always behind. Life has entered power's sphere of intervention and knowledge's field of control, yet from the expert's perspective, power is imperfect and knowledge incomplete. Failure therefore is inevitable and crisis a natural condition. Lethal strains are looming in the shadows; they are constantly mutating; they are constantly recombining. Of course, the goal of biopolitical rule, the idea of governing the life of bodies and populations through power and knowledge, has not vanished. But this effort now has a parasite attached to it, a parasite that derives its force from projects of protection that are assumed to be insufficient from the start. In today's scenario, because everything that can go wrong will go wrong, the message of preparedness is to prepare for disappointment. The notion of emergent viruses has brought about a shift of emphasis from bold dreams of control and eradication to modest schemes of response and relief.

In 2009, a swine flu virus emerged, causing a global outbreak of disease. Yet commentators called the outbreak a "false pandemic." In the next chapter, I explore the category of pandemic influenza. What is the fate of this category in the cosmology of mutant strains?

THREE

Casualties of Contagion

ON APRIL 24, 2009, Mexico's government responded to an unexpected eruption of swine flu by activating the National Pandemic Preparedness and Response Plan and announcing school closures in the capital. Once cases of the disease were detected in the United States, American officials declared a public health emergency of international concern. Experts predicted that two billion people could contract the contagious germ once it spread worldwide. Americans panicked over possible symptoms and flooded hospital emergency departments. In an editorial, the *New York Times* wondered whether "the new swine flu virus that has killed many people in Mexico and has spread to the United States and other countries [represents] the start of a much feared pandemic?"[1] Or was it, on the contrary, a false alarm—"the latest in a long history of worrying that some day a hugely lethal flu strain might sweep through the world and kill tens of millions of people?"[2] The virus, at any rate, continued to infect people, but the illness that it caused was mild. Government officials urged Americans to keep calm, to wash their hands, cover coughs, and stay at home if sick. In June, the WHO declared that the criteria for a pandemic had been met. This statement was important not least because it triggered advance-purchase agreements between governments and the pharmaceutical industry, which secured priority access to vaccines.

Over the following months, WHO's pandemic declaration was scrutinized intensively. "We see that the population is exposed to a mild flu. People fall ill as they usually do in winter season. Some have even respiratory symptoms. But the extent of all this is considerably less than in most of the previous years," observed Dr. Wolfgang Wodarg at a public hearing organized by the Council of Europe in January 2010 to discuss the WHO's pandemic declaration.[3] According to Wodarg, a German doctor and chairman of the

82

Council of Europe's Committee on Health, WHO's declaration had transformed a mild flu into a global pandemic. The declaration had far-reaching consequences, but it was not, Wodarg underscored, "justified by any scientific evidence."[4] It diverted resources from an already strained system, forcing health care providers to limit other services.[5] How had the declaration come about? Did the pharmaceutical industry play a role in its creation? In his statement, Wodarg urged the Council of Europe to investigate allegations that pharmaceutical companies may have pressured health officials to waste scarce resources on a pointless vaccination campaign.

During a press conference at WHO's headquarters in Geneva, Dr. Keiji Fukuda, WHO's Special Advisor to the Director-General on Pandemic Influenza, responded to these charges: "At this point let's not play word games and let's not be indirect about this matter. . . . The world is going through a real pandemic. . . . The allegation that this is not a pandemic is scientifically wrong and historically inaccurate."[6] In his comments, Fukuda was responding to growing concerns that the international health organization may have exaggerated the threat of swine flu, promoting the use of "a sledgehammer to crack a nut," as a pundit in *The Lancet* provocatively phrased it.[7] It is always easy to be smart after the fact, the commentator admitted, but he nevertheless wondered whether the dramatic label was justified given the low level of morbidity and mortality that the virus caused. "If this turns out to be the weakest pandemic in history," he continued, "it will pose some tough questions for the scientific community."[8]

For many observers, the pandemic looked more like the usual flu than pandemic flu: It was indistinguishable from seasonal outbreaks. Indeed, the 2009 pandemic was a far cry from the terrifying specter of widespread disease that experts had been evoking. Insisting that pandemic influenza is a catastrophic event, public health officials suggested that it would require a decisive response to cope with the consequences. Forecasts predicted that billions of people would be affected and the world economy would shut down, but the 2009 pandemic did not affect billions of people and it had no significant impact on the economy. Officials estimated that 15,000 people died worldwide, far less than during seasonal outbreaks of regular flu.

Pandemics are presumed to be exceptional, and for that reason, they require exceptional approaches. But when the swine flu virus appeared, the exceptional character of the pandemic was hard to notice and officials came under scrutiny. They were accused of having produced a public health emergency where there was none. The disease was anything but catastrophic;

journalists exposed the pandemic as a nonevent and called the official declaration a negligent contribution to pharmaceutical marketing. It seemed as if those who first predicted the coming plague later chastised officials for their deception. The prophets of pandemic influenza were in deep trouble.

In a statement made on behalf of the WHO at the hearing conducted by the Council of Europe, Fukuda vehemently defended the pandemic declaration. The pandemic was real, not fake, and the health organization had no intention to cheat the public. Influenza, Fukuda explained, causes "both seasonal epidemics of disease, and on occasion, much larger global outbreaks of disease, known as pandemics."[9] According to the special advisor, "pandemics occur when a new influenza virus appears and spreads around the world in populations which previously have not been exposed to the virus."[10] In his closing remarks, Fukuda emphasized that the event was a real event: Swine flu was "a scientifically well-documented event in which the emergence and spread of a new influenza virus has caused an unusual epidemiological pattern of disease throughout the world," the public health official maintained.[11] Was it really a pandemic? "Here the answer is very clear: yes."[12]

Confronted with allegations that health officials manufactured an event, providing pharmaceutical companies with a splendid opportunity to promote their products, expand their markets, and increase their profits, Fukuda referred to the authority of the microbiological laboratory and invoked the rhetoric of scientific objectivity. The process of identifying a pandemic, he suggested, is not an "arbitrary matter of word-smithing."[13] On the contrary, the concept of pandemic influenza is well defined; it has a clear and distinct meaning, and it commonly refers to a global outbreak of infectious disease caused by the appearance of a new virus. Intensive laboratory testing had unmistakably demonstrated that the swine flu virus was "genetically and antigenically very different from the normal human influenza viruses circulating around the world."[14] Countering accusations that pharmaceutical companies may have influenced important decisions at WHO, Fukuda underscored that effective procedures, which required all experts to declare their financial interests, were in place to protect the integrity of the scientific advice given to the organization.

The sudden spread of the virus caused confusion about the meaning of the pandemic category. Pandemic influenza had become an increasingly contested term in public debate. This debate, however, focused almost exclusively on the question of whether conflicts of interest may have influenced key decisions of public health officials. Although the pandemic declaration was frequently

FIGURE 12. "It's not flu as usual. Key differences between annual flu and pandemic flu." Time and again, experts and officials urged people to prepare themselves for the catastrophic event, emphasizing the fundamental difference between regular seasonal flu and pandemic flu. Flyer and fact sheet published by the Trust for America's Health.

questioned, the category itself was never scrutinized: Both sides of the debate typically took it for granted as a matter of course. Even critics of the pandemic declaration presumed that they knew what a pandemic is, and they believed that it was easy to recognize an event when it happens. Conversely, if the concept of pandemic influenza was as well defined as health officials pretend, then why was a public declaration required in the first place? In the context of preparedness, the classification of infectious disease has enormous social, political, and economic consequences (not least because of advance-purchase agreements between governments and pharmaceutical companies), and it is therefore essential to analyze how the category of pandemic influenza is constituted.

This chapter takes as its starting point the limits of a debate on pandemic influenza, framed predominantly in terms of possible conflicts of interest. It suggests that a debate framed in such narrow terms implicitly promotes the problematic assumption that pandemic influenza constitutes a distinct category and objectively definable condition. But, on the contrary, the category is remarkably ambiguous and the condition difficult to determine. Paradoxically, it is the very effort to define the category that has made it ambiguous in the first place. The chapter examines how microbiologists defined pandemic influenza in ontological terms. The isolation of a growing number of viruses over successive seasons allowed microbe farmers to conduct comparative studies with multiple strains and identify shifts in them. Eventually, microbiologists realized that the influenza virus was changing from season to season and that these shifts were important for immunological reasons. The more a virus changes, the less immunity it is likely to encounter in its host population. This view of a changing virus escaping the immunity of its host population produced a new object: the pandemic virus. In the case of influenza, microbiologists suggested that pandemics are caused by a form of microbial variation that sporadically and unpredictably results in the emergence of an entirely "new" virus. The microbiological concept of the pandemic virus thus appeared as an explanation for the observation of worldwide pandemics; hence, the peculiar constellation distinctive for the contemporary configuration of disease in which pandemic influenza has come to mean both a particular agent—the new virus—and a particular condition—the global eruption of disease.

Microbe farmers took up the epidemiological distinction between epidemic and pandemic outbreaks to propose an etiological explanation for the changing patterns of disease. As a result, the category of pandemic influenza was reconfigured in the context of an ontological understanding of the normal and the pathological. At the source of a pandemic was a particular kind of virus, which was believed to be responsible for the observed event. "Every decade or so," Andrewes remarked in 1978, the virus effects a "protean change, which enables it to start up a fresh pandemic."[15] A new virus comes into existence, and the human population has no or little immunity to it. The microbe sweeps across the planet, infecting more and more people, causing explosive eruptions of respiratory illness; this is the dramatic event of pandemic influenza that has become so familiar today.

According to microbe farmers, the emergence of a new virus explains the occurrence of a global pandemic. But what is a new virus? How much difference is necessary for a virus to count as new? What might "protean change" mean in a context of constant change? These questions are inevitable in a cosmology of mutant strains in which viruses are assumed to evolve all the time. The hemagglutination inhibition assay has played a key role in the effort to compare strains of the influenza virus with one another and determine whether a strain is new or not. But how exactly are identity and difference made concrete by this test? And what is the role of the test for the identification of pandemics? Can microbiologists distinguish between true and false pandemics? Can they tell us what is a real event and what is not a real event? What exactly is it that the prophets of pandemic influenza are predicting?

This chapter examines how microbiologists developed a test to substantiate the category of pandemic influenza. Tracing the use of this test, the chapter highlights the difficulty of defining pandemic influenza by technical means and rational calculation. Occasionally, the most reliable test delivers inconclusive results, producing not less but more questions about the novelty of a microbial creature. I argue that the pandemic became a pandemic in 2009 because of ambivalent test results. Let me begin this next section with a straightforward question: What is a virus?

IDENTITY TROUBLE

"It's a mixture," Dr. Anice Lowen, a postdoctoral fellow in the Palese lab at Mount Sinai, explained to me one afternoon in response to my question about the influenza virus that she and her colleague, Dr. Samira Mubareka, used in their experimental research.[16] In a series of elegant studies that garnered public attention and were covered in a *New York Times* article, Lowen and

Mubareka were exploring the role of humidity, temperature, and radiation in the seasonal transmission of infectious disease.[17] "In a given sample," Lowen observed, "you probably have millions of different variants because the influenza virus is very error prone." The casual remark instantly reminded me that the rapidly mutating and relentlessly recombining virus was constantly making itself different from itself, provoking the troubling question of whether it is actually possible for the ever-changing, ever-shifting microbial creature to have a consistent identity.

If a sample inevitably consists of millions of different variants that are constantly replicating, mutating, and recombining, then how are microbiologists able to identify a virus at all? What allows microbe farmers to attribute a consistent identity to such an ephemeral entity that apparently lacks the necessary means to maintain a stable biological form? What does it concretely mean to identify a virus that is extremely error prone, and how is it done in the laboratory? In a thoughtful contribution to a landmark publication on emerging viruses, Kilbourne highlights the strange nature of the virus. According to the microbiologist, a virus sample is commonly thought of as something homogeneous, but it actually represents a heterogeneous population of mutant strains. It really is, Kilbourne suggests, "a statistical consensus of a genetically heterogeneous population . . . in constant flux."[18] What Lowen used for her experimental study and what she called a "mixture" in response to my question ultimately is, in Kilbourne's terms, a heterogeneous population of mutant strains in constant flux.

"Viruses," biochemist Manfred Eigen notes, "have the ability to mystify laypeople and experts alike."[19] Early on in their experimental investigations, microbiologists "became puzzled by the high mutation rates they observed: the magnitudes indicated that viruses must evolve more than a million times faster than cellular microorganisms. If that were true, how could viruses maintain their identities as pathogenic species over any evolutionarily significant period?"[20] Viruses mutate and recombine relentlessly. Not surprisingly, the scientific attempt to produce objective knowledge about these strange creatures continues to be a challenge because the object in the test tube is constantly changing. Under such peculiar circumstances of constant change, what then comes to count as a new virus—the cause of a global pandemic? What, in other words, makes a microbe new when it appears to be new all the time because it mutates so often and so quickly?

Let us move to the laboratory and explore in more detail how microbe farmers cope with the challenge of constant change. This section examines how microbiologists identify viruses in the test tube, the kinds of technologies available, and the role of these technologies in constituting pandemic influenza as an exceptional event that requires an exceptional response.

On a Saturday morning, in May 2008, Dr. Qinshan Gao, a postdoctoral fellow in Palese's laboratory, greeted me while holding a large tray of white chicken eggs in his gloved hands. Over the course of my research on pandemic influenza, I had become increasingly interested in essential but routine microbiological tests. I was especially curious about and intrigued by the complex ways in which these tests were linked with the predicted pandemic that was looming on the horizon. What might these tests be able to tell us about the specter of disease? Have they made it possible for microbiologists to define the category of pandemic influenza?

Gao was using one of the most important tests in the modern history of influenza research, the hemagglutination inhibition (HI) assay. Gao assembled the serological test to measure the approximate amount of recombinant virus that he had been able to grow in fertilized chicken eggs, which had spent the past two days in the controlled conditions of a mechanical incubator, a device used to maintain optimal temperature, humidity, and oxygen. Hatched under special safety precautions in commercial factories, fertilized chicken eggs containing a living embryo eight to eleven days old are commonly used as the primary medium to isolate and grow influenza viruses in the laboratory. Every week, the laboratory received a new shipment with dozens of eggs ordered for various research projects. While telling me that he was not particularly optimistic about the outcome of his most recent experiment, Gao placed on the lab bench two specially designed and commercially produced hemagglutination plates, each containing ninety-six tiny wells with rounded bottoms. Using his pipette, Gao transferred the virus sample serially into the tiny wells and diluted it with a sterile solution. He mixed the dilutions with a small amount of bottled red blood cells industrially harvested from laboratory chickens and then waited a couple of minutes for the desired effect to occur.

What surprised me about the test were its stunning simplicity and its origin. As I learned over the period of my fieldwork, the test emerged on the stage of microbiological research in the twentieth century and has not changed much over the decades. Despite the fact that it is very simple and old, it has remained the test of choice until today. In an age of supercomputers, smartphones, and reverse genetics, microbe farmers continue to depend on chicken eggs and chicken blood, the nuts and bolts of scientific research.

FIGURE 13. The standard medium. A tray with white chicken eggs containing a living embryo eight to eleven days old. Microbe farmers grow influenza viruses in fertilized chicken eggs, the standard growth medium in today's influenza research. Photograph by author.

The invention of the test in 1941 is itself intriguing. Conducting experimental research in the laboratories of the International Health Division of the Rockefeller Foundation in New York, a young microbe farmer by the name of George K. Hirst accidentally discovered that the red blood cells of chicken embryos gradually begin to clump when brought into contact with an influenza virus. It is this remarkably simple and easily recognizable immunological reaction that lies at the heart of the HI assay used in laboratories today. Here I want to examine how microbiologists deploy this surprisingly simple and incredibly important test to establish pandemic influenza as an objectively definable category. As it turns out, the serological test operates as a bodily system of recognition, to borrow Donna Haraway's phrase, both stabilizing and destabilizing the category of pandemic influenza as an exceptional event.[21] The test matters to the larger argument of the book because it highlights what is taken for granted in pandemic prophecy; namely, that we already know, or assume to know, what a pandemic is.

In early 1941, George K. Hirst, at the age of thirty-two, sterilized the shell of a white chicken egg with some alcohol in his laboratory in New York City.

The chicken egg contained a living eleven-day old embryo. After rubbing the shell clean, Hirst made a small puncture with a blunt needle over the air sac. Into the tiny hole he carefully inserted a sterilized syringe, injecting a small amount of an influenza virus into the nutritious liquid that was feeding the chicken embryo. He then sealed the hole with some wax and stored the egg in a mechanical incubator at 37 degrees Celsius. Two days later, the microbiologist removed the egg from the incubator, placed it on the lab bench, cracked the shell open, and cautiously removed the cloudy fluid presumably containing the grown agent. During this procedure, Hirst inadvertently damaged the blood vessels of the chick embryo and made a simple but important observation. To Hirst's great surprise, the red blood cells leaking into the infected fluid instantly began to stick together as if they were trying to defend themselves against the virus particles to which they were exposed. The microbiologist called this basic reaction "agglutination," a term proposed by bacteriologists Herbert Edward Durham and Max von Gruber in 1896 for any physical action resulting in blood cells sticking together. Later on, the term "agglutination" was replaced by the more specific term "hemagglutination."

Hirst immediately realized the significance of his accidental observation and seized on its potential. As he wrote in a 1941 article, if the "embryo had been infected with influenza virus, macroscopic agglutination of the red cells occurred within 15 to 30 seconds. . . . If the agglutination did not appear promptly, it usually did not occur at all, and the differentiation between positive and negative eggs was easy."[22] The virus, in other words, caused red blood cells to clump. Hirst thus accidentally discovered a surprisingly simple immunological reaction that allowed researchers to determine whether an influenza virus was present in a sample obtained from hospital patients—a crucial advance given the fundamental invisibility of the agent. The discovery of hemagglutination was a significant practical advancement that simplified and accelerated microbiological research and contributed to the consolidation of the laboratory's diagnostic authority. No sneezing ferrets with dangerously sharp teeth were required anymore. Microbe farmers began to use the test on a regular basis and became ever more confident that they would eventually be able to identify the cause of pandemics. But how successful have these attempts been? Has the test fulfilled the expectations? Has it allowed microbiologists to define what a pandemic is? The matter is a complex one.

Let us return to Dr. Gao and see how he is making use of Hirst's test. Gao has just removed two fertilized chicken eggs from the incubator. To measure

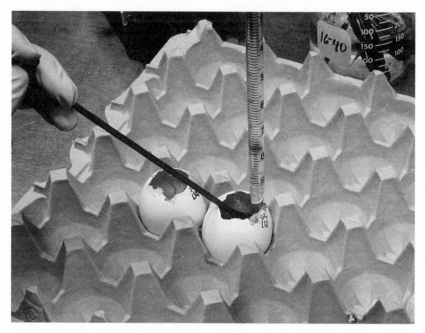

FIGURE 14. The harvesting. A microbe farmer isolates a virus that has grown in two fertilized chicken eggs. After the procedure, the contaminated chicken eggs are disposed of in special biohazard waste bags. Photograph by author.

the amount of virus that he has been able to grow in these eggs, Gao sets up the test. He puts two specially designed hemagglutination plates containing ninety-six wells with rounded bottoms on the lab bench. A small bottle containing red blood cells derived from a living chicken sits in a bucket of ice. On the right side of each ninety-six-well plate, moving from top to bottom, Gao jots down the twelve different samples of influenza virus that he has grown. On the top side of each plate, moving from right to left, Gao notes the different dilutions that he will produce. The dilutions—which, in this case, are very low—are 0 / 2 / 4 / 8 / 16 / 32 / 64.

Gao now uses a multiple-channel pipette and adds 25 ml of phosphate-buffered saline (PBS) to each well in each row, except for the first vertical row on the right side of the plate, which will contain undiluted virus. He then takes a one-channel pipette and adds the different virus samples into the wells of the first vertical row. Next, Gao grabs the multiple-channel pipette and begins to transfer virus from the first vertical row to the next, moving from right to left. Because he transfers the virus samples with the pipette from one vertical row directly to the next, the virus is serially diluted with PBS. The concentration diminishes from row to row. The last vertical row on the left side, therefore, will contain the highest dilution and thus the smallest amount of virus. Gao then adds a small amount of chicken red blood cells to each well containing the various dilutions of virus of the twelve different samples. He shakes the plate to mix the virus well with the cells, puts the plate on ice, and waits thirty to forty-five minutes for the mixture to settle.

Because of the specially designed rounded bottoms of the wells, the cells that do not agglutinate form a distinct button at the bottom of each well. Cells that do agglutinate cover the wells evenly. Therefore the HI assay reverses Hirst's original observation. Hirst, as we saw, noticed how cells began to stick together in the presence of virus, forming a distinctive clump. By contrast, the assay as it is used today in the laboratory renders the nonagglutinated cells visible. It is the lack of clumping, the absence of the reaction, that is rendered visible: Only nonagglutinated cells sink to the bottom of the wells and form a tiny, clearly visible button.

The practical advantages of the assay are obvious. It is simple, rapid, and reliable, as Gao explains, which is why he depends on the assay for most of his experiments. It requires some influenza virus derived from a human or animal source, delivered to the laboratory and then stored in the freezer. It also requires a couple of fertilized chicken eggs and a few droplets of chicken blood, which is purified, bottled, and distributed by commercial suppliers. At the core of the test, as we have seen, is a particular effect: In the presence of an influenza virus, red blood cells begin to clump. Cells that fail to clump slowly precipitate to the bottom of the wells. The precipitation also serves as a visible index of virus concentration: If cells fail to form a button at the bottom of the wells only after multiple steps of dilution, the concentration of the given virus sample is correspondingly high. Conversely, if cells precipitate after a twofold or fourfold dilution of the given virus sample, the concentration of the virus in the sample is low; there is, in other words, not a lot of virus in this particular sample. The routine test provides microbe farmers with an approximate measure of virus concentration. Thus, it is not just diagnostic but also quantitative, and as a quantitative test, it tells researchers how much, if any, virus is present in a given sample. But how, I ask Gao, does a measure of *concentration* become a measure of *relatedness*, meaning how much one strain is related to another strain of the virus? How, in other words, does the test make identity and difference visible? How can the quantitative test produce qualitative results and determine whether a virus is different and therefore new?

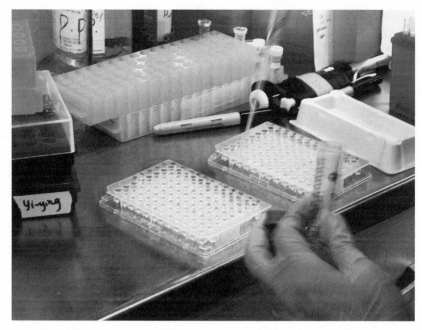

FIGURE 15. The serological test. Two hemagglutination plates containing ninety-six wells with rounded bottoms. Here Qinshan Gao mixes the influenza virus with red chicken blood. Photograph by author.

Already by 1941, Hirst realized that he could use fertilized chicken eggs for neutralization tests, as Smith, Andrewes, and Laidlaw had discovered with ferrets in their celebrated 1933 experiments. The British scientists concluded that the serum of a recovered ferret contained antibodies that could neutral-ize the virus completely.[23] Using a mixture of neutralizing antiserum and virus, Hirst observed that it disabled the clumping effect too.[24] Antiserum—blood containing influenza antibodies—was usually derived from either chickens or ferrets that had been infected with an influenza virus. Two weeks after infection, the immune system of these laboratory animals developed an-tibodies that could neutralize the virus. The animals were then bled, and the blood was filtered, purified, centrifuged, and used as antiserum in experi-ments. Significantly, the inhibition of the hemagglutination reaction is specific. That is, if changes occur in the immunological properties of a given virus, it no longer reacts to the same degree to antibodies. Antibodies, as historians Muriel Lederman and Sue Tolin aptly put it, were therefore able to function as "a mirror of the virus."[25] The more a virus changed and became different from its parent, the less it reacted with antibodies produced against that parental strain. Drawing on this bodily system of recognition, the test thus became valuable, making identity and difference specifiable in immunological terms, even though the underlying biological mechanisms were almost completely unknown.[26] It is important to note that some parts of the influenza virus change faster than others. For example, proteins on the surface of the virus are more variable than proteins on the inside of the virus envelope. The focus of the test is exclusively on the surface proteins, which play an important immunological role.

The HI assay is today's test of choice; it concentrates on the surface proteins, which are highly variable, and offers microbe farmers a simple and quick way to map the relationships between samples of the virus. The test relies on two distinctive reactions: the hemagglutination reaction and its inhibition by the antigen-antibody reaction. Of central importance is the specificity of the immunological reaction. If the clumping effect is inhibited by antiserum in dilutions as high as 1:1024, as Gao explained to me, it indicates that the two strains—the one being tested and the original strain that was used to produce the neutralizing antiserum—must be very similar in immunological terms. The higher the dilution required to inhibit the hemagglutination effect, the more closely related are the two strains. Conversely, if even a low dilution cannot stop the red blood cells from clumping, the strains are not closely related. The relationships between influenza viruses are thus measured in immunological terms and are called "antigenic." Microbiologists have deployed this test as a way to classify specific outbreaks of infectious disease as either epidemics or pandemics, but not always successfully. In fact, the effort to transform pandemic influenza into an objectively definable category has turned out to be more complex than it seemed at first sight. Although the serological test was developed with the promise of producing conclusive results, such results have not necessarily been the rule.

ON THE THRESHOLD OF AN EVENT

In November 2010 Palese drew my attention to a newspaper article that he had published in the *Wall Street Journal* at the outset of the swine flu pandemic. "As swine flu continues to spread," Palese observed, "concerns are mounting about a serious pandemic. Yet based on history and what we know about the flu virus, the threat is not as bad as it may seem."[27] In the article, Palese again assumed the role of the counter-prophet. As he noted, because "people have been exposed to H1N1 viruses over many decades, we likely have some cross-reactive immunity against the swine virus. While it may not be sufficient to prevent illness, it may very well dampen the impact of the virus on mortality."[28] In our 2010 conversation, he told me,

> I suggested in this article that the virus wouldn't be as virulent as some people thought. So this was, you see, May 2nd [2009], so that's very early . . . and it turns out that this is really what actually happened, and so I am pretty proud of that article because at that time I was sticking my neck out. I was pretty sure the virus wouldn't acquire some additional virulence. One reason is that we all have some H1N1 antibodies, so there was some dampening, even though we didn't know the extent.

When I asked Palese what he thought about the classification of the virus as a pandemic virus, he responded,

> It's not a full pandemic virus in the classic definition. "Pandemic" means it's a global epidemic, but the additional definition, which we use for influenza, is that it has also to be a change in subtypes. So in this case, yes, it was a global epidemic influenza virus, but it hadn't changed its subtype, so that's why sometimes I call it the 0.5 pandemic virus. It's not a full pandemic virus in the classic definition where first it has to be global and second it has to change its subtype.

"So you would actually not have called it a pandemic because the virus did not represent a new subtype?" I wondered. "No, I would not have called it a pandemic," Palese answered. "That's what the WHO did. . . . I mean, I have no problem with calling it a pandemic, but with the understanding that one also changes the definition of it. So I would probably have called it a new H1N1, or something."

Originally, the term "pandemic influenza" referred to the worldwide spread of disease. This important part of the definition continues to be crucial. "Pandemic," as Palese phrased it, "means it's a global epidemic." The virus travels from country to country and from continent to continent, affecting people in all walks of life. Thus, the notion continues to refer to the global nature of the event. It is the geographical distribution of disease that defines the notion of pandemic. For medical observers of the nineteenth century, who were uncertain about the cause of disease, the notion primarily operated in analytical fashion, but the distinction between epidemics and pandemics remained vague and elusive.[29] The question of how to set criteria in terms of spread, which would allow officials to distinguish systematically between an epidemic and a pandemic, turned out to be a normative problem almost impossible to resolve on the basis of observation alone. The problem was this: Because influenza sweeps across the world year after year, which episode should be considered an event? If the global spread of influenza occurs every year, then what counts as a pandemic? The flu is a regular seasonal infection that occurs annually. The ontological understanding of infectious disease that the masters of microbe farming promoted promised to resolve the problem of definition by focusing on the pathogenic agent and determining the cause of the disease. A pandemic occurs when a protean change happens and a new virus emerges, microbiologists suggested.

But this attempt to define the event and determine the disease in the laboratory has not been entirely successful. Ironically, it was the very effort to eliminate ambiguity that produced it. Palese's reference to the swine flu virus as a "0.5 pandemic virus" shows how the serological test has itself become a source of ambiguous perceptions. Although microbe farmers reformulated the problem of influenza's identity in ontological terms—the concrete pathogenic agent and its distinctive immunological properties—the etiological focus of microbiological research struggles with the same fundamental questions: How much difference makes a difference? What constitutes "protean change"? When is a virus new? If the influenza virus is rapidly mutating and relentlessly recombining, if it is constantly making itself different from itself, then how much difference is required for a virus to count as new? Attempts to answer these questions face the limits of the serological test and, more generally, of the germ theory of disease and its reductionist ambition to make the virus the determining factor. What this serological test is able to tell microbe farmers is how different a particular strain is in comparison to another strain, but whether that difference is sufficient, whether that difference matters, and to whom, it cannot say. Though it offers microbiologists a quantifiable measure of difference, it is ultimately unable to resolve the normative problem of defining pandemic influenza as a distinct event.

Not surprisingly, microbiologists decided to resolve the problem by convention; that is, by organizing a meeting at the WHO headquarters in Geneva, where they decided to classify the influenza virus according to specific subtypes. For microbe farmers, a new virus is a virus with a new subtype. The definition used for pandemic influenza, as Palese explained, "is that it has . . . to be a change in subtypes." The virus is changing constantly, but new subtypes emerge only occasionally: That subtype emergence is the protean change. Currently, microbiologists distinguish among eighteen hemagglutinin subtypes

(H1–H18) and nine neuraminidase subtypes (N1–N9). According to this definition, a pandemic occurs when a new subtype of the influenza virus appears and begins to circulate in the human population. For instance, in 1957, the H2 virus replaced the H1 virus and triggered a pandemic. A decade later, in 1968, the H3 virus replaced the H2 virus. These two subtypes (H2 and H3) had not been circulating in human populations before. The H1 virus, which circulated until 1957, returned in 1977, but in this case the outbreak was not classified as a pandemic because H1 viruses had been circulating until 1957. The virus, in other words, was new, but only for people born after 1957.

The swine flu virus posed a similar problem. As Palese remarked, the virus does not represent a new subtype. It belongs to the H1 group of influenza viruses, and as part of this group, it is not new. According to the microbiological definition of what constitutes a new virus, the swine flu is "not a full pandemic virus in the classic definition where first it has to be global and second it has to change its subtype," as Palese phrased it. The swine flu virus is different from other strains, to be sure, but does not represent a change of subtype.

Recently, microbiologists proposed that pandemics can be caused by the same subtypes as regular annual flu.[30] The suggestion seems provocative, but it runs the risk of creating even more confusion, blurring a distinction that is fundamental for preparedness. Can the same subtype cause annual seasonal flu and pandemic flu? How can one prepare for pandemic influenza when it is not clear what it is? Given the precarious constitution of the category and the difficulty of defining pandemic influenza, what are the prophets of pandemic influenza actually predicting? When I mentioned the press conference in which Keiji Fukuda, the WHO official, affirmed that the "world is going through a real pandemic" and that the "allegation that this is not a pandemic is scientifically wrong and historically inaccurate," Palese responded, "Yes, but that's just one voice." Palese was technically correct, because the health organization represented just one voice among others. And yet this voice was trying to speak with performative force, claiming for itself the power to identify events, declare pandemics, and institute the reality of which it speaks.

WHEN IT MATTERS

The question of the "new" virus became so important in the laboratory of the twentieth century because microbiologists thought it could provide a possible explanation for the changing nature of disease. How was it possible for the influenza virus to infect a few people in one year and kill millions in another year? Gradually microbiologists became aware of the existence of a considerable degree of microbial variation in the world of influenza viruses. This was fundamental in experimental investigations designed to attenuate bacterial organisms and viral particles for use in human vaccination.[31] After the first isolation of an influenza virus from a human body, accomplished in 1933, microbe farmers quickly began to produce attenuated strains by serial passage through animal bodies and tissue cultures. Yet microbial variation was not only manufactured in the laboratory by artificial means to manufacture vaccines but it was also observed under natural conditions. After isolating a growing number of influenza viruses from human populations over successive seasons, it increasingly became evident that the causative agent responsible for the communicable disease was changing because of its reproductive infidelity. The notorious error frequency of the virus was staggering; infidelity seemed to be its only loyalty. Scientists reluctantly realized that the virus existed not in the singular but in the plural. Microbial variation eventually emerged as a subject of lively debate and intensive research because it "came to be seen as the most likely explanation for both the regular waxing and waning of epidemics."[32] It was considered a possible explanation for the occasional occurrence of devastating pandemics. A particular kind of epidemiological observation was reformulated as an etiological problem, which was then explored in the context of laboratory medicine.

Let me return here to a question that I posed in the course of this chapter. What, in fact, is a virus? What, more specifically, is a new virus? If anything, this chapter reveals the false concreteness that we tend to attribute to the idea of the new. The new matters, the new is important, the new is exciting, the new is different, but what exactly counts as new? In a contribution to a book on emerging viruses, Kilbourne wondered how microbiologists might actually define what is a new virus. To provide such a definition is difficult given the fact that "a virus really is a statistical consensus of a genetically heterogeneous population, which . . . is in constant flux," as he pointed out.[33] Celia Lowe phrased it nicely: Viruses exist in a "state of indeterminacy."[34] It is thus not surprising to find scholars attributing a certain "taxonomic untidiness" to these promiscuous creatures.[35] Whenever scientists think they have identified a virus, it seems to have already made itself different from itself.

In his contribution to the emerging viruses book, John Holland pondered this question: When is a copy of a virus not really a copy? His answer: when it is a copy of an influenza virus. As Holland explained, "With error frequencies per site averaging 10^{-5} or greater, we cannot envision an RNA virus as 'a virus' nor an RNA clone as 'a clone' (i.e., a collection of identical virus genomes)."[36] No copy of an influenza virus is really a copy.

Influenza viruses replicate rapidly but inaccurately. Their extreme error rate is fundamental for "survival" because it allows the germ to escape the immunological defense operations of the host. Scientists wondered whether it might be possible to take advantage of the error rate, push the virus over its threshold of tolerance, and drive it into an "error catastrophe." A "suicidal" error rate would make it impossible for the pathogenic agent to replicate its genetic information.[37] Random errors, which happen in the process of replication, allow the virus to adapt and adjust, but too many errors could be "lethal" for a viral population. There is a limit even for influenza in terms of its tolerance for error.

In a context of extreme evolution and relentless change, the "definition of what is really new becomes quite arbitrary and, I think, quite important," wrote Kilbourne.[38] What, then, counts or qualifies as a new virus in the cosmology of mutant strains? Kilbourne posed the question to Joshua Lederberg, the chief promoter of the emerging infectious disease worldview. His response is striking because it is simple and straightforward. A virus is new, Lederberg argues, "when it matters." Lederberg's suggestion is not quite what we would expect from a Nobel Prize-winning scientist, nor after almost a century of tireless microbiological research in the laboratory. Lederberg offers no definition, provides no criteria, refers to no numbers, invokes no threshold, presents no algorithm, points to no assay. What he says ultimately runs the risk of undermining the authority of the microbiological laboratory and its battery of tests. Lederberg's response sparks a whole range of questions, among them two important ones: If a virus is new when it matters, then who determines what matters? WHO takes on the burden of declaration?

The microbiological laboratory, with its founding ambition to reduce the disease to the presence of the virus, arose as the final arbiter of influenza's identity. However, the methods of microbe farming produced a series of difficulties that made it necessary for microbiologists to look beyond the test tube and correlate epidemiological observations with shifts in the virus. The aim was to align these shifts with observed patterns of disease. These retrospective correlations of "cause" and "effect" resulted in definitions of types and subtypes of the influenza virus, but they were not necessarily straightforward;

borderline events required discussion and debate. Lederberg's response highlights the negotiated character of influenza's identity.

Lederberg's response also reveals a fundamental assumption operating at the heart of pandemic preparedness: Pandemics matter. They matter because they can be catastrophic, because they can cause widespread sickness, because they can disrupt everyday life, because they can be important global events, because they can shut down economies overnight. This is the rationale for preparedness—the key motivation for the development of plans, the consideration of scenarios, the production of vaccines, the mobilization of experts, the allocation of resources, the review of policies, the funding of research, the training of staff, the declaration of emergencies, the adjustment of a response to a disease that is supposed to be different from ordinary seasonal flu. In short, pandemics matter because they are extraordinary events, because they are not flu as usual.

The current definition of pandemic influenza is contingent on test results, but these test results can be inconclusive. Such inconclusive results make it necessary to examine the situation, consider the options, make announcements, and declare pandemics. Expert deliberations and official statements are assumed to solve the problem. The swine flu virus, which was new even though it was not new, required health officials to negotiate a response. The event did not simply happen; the virus was detected and the pandemic was declared. It was the microbe that microbiologists studied in the laboratory that caused the concern in the first place, not the illness, which was mild. The virus was partially new, to be sure, but it did not represent a new subtype and thus lacked distinction compared with previous pandemics. It failed to fit with the microbiological definition of the new. Health officials were confronted by an ambiguous biological entity. What should they call it? How should they classify it? How dangerous would it be? They faced an irregular virus that produced a crisis in meaning. The pathogenic agent exposed the conventional grammar of identity and difference that microbe farmers used. The virus was irregular, uncommon, and atypical, but primarily because it escaped microbiology's understanding of the regular, the common, and the typical. The virus did not fit well into the established grid of sameness and difference.

The effort of testing the virus to determine what it is turned the germ into a borderline case that caused concern because it had no intention of crossing the border and settling on one side or the other. A decision was necessary to resolve the problem. WHO's declaration was based on the view that health officials are charged with the responsibility to protect populations from possible harm. Thus, officials must have a high level of tolerance for error, just as the influenza virus does, and choose a course of action that may turn out to be exaggerated. Health officials must err on the side of caution. At the start of the pandemic, when public health authorities were dealing with the situation, "they had to make a lot of decisions about what to do," explained Fukuda. "And this is when many of the hardest decisions were coming up during the pandemic."

Microbiology's serological test intensified the uncertainty about the virus and whether it could possibly trigger a serious form of disease. The test deprived the world of confidence and created confusion about the category of pandemic influenza. The result was a vaccination campaign—what some pundits called an inflated response to control the circulation of a virus that caused only mild disease. Initially, the notion of pandemic influenza came into being as a designation for an extraordinary eruption of disease. But what health officials encountered in 2009 was not extraordinary severe at all. What they encountered was an ambiguous biological entity, suspended in a grammar of sameness and difference. In the end, the WHO declared an event that did not feel like an event.

Health officials raised the specter of pandemic disaster to mobilize the population in the struggle against the coming plague. In so doing, they reproduced a narrow understanding of pandemic influenza as a catastrophic disease, ignoring the fact that the category is primarily a convention, one that is based on a microbiological test. The genre of dramatic disease was powerful, persuasive, and valuable for public health advocacy as long as the pandemic was looming on the horizon as a threat. Officials relied on the prophetic perspective, overlooking the precarious constitution of the category. Emphasizing the necessity of preparedness, officials became so intimate, so comfortable with the prediction that it began to stick to their skin like a shadow. In 2009, officials realized that it had become impossible to dispel the specter of catastrophic disease, that it had acquired a life of its own. The pressure was mounting. The virus was not as new as expected. Officials were concerned and declared a pandemic, insisting in vain that the disease might be mild. They explained that a pandemic is not inevitably catastrophic, that large numbers of deaths and serious social, political, and economic consequences would be unlikely. The event might perhaps not look like an event, but it was real nevertheless, they said. Of course, these officials were arguing against the sense of prophetic expectation that they had produced for more than a decade. They had invoked the H5N1 virus with its staggering mortality rate to associate the notion of pandemic influenza with the daunting image of a catastrophic event. Now the prophetic vision of their own making was hanging over their actions, casting a dark shadow over their words. The prophetic scene of pandemic influenza encouraged observers to scrutinize what experts were saying. Public declarations carried little force when the event was other than expected.

At stake in the controversial debate was the credibility of the public health message. The vaccination campaign was exposed as unnecessary. Officials were charged with overreaction, even corruption. They were accused of abusing scientific authority, of creating an event where there was none. This was flu as usual, not pandemic flu; there was no justification for the dramatic declaration of a public health emergency. The prophetic orientation, which seemed to have made communication with the public so effective, was making it difficult now. But then again, what else are prophetic words supposed to do? They are made to irritate.

FOUR

Experiments of Concern

Prophecy is living mimicry.

MAURICE BLANCHOT

IT WAS AT THE INTERNATIONAL OPTIONS for the Control of Influenza conference in Toronto, in June 2007, where I first learned about the quandary in which Dr. Taronna Maines found herself. Mobilized by the threat of a global pandemic, a record attendance of 1,600 delegates from more than sixty-six countries had gathered to discuss measures for influenza detection, containment, and prevention. I had already encountered Maines, a microbiologist and influenza researcher, a few months earlier when I visited her lab at the CDC in Atlanta. My visit was occasioned by a research article that Maines and her colleagues at the CDC had recently published in a prominent journal, the *Proceedings of the National Academy of Sciences*. In the article, the scientists reported the preliminary results of a series of experiments conducted with a set of genetically engineered influenza viruses.[1] According to Maines, the main purpose of the research was to evaluate the pandemic potential of the H5N1 avian influenza virus that was rapidly sweeping across Asia, Europe, and Africa at the time. What biomedical scientists and public health specialists feared was that the notoriously unpredictable virus might exchange genes with an ordinary human virus, obtain the transmissibility of regular seasonal flu, and become a highly contagious agent causing a global pandemic.

Within this historically distinctive context marked by an uncertain biological entity, growing political pressure, and an acute sense that the future was at stake, Maines and her colleagues designed an experimental system to test under controlled conditions what might actually happen if the avian virus suddenly mixed its genes with a highly transmissible human virus. Addressing an important question investigated in contemporary microbiological research, Maines and her colleagues wondered why some viruses pass more easily among humans: "What are the molecular factors that affect the ability of the influenza virus to transmit?" That was the big question. Invoking the H5N1 virus that she was investigating in the laboratory, Maines told me, "We're trying to predict what will happen in nature, and that's a difficult thing to do." The project garnered public attention and was covered in several newspaper articles.[2]

Deploying a sophisticated technology of reverse genetics originally developed by the group of microbiologists headed by Palese at Mount Sinai in New York, Maines carefully constructed a number of hybrid strains in the test tube. These genetically engineered strains contained genes from both avian and human influenza viruses. Not surprisingly, most of the genetic combinations produced microbial creatures that were not viable at all, and the main technical challenge was to find genes "that are happy together," as Maines phrased it. "Because you're taking two very different viruses, and you're mixing their genes, and a lot of the combinations just produce a virus that is not viable," she explained. The pandemic potential of those genetically engineered viruses that were viable and that replicated efficiently and grew well under laboratory conditions was then investigated in an animal model.

In early 2006, Maines received a fresh stock of ferrets, six to twelve months of age.[3] In the laboratory, twelve animals were infected with a low dilution of the genetically engineered avian-human flu strains. The microbe farmer observed the ferrets closely over the next few days, though no transmission took place across the perforated walls separating the animal cages. None of the hybrid strains, whose genes were "happy together," appeared to be able to spread easily from animal to animal, despite genetic combination with influenza viruses known for efficient transmission. In its current state, Maines and her colleague, Dr. Terrence Tumpey, observed that the avian virus seemed to require further adaptive steps to trigger a pandemic. Yet the scientific response to the pressing question was no reason to become complacent about the threat. "We really try to stress that the findings of the study are limited to the particular strains that we used," said Tumpey. "We only looked at certain combinations." Many other combinations were possible, and therefore the research results were only provisional. There was no reason to think, "Oh, it's not going to happen because it just didn't happen with these particular strains," emphasized Maines. What the oracle offered was neither verification nor falsification: The threat continued, and more testing was required. Maines stressed that it was important to carry on, construct new strains, and test them in the animal model.

With these provisional results on the table, Maines found herself entangled in a difficult quandary, as she explained to me at the Options for the Control of Influenza meeting. As long as it remained impossible for her to construct hybrid strains that pass in the laboratory from ferret to ferret, it would not be feasible for her to publish more research about the virus. A journal would only publish positive experimental results. However, it would be equally difficult, if not impossible, to publish an article that would demonstrate how the virus could be transformed into a contagious agent dangerous for humans. Even though it would provide important scientific information regarding the pandemic potential of the virus and possibly reveal some of the molecular factors responsible for its spread, such an article, Maines explained, would inevitably elicit serious security concerns among government officials, and perhaps rightly so. At stake for Maines were not just the fate of a research project but also the very possibility of participating in the moral economy of scientific exchange.[4] No matter what her work would eventually produce, be it positive or negative results, Maines felt that her research was inextricably trapped in an expanding script of security. Growing concerns with security, as I gradually came to realize over the course of my fieldwork, loomed large over the work of microbe farmers in the United States. Paradoxically, as Maines's project vividly demonstrated, these concerns were both enabling and disabling, opening up and closing down promising avenues in the competitive world of cutting-edge science.

This chapter examines a set of intensive security debates about infectious disease research. As Ronald Atlas and Judith Reppy remarked in a sweeping 2005 publication, "in the current paradigm, all infectious disease research is potentially relevant to bioterrorism and may be implicated in controversies over the motivation and possible uses of the research."[5] According to Gerald L. Epstein, infectious disease research has become "contentious research" because it may generate information "that could have immediate weapons implications."[6] The fear was that anticipatory research might generate what it anticipates.

Concerns with security are not new, to be sure. In fact, infectious disease research has always been politically charged in many respects, but it is now even more so and in a very particular way. My aim here is to explore how concerns over security have sparked a contentious debate about experimental research and its mandates, responsibilities, and accountabilities over the past decade. This debate has underscored the need for microbe farmers to address the possibility of a self-fulfilling prophecy.

Drawing on Foucault's lectures at the Collège de France, I first examine the concern of security and its constitutive problematic of circulation. I specifically suggest that, within the context of infectious disease research, security experts have *not* been primarily concerned with the circulation of biological matter, as some scholars have argued in their examinations of contemporary biosecurity formations.[7] Of course, experts still worry about the dissemination of biological matter and technological equipment— potentially dangerous scientific information is worthless, after all, without simultaneous access to the complex and sophisticated material infrastructure necessary to manipulate viruses in the test tube. Yet these experts, I propose, have begun to focus more on the exchange of scientific information. The concern with scientific information that has been expressed over the past decade in relation to contemporary infectious disease research has affected the biopolitical economy of security in distinctive ways.

Although the focus on scientific information as a security threat is new in the context of infectious disease research, it is not new, of course, in the context of the nuclear program, where security experts have always been concerned with both dangerous matter *and* sensitive information.[8] What is specific to the biological sciences, however, is that—in contrast to the physical sciences—it is matter *itself* that is increasingly understood in informational terms.[9] Modern information and communication technologies have affected scientific understandings of biological life. Viruses are now theorized as "vectors" that "transfer" genetic "information" from one host to another. This genetic information can be rearranged and recombined to create new microbial creatures, whose genes are "happy together." Probing the cosmology of mutant strains, biologists have increasingly become biologists of information. My aim, consequently, is to attend to the historically distinctive effects of this informational redefinition of biological life for the biopolitical economy of security.

INFORMATION COMES TO MATTER

"Deadliest Flu Bug Given New Life in U.S. Laboratory," a *San Francisco Chronicle* article's headline announced in early October 2005. The article reported that U.S. scientists had re-created in the laboratory "a living copy of the deadly flu bug responsible for the catastrophic 1918 Spanish influenza epidemic."[10] The strain of the virus that triggered the pandemic had never been isolated in the laboratory. It quickly disappeared from the human population and was replaced by other, less virulent strains of the virus. Descendants of the virus have been present in pig populations since 1918, but they changed over time. Then, almost a century later, a team of American scientists successfully reconstructed the original virus in the test tube, rebuilding the pathogenic agent from its recovered genetic sequence. According to the scientists, the reason for resurrecting the 1918 virus was to examine the biological mechanisms that may have contributed to its extraordinary lethal power. Such research, the scientists suggested, might eventually lead to effective forms of public health protection against future eruptions of disease.[11]

As Palese recalled, the research that he conducted with his colleagues, Dr. Jeffery Taubenberger of the Armed Forces Institute of Pathology in Rockville, Maryland, and Terrence Tumpey of the CDC, began in 1995. Small samples of infected human tissues soaked in formalin and sealed in paraffin at the Armed Forces Institute, in addition to a few specimens recovered by a certain Johan Hultin from a frozen corpse of an Inuit woman in Brevig Mission, Alaska, allowed Taubenberger to sequence bits and pieces of the virus's genetic information.[12] By means of a sophisticated technology known as reverse genetics, which Palese adapted for influenza research in the late 1980s and frequently used in his laboratory, the researchers were able to replicate the actual virus in the test tube. First, they constructed plasmids at the Mount Sinai lab on the basis of the sequence information Taubenberger provided. In cell cultures, the genetically engineered plasmids generated proteins, which then assembled into functional particles. Following stringent biosafety procedures, the genetic information was turned into viral matter and given life in Tumpey's laboratory at the CDC in Atlanta. Tumpey finally injected the fully functional virus into fertilized chicken eggs, and then he infected ferrets and mice with the agent. On October 7, 2005, *Science* published the results of the reconstruction.[13]

As Palese told me, on September 27, 2005, just ten days before the article was published, the editorial board of *Science* received an unexpected call from the office of the secretary of the U.S. Department of Health and Human Services (HHS). In this call, the department signaled its serious security concerns regarding the forthcoming research article. A flurry of conference calls and electronic messages followed in which Assistant Secretary Stewart Simonson eventually declared that the secretary of the department insisted on an additional review of the article by the recently established National Science Advisory Board for Biosecurity (NSABB)—a permanent federal body of twenty-five voting members who are considered experts in the fields of science, medicine, and security and whose prime function is to recommend policies in the area of biosecurity. As the issue of *Science* was being printed, Simonson announced that he had ordered the advisory board to be polled. The advisory board "gave the paper an unusual last-minute review to make sure the merits of its publication outweighed the risks of releasing potentially dangerous knowledge."[14] The NSABB voted unanimously in favor of publication, requiring the journal to add a special note explaining the general purpose of the research.

A series of newspaper articles about the resurrection of the virus had already appeared before the scientific experiments were completed, establishing a space of "scandalous publicity," to borrow Lawrence Cohen's term; a space, in other words, in which a public is formed "in the enunciation of scandal" and in which there is growing political pressure to take a stance and either defend or denounce the matter at stake.[15] Scandals are trials for the public affirmation of collective values.[16] Framed as a narrative of scandal, the story about the resurrected virus affirmed the authenticity of pandemic prophecy; it made concerns about a catastrophic event credible and shaped public attitudes toward contemporary microbiological research. Rather than prevent the event, microbe farmers seemed to have produced the conditions of possibility for the prophecy to be fulfilled.

In an April 2005 *Washington Post* article, Wendy Orent suggested that "the feverish anxiety of public health officials to head off a new influenza pandemic may be generating the greatest influenza threat we face."[17] As Orent reasoned, once the genetic information is in the public domain, "the entire 1918 flu could be built from scratch by anyone, anywhere, who has sufficient resources and skill." She added, "It is quite conceivable that resurrected 1918 flu could someday be used as a bioterrorist agent." Charles Krauthammer, a syndicated *Washington Post* columnist, referred to the reconstruction of the 1918 virus as a "scientific achievement of staggering proportions."[18] Yet beyond the semblance of scientific brilliance "lies the sheer terror," cautioned Krauthammer. "We have brought back to life an agent of near-biblical destruction," he wrote, accusing the researchers responsible for "the most momentous event of our lifetime" of having opened the "gates of hell" by publishing the entire sequence of the virus "for the whole world, good people and very bad, to see." In a *New York Times* article, computer scientists Ray Kurzweil and Bill Joy concurred, arguing that it was "extremely foolish" to publish the genetic information of the virus, because it was "essentially the design of a weapon of mass destruction."[19] They warned that it would be "easier to create and release this highly destructive virus from the genetic data than it would be to build and detonate an atomic bomb given only its design, as you don't need rare raw materials like plutonium or enriched uranium." The spread of a contagious virus would be far worse than a nuclear attack, killing hundreds of millions worldwide. According to Kurzweil and Joy, it was vital to develop defenses for such "killer flu viruses." What the world needs is a "new Manhattan Project to develop specific defenses against new biological viral threats, natural or human made." Modern scientific research was responsible for the existential threat, but it was also humanity's only source of hope.

A few days later, the *New York Times* featured a reader's response to the editor. In the response, Karin Tzamarot accused Kurzweil and Joy of giving "only more life to the makings of a potential debacle."[20] As Tzamarot noted, it was the *New York Times* article that should never have been published because it explained and simplified for millions of readers worldwide why the reconstruction of the virus is so dangerous and why it might be "the preferred method of mass destruction rather than, say, an atomic bomb." Terrorists may not consult specialist journals, such as *Science* or *Nature*, but they may well have access to sources like the *New York Times*, where they can read "recipes for destruction," the title of Kurzweil and Joy's article. It was this kind of mass publicity that was responsible for the threat. The reader's letter addressed the public with a plea for silence: "Let all discussion of this matter end here!"

What this episode in the public life of pandemic influenza highlights is the scandalous publicity that has become so powerful in shaping the contemporary perception of infectious disease research in the United States. During my fieldwork, I encountered a series of scandalous stories related to scientific research that reinforced the view of pandemic influenza as a catastrophic threat. At the heart of the stories was the assumption that it is "the spread of information rather than microbes that poses the biggest bioterrorism threat today," as one article put it.[21] The circulation of information seemed more dangerous than the circulation of microbes. Stories about the dangerous spread of information typically referred to terrorist groups that might abuse scientific research. These stories drew on apocalyptic tropes of death and destruction, invoked the nation's traumatic experience of 1918, and created fears about a future in which a prophecy was fulfilled. "You have to alarm people because until people are sufficiently alarmed they're not going to listen to what has to happen," argued journalist Ted Koppel in a 2005 edition of NBC's *Meet the Press*. Scandalous stories about scientific research kept the public's attention focused on the future. These stories confronted people with the irony that pandemic prophecy might have increased the probability of the predicted event happening.

The key aim of scandal is to disclose real or imagined actions "involving certain kinds of transgressions which become known to others and are sufficiently serious to elicit a public response."[22] Significantly, such dramas of revelation often remain indifferent to the question of conclusive evidence. "A scandal has public effects regardless of a final determination of its truth or falsity, and it captures public attention only to the extent that such a determination is deferred."[23]

The prime function of scandal in this case was to perform dramas of revelation to feed the public imagination of pandemic influenza as a catastrophic disease. In these dramas of revelation, scientists appeared as ambivalent figures, capable of making ominous predictions come true. Infectious disease research was a suspicious undertaking, especially when scientists became overzealous. "The cure may prove worse than the disease," warned Orent.[24] For Krauthammer, the reconstructed agent was a "destroyer of civilizations."[25] Thus, infectious disease research became a subject of scandalous revelations, and these revelations contributed considerably to the publicity surrounding the pandemic in the United States.

At the center of the discussion about the resurrected virus was the circulation of scientific information. Having dangerous information in the public domain was considered dangerous because malicious actors might misappropriate it. Of course, whether such abuse was likely or not was difficult to determine. Even if it was unlikely, it remained a possibility with potentially catastrophic consequences. At stake more generally was the nature of prophetic speech and how it might have contributed to bring about what it foretold. In the next section I explore how security experts conceived the abuse of scientific information in the context of a more general problematic of circulation. To do so I turn briefly to Foucault's work on security.

SECURITY AND THE PROBLEMATIC OF CIRCULATION

Foucault's approach has the general advantage of avoiding the reduction of security to a set of mechanisms for the prevention of war. In Foucault's analysis, security comes into view primarily in relation to a historically distinctive problematic. As he argued in *Security, Territory, Population*, security is mainly concerned with the optimal circulation of people, goods, and things.[26] In contrast to both the apparatus of sovereignty and of discipline, security operates within a field of heterogeneous objects that must be modified in accordance with their intrinsic qualities and tendencies. For Foucault, a security intervention does not seek to transform all the material givens it encounters in the world; it instead operates by rationalizing the maximization of positive elements and the minimization of negative elements. The problem, Foucault points out, is no longer that of "fixing and demarcating the territory, but of allowing circulations to take place, of controlling them, sifting the good and the bad, ensuring that things are always in movement, constantly moving around, continually going from one point to another, but in such a way that the inherent dangers of this circulation are cancelled out."[27] For security, circulation thus constitutes the target of intermittent intervention, not total reformulation. Security's approach is often flexible and adaptive, advancing in response to changing conditions. It is only when certain forms of circulation begin to destabilize other forms that they must be controlled and curtailed. The crucial question, as Foucault puts it, is thus the following: "How should things circulate or not circulate?"[28]

Given security's concern with the regulation and modulation of circulation, it is hardly surprising to find that security experts have taken up the problem of infectious disease. In a world that has increasingly learned to describe itself in terms of globalization[29] and in which the metaphor of "flow" has become "global common sense,"[30] concerns with the threat of spreading germs have appeared at the center of a new order of "post–Cold War terrors."[31] Among the key issues for public health professionals who have begun to address the problem of emerging viruses is how to facilitate the flow of people, goods, and things without stifling exchange in the name of security. Thus, endemic to the apparatus of security is a fundamental tension between the necessity to promote and facilitate exchange, on the one hand, and the imperative to regulate and modulate circulation, on the other. My aim here, however, is not so much to analyze the constitutive tension at the heart of security in a world of globalization and deregulation, but to track how security affects experimental science.

Today, security experts focus not only on emerging viruses but also on efforts to promote particular kinds of research. Scientific research itself, in other words, is now considered a threat, the potential cause of a catastrophic event. The successful reconstruction of the 1918 virus is one of many examples demonstrating how scientific research is perceived as a source of sensitive information.[32] The accidental release of a pathogenic agent from a laboratory has always been an issue, to be sure, but the crucial problem is increasingly located elsewhere. What drew the most attention over the past decade was not so much the potential circulation of dangerous biological *matter* but rather the exchange of sensitive scientific *information*. What has come into being as a result of this concern with the mobility of information is a "map of misreading."[33] It is to this map that I now turn.

THE MAP OF MISREADING

In the aftermath of September 11, 2001, and the subsequent anthrax scare, biologists faced growing concerns that scientific information generated in the name of public health and its protection might be exploited by terrorists for malicious purposes.[34] Facing growing political efforts to promote a new category of information termed "sensitive but unclassified," scientific publishers and editors convened a meeting in January 2003 to discuss the potential security implications of biological research.[35] Increasingly embroiled in politically charged struggles over the legitimacy and accountability of biological research, leading journals responded to the political pressure in late February. Both *Science* and *Nature* released editorial statements on scientific publication and security, recognizing that "the prospect of bioterrorism has raised legitimate concerns about the potential abuse of published information."[36] In their statements, the editors vehemently rejected a formal role for the federal government, instead advising journals to take seriously their responsibility to determine what constitutes sensitive information by designing appropriate procedures to identify potential risks. In October of that year, the National Research Council of the National Academies published *Biotechnology in an Age of Terrorism*—also known as the Fink report—about technological advances that could be abused for nefarious purposes.[37] The report recommended steps to address potential abuses, among them a systematic review of biological experiments and scientific publications for potential security implications.[38]

At the center of these concerns was the possible misappropriation of scientific information. In this context, security experts began to address the problem of "dual use," and in so doing they simultaneously promoted a distinctive linguistic model. Whatever the intended audience of scientific information, it can always come under the influence of unforeseen readers. There is, in other words, forever the possibility of other contexts and other circumstances in which other meanings may prevail. Foregrounding the fundamental capacity of information to break from its original context of production, this linguistic model, increasingly operating at the heart of security, seems to reject the premises of a theory of language, in which the consciousness of the speaking subject is made the prime source of meaning. Significantly, this model also recognizes the possibility of failure; that is, the inescapable risk of infelicity, uncertainty, and ambiguity to which every enunciation remains liable. It is important to underline that the determination of meaning nevertheless continues to be context bound in this model. As Jonathan Culler astutely observes, "meaning is context-bound, but context is boundless."[39] What remains impossible is to limit context, so as to determine the true meaning of information.[40]

In the world of security, information increasingly comes into view as an object acquiring its meaning not from its present but from its future use. What comes into existence as a result of this perception is what we might call, with literary critic Harold Bloom in mind, "a map of misreading."[41] Today, terrorists are imagined as malicious agents who deliberately exploit the results of experimental research, misappropriating the immaterial products of scientific labor. The challenges of security are therefore to anticipate abuse and to mitigate the vulnerability of scientific publication. At the heart of these growing concerns is the semiotic logic of *iterability*: the ability of the sign to break from its context and acquire a new meaning. Scientific information, in this view, appears to be driven by a natural "force of rupture" and is never absolutely anchored in a given context; it can, on the contrary, always be used in other ways and always be appropriated for other purposes.[42]

SECURITY AND THE BODY IN-FORMATION

The characteristic features of the contemporary politics of security have recently been examined in a set of sweeping articles published by a group of critical thinkers.[43] Bruce Braun, Melinda Cooper, and Michael Dillon roughly share a diagnosis that lies at the core of their theoretical interventions. What is at stake is, most broadly stated, the politics of life in the philosophical tradition of Foucault. In his lectures, Foucault developed his productive notion of security, at least to some extent, in relation to the epidemiological thought and practice of the late eighteenth and early nineteenth centuries.[44] The ascendancy of molecular biology marks a significant break in the scientific understanding of infectious diseases and their causes. This break suggests that a reconsideration of Foucault's account of security is overdue. Political struggles in which pathogenic agents figure as objects of contestation have increasingly taken a different shape because scientific understandings of biological matter have changed in significant ways.

For Braun, Cooper, and Dillon, molecular biology has fundamentally transformed the idea of biological life. Not only has biological life been molecularized, as Nikolas Rose notably proposed, but it has also become contingent, unpredictable, and emergent.[45] "Molecularized life is . . . contingent life," Dillon argues.[46] In the molecular age, "life" appears as relentlessly emerging and intrinsically expansive; "its field of stability is neither rigorously determined nor constant."[47] Far from generating a stable form of existence, biological bodies now appear as if they were "thrown into a chaotic and unpredictable molecular world filled with emergent yet unspecifiable risks."[48] For Braun, Cooper, and Dillon, the "precarious body" constitutes a new challenge for the apparatus of security, posing the crucial question about how this body should or should not circulate. The contemporary concern with biological threats represents a response to the indeterminate, contingent, and unpredictable character distinctive of the biological body.[49]

The work of Braun, Cooper, and Dillon opens up a promising line of inquiry and scrutiny, enabling scholars to explore reconfigurations of security beyond Foucault's account. Such reconfigurations are occurring today not least because biological bodies have been transformed by an "art of continuous modulation, in which form is plunged back into process, becoming continuously remorphable."[50] As Donna Haraway underscores in her seminal essay on the biopolitics of postmodern bodies, the destabilization of the hierarchical, localized, fixed organic body as a principal anchor of biopolitical practice has resulted in a different kind of biopolitics, one of postmodern bodies.[51] It is precisely such a postmodern body that is at the heart of the economy of security today, a body that is just as much semiotic as it is corporeal. As a result of the ascendancy of molecular biology and its "biotechnical touch," to use Hannah Landecker's felicitous phrase, biological bodies have increasingly begun to circulate in informational forms, rather than corporeal ones.[52] The biological body is a body of information. The fact, however, that the biological body is circulated and exchanged in informational forms does not imply that it is somehow not material; the body in-formation has, on the contrary, its own distinctive materiality.[53]

We can now see that the changing ontological form of the biological body—which increasingly finds itself entangled in a permanent process of formation and reformation and is problematized in terms of a generalized economy of exchange and circulation—has affected the biopolitics of security in the United States, both stabilizing and destabilizing it. In what follows, I want to bring into sharper relief the tensions, contradictions, and contestations that have begun to manifest themselves in recent years and that are not explored in the accounts of Braun, Cooper, and Dillon. What I refer to here as "iterability" permits a detailed analysis of the fissures and fractures in today's economy of security.

CONTEXTUALIZING BIOLOGY

Aware of the many ways in which information can be detached from its original context, security experts have become concerned with the public circulation and potential misappropriation of sensitive information. Such information now seems to pose a bigger threat than viruses.[54] Nevertheless, in the conversations that I conducted and in the debates that I witnessed during my research, information was simultaneously recontextualized. This should come as no surprise at all, because "one cannot do anything, least of all speak, without determining (in a manner that is not only theoretical, but practical and performative) a context," as Jacques Derrida observed.[55] The moment of detachment, in other words, is always also a moment of reattachment, and the logic of iterability therefore constitutes the condition of possibility of both decontextualization and recontextualization.

Over the course of my research, I increasingly realized that biologists of information frequently responded to security demands with a biology of context.[56] What eventually came into view was not so much a situated science but a situating science—not a contextualized biology but a contextualizing biology. When I asked Palese about the publication of the controversial article in 2007, he stated, "We felt very strongly that the paper should be published. There was no reason that it shouldn't. At the time, we already knew for example that the 1918 virus can be inhibited by anti-influenza virus drugs, which, I think, is very important." In our conversations, Palese always insisted that the perception of the microbial creature as a "killer virus" was misleading. His view was based on a series of experiments conducted in advance of the article's publication. These experiments were designed to assess whether vaccines for regular seasonal flu would provide protection against recombinant viruses, which contained the immunologically relevant genes derived from the 1918 virus. They were conducted to contextualize the virus in contemporary circumstances, and they confirmed Palese's assumption that current vaccines would protect against it, in part because the 1918 virus belongs to the same subtype of the influenza virus (H1N1) that is currently circulating in the human population. In addition to these experiments, the scientists tested the efficacy of four antiviral drugs, which also proved effective against the 1918 virus.[57]

In his characteristically blunt and plain-speaking manner, Palese proposed that there was no justification for classifying the 1918 virus as a "select agent," for making it as dangerous as anthrax and smallpox.[58] The public perception of the scientific publication as a "recipe for destruction" was inaccurate.[59] As Palese told me,

> Very recently we have published a paper where we showed that you actually can protect against the 1918 virus with the current vaccine for the H1N1 influenza virus. With an influenza virus that is fairly similar to the 1918 virus, we already have a population which is almost completely protected against the 1918 virus. The fact that the regular vaccine formulation protects against the 1918 virus brings this virus into the realm of regular influenza viruses and does not justify people making it a select agent and preventing researchers from working on it. It's completely unjustified. Drugs work, vaccines work, I mean, what else do we have to have?

Nevertheless, security experts continued to refer to the article as an illustration of the security implications of contemporary biological research. It had become an instructive case, spectacular enough to draw attention, highlight the problem, and generate a sense of urgency. The fact that both regular antiviral drugs and regular flu vaccines had been shown to work against the virus was rarely taken into account in discussions of the case. Palese also emphasized that the entire human population was now carrying a partial immunity to the 1918 virus, especially after the 2009 pandemic, which was caused by a similar strain of the H1N1 virus. "So by learning all this, by knowing all this, I think this is very important information," he underscored. Microbiologist Dr. Richard Elbright, who questioned Palese's research in 2005, agreed, explaining in an interview that his critical comments about the resurrection of the 1918 virus "only apply to the situation as of October 2005, when the reconstruction of the 1918 virus was published." These comments, he continued, "may not fully apply to the situation after

October 2009, due to the immunological impacts of the H1N1 pandemic." Despite these qualifications, the virus was classified as a "select agent" by the U.S. government.

The public debate about the potential threat created its own performative effect. The very fact of a public discussion about a potential source of danger seemed to magnify the threat and make the security intervention necessary to prevent the fulfillment of a prophecy. The global media coverage made the "recipe of destruction" public, which terrorists in foreign countries might appropriate now. As a result of the publicity, the nefarious use of the scientific information seemed more likely. Meanwhile, the microbiologists at Mount Sinai had to deal with the FBI and pass a background check to resume their work with the virus.

It is important to note that Palese should not just be seen as a biologist of information but also, and perhaps primarily, as a biologist of context. In our conversations about pandemic influenza, he was always careful to consider the pathogenic agent in its biological milieu, emphasizing its relationships with other entities. In so doing, he systematically avoided the reification of the virus as an organic totality set apart from other organic totalities. For Palese, the 1918 virus's resemblance to other strains of the virus, its susceptibility to antiviral drugs, and its responsiveness to current vaccines were essential to determine its dangerousness. It was impossible to talk about the resurrected virus without simultaneously talking about its hosts. It seemed difficult for the virus to have an identity before being brought into relation with other bodies, human and nonhuman. What I learned from Palese is to understand the pathological as an encounter and, therefore, as a relative value. In the world of infection, disease must be conceived of as an ever-shifting, ever-changing relationship.

Iterability is the general condition that has made the decontextualization of microbial bodies in-formation possible. Yet it has concomitantly made the recontextualization of these bodies necessary, biologically as well as politically; that is, biopolitically. The articulation, contestation, and negotiation of the security demands that have been proposed over the past years take place now in terms of a biology of context or, as Landecker might phrase it, in terms of a "relational biology": "Rather than pursuing the qualities and quantities intrinsic to living things—their genetic sequences, their functional structures—these relational approaches are more likely to focus on the biology of the in between."[60] For microbe farmers, it was this space in between that was most productive, scientifically as well as politically. But this space was also generative for security experts because it revealed the limits of an economy of security preoccupied with stable genetic sequences and functional properties. In the next section I explore how security experts determine "sensitive information" in the context of contemporary infectious disease research. How exactly is sensitive information distinguished from other, presumably less sensitive information? How is the infinitely expandable category of sensitive information defined? What principles for the containment of the category are mobilized in today's economy of security?

TAXONOMIC TROUBLE

What may be the most informative research . . . must surely be the most dangerous as well.

JAMIE SHREEVE, *New York Times*

In early 2006, the U.S. government charged the NSABB with examining the potential risks posed by the synthetic construction of biological agents in research laboratories.[61] Specifically, the board was asked to assess whether microorganisms generated by means of reverse genetics (such as the 1918 virus) escape the purview of the existing regulatory system established under the Public Health Security and Bioterrorism Preparedness and Response Act of 2002. As the NSABB noted in its report, technologies such as reverse genetics and the open availability of genomic information on public data banks "have raised concerns in the scientific community and general public regarding the possible use of this technology and information to generate biological agents that could threaten public health."[62] The board further reported, "Approaches based on *de novo* synthesis avoid any need for access to the naturally occurring agents or naturally occurring nucleic acids from these agents."[63] Significantly, the genomic information that enables researchers to synthesize these pathogenic agents in the laboratory by means of reverse genetics is available online. Given the new technological capabilities, experts concerned with security have argued that it is necessary to establish a new regime of governance that reaches beyond the current regulation of dangerous matter.[64] What must be controlled and curtailed are not only the circulation of dangerous biological matter but also the exchange of sensitive scientific information made possible by the availability of the technology.

The simplest and cheapest way for a scientist to design and construct (or redesign and reconstruct) a body in-formation is to order a gene or a full genome online from a commercial firm. As of 2013, approximately forty-five private companies were providing researchers with this essential service. Typically, researchers place orders for several small pieces of DNA that they then assemble on their own. In the laboratory, experimental work with bodies in-formation often drew the microbe farmers I worked with into lively discussions about the quantity of plasmids, the quality of reagents, the purity of cells, the temperature of agar, and the fate of "bad hands." The technical procedures required to sustain this peculiar type of biological materiality are inevitably fraught with considerable contingency and create a certain anxiety, especially among graduate students in the laboratory. The techniques to culture bodies in-formation remain remarkably difficult and seem to require what Evelyn Fox Keller once identified as a "feeling for the organism" and what we might call a sensibility for its milieu.[65] Although it is a routine procedure in research laboratories, the construction of a virus in the test tube is neither simple nor straightforward. It is, on the contrary, a complex technical craft, fraught with failures. It is based on highly skilled labor and requires patience, experience, and luck. Simply following the standard protocol others have developed is no guarantee of success. Creating the right milieu in the laboratory turns out to be essential for the successful animation and circulation of bodies in-formation.

In their efforts to determine what kind of information might present the greatest concern, security experts initially suggested that scientific information about the most dangerous viruses was also the most sensitive information. Here, then, a classification of dangerous biological matter served as a model for the classification of sensitive scientific information. Experts thus invoked the presumably stable ground of dangerous biological matter and its current taxonomical classification. However, as the NSABB report noted, genomic research has increasingly begun to challenge such classifications:

> Studies of human pathogens using genomics-based approaches have revealed an enormous level of strain diversity that has challenged our notion of microbial species as discrete entities with well-defined properties. This diversity in large part reflects the fact that microbial genomes are dynamic entities shaped by multiple forces, including acquisition of new functions via lateral gene transfer. One implication of these observations is that in some instances the assignment of a genus/species name to an organism may be difficult, and of limited utility, in predicting the phenotypic properties of a particular isolate,

in particular with regard to virulence, infectivity and pathogenicity. There-fore, the genus/species based approach that is currently used in Select Agent classification is imperfect since it does not take into account the great degree of genetic variability that can exist within species as they are currently defined.[66]

The fact that microbe farmers are constructing and reconstructing viruses in the laboratory on a regular basis using combinations of genetic materials derived from different species has gradually begun to reveal the limits of a biopolitical economy of security, which is based on tidy taxonomic definitions, permanent organic substances, and stable genetic essences. New microbial creatures, which blur the boundaries of species—and thus challenge the very concept of the "species"—are potentially equipped with the same properties as select agents, but they may not necessarily fit into the taxonomic tables of the classical Darwinian sort. Such creatures increasingly seem to become il-legible in a regime in which legibility primarily depends on affixing a genus or species name to a virus. Here, then, the experimental practice of reverse genetics—or the ability of researchers to take advantage of the cosmology of mutant strains and replicate, recombine, and rearrange bodies in-formation by technical means—appears to have destabilized a regime, which derives its standards of evaluation from a taxonomic system of classification. Taking into account that microbial genomes are now considered dynamic, ever-shifting entities shaped by multiple forces, both natural and technological, tidy taxo-nomic tables increasingly prove less than adequate to reliably predict patho-genic effects.

Reverse genetics is a powerful cut-and-paste technology taking advantage of the logic of iterability. Relentlessly replicating, recombining, and rearrang-ing genetic materials in the test tube, and thereby constructing and recon-structing viruses in the test tube, researchers have successfully tied repetition to alterity and turned iterability into a generative principle of experimental practice. Genetic sequences are decontextualized and recontextualized on a regular basis, and new bodies in-formation with "uncertain ontologies" are produced along the way.[67] These new viruses, whose genes are happy together, call for a relational biology and increasingly disrupt conventional efforts to provide biological bodies with a proper name and a proper place in an evolu-tionary genealogy of microbial descent. Bodies in-formation do not suit the classifications into which security experts hope to cage them.

It would be a mistake, however, to suggest that iterability can be observed only inside the laboratory. The logic of iterability is at the heart of both a technical procedure and a natural mechanism. As scientific studies have shown, microorganisms receive genetic materials not only from their ancestors but also from other organisms without necessarily being their offspring.[68] Genes, in other words, are also transferred horizontally between organisms that are only distantly related. Stefan Helmreich explores such horizontal gene transfer in a 2003 article, where he argues that the lateral exchange of genetic material among viruses observed in the extreme ecologies around hydrothermal vents may contribute to the dissolution of the traditional relation between genealogy and taxonomy. In the case of viruses, the discovery of horizontal gene transfer is now encouraging scientists "to give up the notion of species for recombining microbes," as suggested in a recent account on the epistemological impacts of horizontal gene transfer.[69] Helmreich underscores that the "taxonomic untidiness such microbes have introduced through their lateral gene transfer reaches beyond issues in phylogeny and molecular systematics into arenas adjacent to kinship concerns and biopolitics."[70] "When genes become information and are made legible through gene sequencing and bioinformatics," Helmreich writes, "the biopolitics that result may well be new."[71]

If the microbiological ontology of the normal and the pathological offered modes of classification and standards of evaluation allowing experts to establish normative principles for the biopolitical economy of security and to determine the kind of circulations that must be controlled and curtailed, then the logic of iterability has profoundly undermined this ontology. The fact that some pathogenic agents are inherently less "dangerous" than others does not necessarily mean that the genetic sequences of these agents are equally "harmless." Because of the high sequence similarity of some select agents with other organisms, the genetic sequence of a harmless organism may ultimately prove just as dangerous as the genetic sequence of an organism officially classified as a select agent. In an effort to define "sequences of concern," the U.S. government released new guidelines in October 2010, recognizing that there are genetic sequences not unique to select agents that may also pose a security concern.[72]

Today, security experts are preoccupied not only with a distinctive practice (the public exchange of information) and with a distinctive problem (information's essential iterability); they are also confronted by a new challenge caused by the disruption of a form of regulation that is based on the taxonomic identification of microbial organisms. Meanwhile, microbe farmers continue to grow new bugs and test new bodies, providing new occasions for discussion and debate.

THE TRUTH OF SCARY VIRUSES

Palese was outraged and upset. He could hardly contain himself. "They should have gone to the press," he told me when I saw him in May 2012. "They should have gone to the press and said: 'Look, we want to make a statement that these viruses that we have produced in the laboratory have lost any virulence in ferrets.' It is absolutely fraudulent, and I think they should lose their NIH grant, as far as I'm concerned. I feel very strongly about it. Because it is dishonest and scientifically fraudulent. Fouchier and Kawaoka: dishonest guys! I think it is really criminal!"

Palese was distressed over a scandal that two research papers caused in the news media. The two papers had been submitted for peer review in October 2011. Dr. Ron Fouchier, a microbe farmer at Erasmus Medical Centre in Rotterdam, submitted a paper to *Science,* and his colleague, Dr. Yoshihiro Kawaoka of the University of Wisconsin, submitted a similar paper to *Nature.* In the papers, the scientists and their teams of researchers independently reported results of a series of experiments conducted with avian viruses that they had modified in the laboratory. Following in the footsteps of Taronna Maines's research at the CDC in Atlanta, they had manipulated the avian viruses to make them more transmissible among humans. The purpose of the research was to identify the pandemic potential of the H5N1 avian influenza virus. In other words, the scientists wanted to know if the virus could mutate and cause a deadly pandemic. The project's ambition was to provide proof to prophecy. It seemed as if such proof could finally confirm their claim to a title—the title of perceptive scientists.

In an ABC News report broadcast on television in February 2012, a journalist declared that "all sides agree that the mutated bird flu virus created by scientists . . . could kill millions if it gets out."[73] Fouchier, who was introduced as a "respected microbiologist," proudly told ABC that his team had crafted "probably one of the most dangerous viruses you can make."[74] Yet the researchers insisted that they were far from being mad scientists. They claimed that they were not trying to fulfill the prophecy and bring about what they had foreseen and foretold. They considered themselves responsible researchers, enabling a better understanding of pandemic influenza. To know more about the potential of the virus seemed to be important for preparedness efforts. The research would reveal the signs by which the coming plague could be recognized. "Does this scare you what you have discovered?" the ABC journalist queried. "What scares me is that this can happen and that it can happen so easily," replied Fouchier.[75] If scientists could mutate the H5N1 virus in the laboratory and make it transmissible, then nature could do it easily on its own. As the microbe farmer and his colleagues remarked in their paper, "Whether this virus may acquire the ability to be transmitted via aerosols or respiratory droplets among mammals, including humans, to trigger a future pandemic is a key question for pandemic preparedness."[76] Without such research "we will be overwhelmed by Mother Nature terrorizing us in the future," maintained Fouchier.[77] From the vantage point of the microbe farmer, nature was the real source of terror.

Kawaoka and his team offered similar justifications for this type of research, arguing that their "findings emphasize the need to prepare for potential pandemics . . . and will help individuals conducting surveillance."[78] The scientists refuted accusations that they were pursuing overzealous research and claimed instead to be contributing to surveillance activities by mutating the virus and exploring its potential to adapt to humans. But what if the information about the mutated strain inadvertently falls into the wrong hands or the virus escapes by accident? The predicted event might occur due to the very effort of preventing it from occurring. Laurie Garrett, of the U.S. Council on Foreign Relations, was interviewed for the ABC report and said, "My first reaction was 'Oh, my God, why did they do this?'" Then she added, "I'm not real comfortable with having this virus exist—anywhere!" Security experts, the ABC journalist noted, "say it's crazy to let these secrets get into the hands of terrorists."

In an editorial, the *New York Times* dubbed the bug a "doomsday virus" that "could kill tens or hundreds of millions of people if it escaped confinement or was stolen by terrorists."[79] Hundreds of journal articles, opinion pieces, newspaper reports, and blog entries offered a broad range of suggestions on what should or should not be done with the research. Commentators underscored that there are limits to scientific freedom and that these limits had been transgressed in this case. Scientists should not be allowed to conduct "deadly research" to contain a "deadly disease." This contribution to preparedness had not delivered on its promise of making the world safer; on the contrary, it seemed to have manufactured a great threat. The research produced precisely the kind of peril that it aimed to prevent. Richard Elbright noted that "it should never have been done" in the first place.[80] The biosecurity advisory board NSABB intervened and recommended that the journals *Science* and *Nature* withdraw key details of the studies that would allow others to replicate the experiments and re-create the virus in the test tube. Government officials contacted the journals, requesting that the editors postpone the publication and redact the papers. In January 2012, microbiologists responded to the public debate and the government's intervention and announced a pause of sixty days on transmission experiments with the mutated strain.

A group of scientists, including Palese, requested that the NSABB reconsider its attempt to censor a publication. "Realistically," they wrote in an open letter, "there is no direct evidence that the specific viruses would even cause disease in humans."[81] Fouchier and Kawaoka, the letter implied, had overstated the results of their experiments to draw attention to their research and highlight the pandemic threat, which they believed was real (though presumably not of their own making). At a panel hosted by the American Society of Microbiology, Fouchier eventually admitted that his research actually demonstrated that the mutated strain created in the laboratory was less lethal and contagious for ferrets than those found in nature. A few months earlier, the same scientist had claimed to have created "one of the most dangerous viruses you can make." Contrary to what he had suggested, the "doomsday virus" discussed in newspapers worldwide turned out to transmit poorly in the laboratory. In fact, the "deadly virus" did not kill any of the ferrets.

Palese thought that such behavior of Fouchier was fraudulent, dishonest, and even criminal. "It's fraudulent when the virus is completely, completely a-virulent and a-pathogenic in ferrets. And [to] not say anything for more than half a year. Not to admit it, not to say it after everyone is up in arms . . . it's criminal." In February 2012 the journal *Nature* joined the debate, announcing that more discussion was needed, but that the papers should be published. Then, in a sudden turnabout, the NSABB in March reversed its original decision and recommended that both papers be published in full. The board's decision making seemed capricious and chaotic. Its recommendation changed completely and with no coherent explanation.

What this story illustrates are intensifying anxieties about the possibility of a self-fulfilling prophecy. Fouchier and Kawaoka were well known among their colleagues for scientific hubris and hyperbolic statements. "They have a history of making extravagant claims," a junior microbiologist told me when we discussed the controversial research. "The good studies don't get attention.

The mediocre studies are pushed and oversold." And yet, the pushing and overselling were not useless, according to the microbiologist: "It's good to keep the interest in influenza research." Security experts, too, considered the panic produced by the mutated strain a valuable thing: It provided another example of dual-use science, illustrating the security implications of infectious disease research. Of course, the mutated strain crafted in the test tube had not killed any ferrets, and the entire debate was based on misleading claims made by scientists eager to emphasize the threat, which they believed was real, create a media spectacle, and justify more research to protect people from "killer viruses" manufactured by nature, the real bioterrorist.

At a forum organized by the Harvard School of Public Health in February 2012, epidemiologist Marc Lipsitch suggested,

> It's good that the research was done. . . . I think it helps us to remember that the H5N1 pandemic threat is a real one. Every year that a pandemic didn't occur, people began to think we were crying wolf and there was some reason to think this threat was diminished. And I think psychologically with the 2009 pandemic, which was not H5N1 . . . a lot of people found it hard to maintain the same level of preparedness. But the threat continues, and I think this is a scientific piece of evidence that it continues. So in that regard, I think it's important.

For these experts, the necessity of constant vigilance and permanent exhortation justified the research.

Bruce Alberts, editor-in-chief of *Science*, argued that as a result of the controversy "people worldwide are now much more aware of the potential threat that this virus . . . poses to humanity."[82] Public awareness was crucial, even if it was catalyzed by false claims about killer viruses that were not quite what they were purported to be. Fouchier, the press-ready scientist and champion of scandalous publicity, said that he would stick by his original comment. "Maybe I'd put it slightly differently next time," he declared in April 2012 at a meeting of the Royal Society in London, "but it is the truth: Flu viruses are scary and if they acquire the ability to go airborne in humans, they cause pandemics." It was undeniable; it was the truth: Flu viruses are scary. Faith in this truth was foundational for pandemic preparedness.

The microbiological laboratory was an important location where pandemic prophecy became living mimicry, where microbe farmers like Fouchier testified by words and deeds. The laboratory was the place where they professed their faith and demonstrated the reality of the threat. In the name of preparedness, they created a mimetic spectacle, manufacturing microbial creatures that were supposed to inform us about a truth: the truth of scary viruses.

INFORMATION INCORPORATED

Viruses inform us . . . much more than they infect us.

DAVID NAPIER

At the heart of the contemporary attempt to regulate infectious disease research is the public circulation of information. As Evelyn Fox Keller, Lily Kay, and others have shown, information is a problematic and confusing concept, especially in the biological sciences.[83] Yet although information appears to be confusing as a concept, it has nevertheless been incredibly productive, perhaps precisely because it is so confusing in the first place.[84] Confusing (and confusingly productive) as it may be, information has operated as a generative "boundary concept," establishing relations between separate and separated domains.[85] The boundary concept of information has become a driving force for dramatic stories. At stake in these stories are the changing relations between science, security, and the state. Today, microbe farmers are drawn into expanding debates about the security implications of their work. This work increasingly involves the publication of informational bodies. Not surprisingly, these bodies have a life of their own once they begin to circulate in the public culture of danger. A biology that has increasingly become informational has attached microbe farmers to the world, to the state, and to the FBI. To conduct microbiological research in the United States now means to pass a background check and submit papers to biosecurity advisory boards for official approval. Microbiologists must prevent scientific information from getting into the wrong hands. They must take responsibility for the bodies of information that they are releasing in publications. Influenza research has received abundant attention in the media over the past decade, and the field has become ever-more competitive. "It used to be a very small universe for flu researchers," observed one microbiologist. Today, with all the publicity, research can be stressful.

In conversations, microbe farmers always insisted on the stringent safety precautions that must be observed, but they concomitantly stressed the importance of publishing the results of experimental research without externally imposed limitations or restrictions. It is their belief that such a strategy of safety and precaution both improves science and protects the public's health. Underwriting this belief is the liberal imaginary of an unrestricted exchange and free sharing of information. This imaginary is, of course, itself a constitutive element of the founding myth of modern science as a public institution. It would be a mistake, therefore, to consider it an adequate description of the actual practice; instead it should be seen, as historian of science Robert Kohler suggested, as the articulation of a moral code.[86] With Kohler's *Lords of the Fly* in mind, it is fair to say that this moral code continues to shape the way scientists perceive themselves today.[87] Based on this perception scientists frequently declare that security concerns and intellectual property rights are increasingly straining the moral economy of scientific exchange in which they are supposed to participate. At stake in these debates are thus questions about the moral foundations of the scientific community. There is no doubt that the notion of information continues to be essential for the relational understanding of the biological that biologists of information are promoting. But the notion also constitutes a central element of their moral identity as scientists engaged in social relationships mediated by the public exchange of scientific information.

As a boundary concept, the notion of information thus structures both a scientific understanding of biology and its moral foundation as a science based on social relationships mediated by a form of generalized exchange. Today's biologists of information are engaged in the difficult effort of constructing a biology of context, reflecting the crucial question of how to access the power of informational bodies.

FIVE

A Real Test

IN AUGUST 2005 a newspaper article reported that health officials in New York City "are working with increasing urgency to develop a defense in case a deadly strain of influenza begins to spread widely."[1] A year later, in July 2006, New York City's Department of Health and Mental Hygiene released its Pandemic Influenza Preparedness and Response Plan. Mayor Michael Bloomberg declared that he was very confident "that the plan will help us detect a pandemic quickly."[2] Because of influenza's notoriously confusing array of symptoms, laboratory testing was considered essential for rapid detection. Emphasizing the need for accurate surveillance, health officials argued that they had to expand the financial, logistical, and technological resources available for the network of laboratories authorized to perform influenza testing in the city. The plan's purpose was to improve the existing infrastructure's ability to provide accurate information in the case of an emerging pandemic situation. As New York City's health officials announced, "regular influenza seasons will be used as preparedness drills to ensure that all components of the laboratory network function optimally."[3] Year after year, the virus would change, and the disease would return. Doctors would collect samples from their patients, putting the laboratory network to the test. Influenza's seasonal nature made it valuable as a proxy for the catastrophic pandemic. "It's the perfect disease for preparedness," a public health professional told me.

In this chapter, I explore the contingencies of diagnostic testing. Responding to concerns about a potentially catastrophic pandemic, the market for rapid diagnostic tests has expanded exponentially over the past decade. Commercial suppliers now offer a large number of products that promise reliable results within ten minutes or less. Such tests, which are used by doctors in their offices, look like home pregnancy tests. A public health official told me,

"They look similar. It's that quick. You take a swab; you put it into the buffer. It's just going to tell you whether it is influenza A or B. You will get a little blue line—that's all it is." In the United States, health officials encouraged the development of such products, but they also maintained that test results could not always rule out infections. Indeed, CDC's interim guidance for rapid diagnostic tests warned that false results are common, and the Food and Drug Administration (FDA) admitted that their level of accuracy is only moderate, ranging from 50 to 70 percent. The predictive value depended on a number of variables, including "the level of influenza activity in the community, the types of circulating viruses at the time, the age of patients, and the adequacy of specimen collection."[4] To reduce the risk of a false diagnosis, it was recommended that negative test results always be followed up with additional tests. Pharmaceutical companies took advantage of the specter of pandemic influenza and brought tests to the market that were not always reliable, making more testing necessary. The large number of products that became available made it important for health officials to assess their accuracy and evaluate their proficiency on a regular basis. New York City's Preparedness Plan underscored that such proficiency testing is crucial to ensure accurate surveillance, and it is now mandatory for clinical laboratories in the United States.

Proficiency-testing programs are intriguing because they reveal a more general feature of pandemic preparedness: its emphasis on the idea of testing. To prepare means not just to make plans but also to put these plans to the test. Preparedness needs to be tested; it cannot simply be taken for granted as a given, and it must be checked constantly. In the United States, hospitals are required to stage at least one exercise per year with a simulated patient suffering from a highly communicable disease. The aim of such testing through exercises and drills is to assess preparedness; that is, to evaluate performance, ensure compliance, maintain vigilance, and improve readiness. Simulated events allow public health professionals to reveal potential vulnerabilities and address gaps in the preparedness and response plan. Tabletop exercises result in after-action reports and improvement plans, where procedures are reviewed and recommendations made.

Emergency consultants argued that the process was more important than the plan as such. "Planning is useful; plans are useless," stated a consultant in a conversation with me. "Your plan is never going to be exactly the same as the situation you're facing," the emergency expert emphasized. But planning as a process was useful because it made sure that people were getting prepared, that people were taking the necessary steps to be ready for the catastrophic future. For hospitals and other health care facilities, the persistent demand to engage in a process of permanent planning and constant testing amounted to an ordeal of its own.

In this chapter, I take the focus on rapid diagnostic tests as a starting point to continue my investigation of the prophetic scene and explore the idea of testing more generally. Not surprisingly, the concerns that officials expressed regarding the accuracy of rapid diagnostic tests have made proficiency testing more important than ever. Rapid tests are known to have limits in terms of accuracy, but they are nevertheless considered essential because they are seen as important tools for quickly detecting pandemics in the making. Scholars trained in the tradition of the social studies of science might say that such tests are fundamental for the constitution of the pandemic as a threat. Yet, in fact, it is not the felicity, but rather the infelicity of the testing that is foundational. In the prophetic scene, the threat becomes a threat not by prevailing in a trial of strength, but by failing.[5]

This chapter tells the story of a test that produced poor results, though it contributed to the sedimentation of the threat. As we will see, inaccurate test results such as false positives are valuable for preparedness. False positives are inaccurate results that indicate that a condition is present when in fact it is not. Significantly, the logic of the false positive reflects the more general intention of preparedness and its emphasis on trainings, exercises and drills, which also encourage people to assume that a condition is present when in fact it is not.

While engaging as a volunteer in various trainings, exercises and drills, it occurred to me that, for preparedness, false positives are much more productive than false negatives, because they can trigger a genuine response. By so doing, they provide practitioners of preparedness with an opportunity to test their plans and check how robust they are in the event of an emergency. In contrast to simulated events, which are typically based on fictitious scenarios that are never able to generate a real sense of urgency among participants, false positives confront the actors with situations that are not announced beforehand. What happens, in other words, is not a simulation. False positives trigger a real response. People proceed under the *false* impression that an *actual* event has occurred. For this very reason, false positives are valuable as tests precisely because they are not marked as tests in advance. They produce the feeling of an actual event, an event that is not seen as a simulation as soon as it occurs. With the help of the false positive, the test becomes more real than the most realistic test. In contrast to the false negative, the false positive is capable of eliciting a reaction and generating a response. What it creates is a dramatic scene, a scene of eventfulness in the absence of events. Paradoxically, the most inaccurate test allows practitioners of preparedness to conduct the most accurate test.

A COMEDY OF ERRORS

The modern territorial state has always been aware of the promise and peril that the growing traffic of persons and things across its borders represents. Over and over, states have been involved in both promoting and channeling, and thus controlling, these flows by a variety of means. Among the numerous items that travel the globe on dry ice are patient specimens.[6] Clinical laboratories, large and small, are at the receiving end of this lucrative traffic. The main task of laboratories is to process high volumes of samples efficiently, perform diagnostic procedures accurately, and turn biological matter into meaningful medical information. Equipped with a relatively simple technical infrastructure of test tubes, centrifuges, microscopes, and a variety of reagents, diagnostic laboratories are not supposed to, nor do they have the means to, detect and determine all known pathogenic agents. Typically, they focus on the most common disorders that affect the population.

Physicians send specimens to clinical laboratories because they need to know what disease it is and what virus a patient has. The CDC encourages laboratories to forward anything unusual or unidentifiable to Atlanta. "We tell them, over and over again, we're the CDC, we never close. We're here to accept that and test that specimen as soon as possible," a CDC official noted. "It's what we do, we keep an eye on the changing of the virus." She also noted that each year the number of specimens delivered to the CDC has grown exponentially because of the growing fears of an impending pandemic. In 2006, the CDC got seven thousand influenza specimens for further analysis. "We received this from all over the world, not just the United States. We received specimens from countries that we had never received specimens from, which is fabulous. It's good to see this surveillance being built up. We're doing a lot of work with India. We're doing a lot of work with South America," the official proudly told me. Such work is valuable to see what kind of viruses are circulating throughout the world. "We want to make sure we are not missing anything."

In February 2005 the specimen of a patient suffering from an undetermined respiratory disease made its way to a clinical laboratory in Vancouver, Canada. A rapid diagnostic test revealed the presence of an influenza virus, but it could not promptly determine the subtype of the virus. Following standard procedures, the specimen was dispatched for further investigation to the National Microbiology Laboratory in Winnipeg, Manitoba, where it was identified as an influenza virus of the H2N2 subtype. This particular subtype had not been seen in people in decades, and its detection in the specimen of a hospitalized patient was troubling, public health officials emphasized. The virus appeared to be similar to the pathogenic agent that had spread in 1957 at the outset of a global pandemic. Confronted with the terrifying prospect of a prophecy come true, Canadian health authorities immediately informed the WHO in Geneva, as well as the CDC in Atlanta.

The H2N2 influenza subtype, also known as the cause of the "Asian pandemic," originally emerged in Asia in February 1957, arrived in the United States a few months later, and then continued to spark epidemics of seasonal flu in humans over the following decade.[7] Then, in 1968, the virus suddenly disappeared from the human population and was replaced by a new subtype of the influenza virus, H3N2, which triggered what is known as the "Hong Kong pandemic." Microbe farmers isolated the H2N2 virus in 1957, stored the pathogenic agent in the freezer, and preserved samples for future research. When the virus suddenly appeared in a hospitalized patient in March 2005, health authorities wondered whether they had just detected an ominous sign announcing the return of an old foe and the onset of a global pandemic.

In the end, the dreadful event failed to occur. Tracking down the origin of the strange sample, the Canadian authorities eventually concluded that the specimen had been drawn from a patient who clearly failed to present the symptoms typically associated with the disease. Yet if the virus was not present in the patient, then why was it in the patient's specimen? How did it get there? Where had it come from? A systematic retrospective investigation revealed that the patient's specimen had been contaminated inadvertently in the course of the analysis in the Vancouver laboratory. As it turned out, it was the panel of proficiency-testing samples manufactured by a private U.S. company that actually contained the H2N2 virus. Due to an accidental contamination the virus had slipped from the panel into the patient specimen, where it was eventually detected.

In the United States and Canada, certified laboratories are required by law to demonstrate on a regular basis that they are able to identify a certain number of pathogenic agents accurately and efficiently. Proficiency-testing programs are compulsory and must be administered by private nonprofit organizations as mandated, in the United States, by the Clinical Laboratory Improvement Amendments of 1988. The oldest and largest provider of proficiency-testing kits is the College of American Pathologists. For example, in September 2004, the nonprofit organization delivered 4,400 panels containing samples of various flu viruses to participating laboratories in the United States, Canada, and elsewhere. Other organizations distributed panels as well that year.[8] In total, the virus was shipped to six thousand laboratories in eighteen countries.

The samples in the panels are chosen to mimic as closely as possible the patient specimens that diagnostic laboratories receive and process on a regular basis. Manufactured by a contractor, Meridian Bioscience of Cincinnati, Ohio, the samples were supposed to contain strains of the two contemporary subtypes of the influenza virus known as H1N1 and H3N2. These strains were then circulating in human populations and were therefore considered "low risk" for laboratory personnel and the public. In 2004 Meridian Bioscience made the decision to include the H2N2 virus in its proficiency-testing kit. According to a spokesperson, Meridian knew what the microbe was, but assumed it was safe because it was classified as a biosafety level II agent, which is considered "low risk," just like any other regular seasonal flu virus. At a press conference, Julie Gerberding, director of the CDC, said, "It was probably a situation where the advantages of using a strain that grows well and can be easily manipulated in the lab were the driving force."[9]

Meridian was primarily focused on cost efficiency and profit, but its decision to include the H2N2 virus was not entirely unreasonable from the perspective of pandemic preparedness. If a key aim of diagnostic laboratories is to contribute to rapid detection, then there might be a legitimate reason to use the H2N2 virus as a testing sample. "In order to control a pandemic, public health laboratories need to be able to identify novel strains," a lab director emphasized.[10] And the H2N2 virus was a novel strain. The panel with the specimen was thus not just a proficiency test but also a test of preparedness, a test of the capability of clinical laboratories to detect new strains.

The contamination that occurred in the lab in Vancouver clearly compromised the test results. As it turned out, there was a virus, but no disease. The whole situation was an incident, not an actual event. Nevertheless, the contamination of the sample and the detection of the virus produced a series of unpredictable effects. The story that seemed to be happening and that caused considerable concern because of the flawed diagnosis became a potential story that might have happened under less fortunate circumstances. The test-kit error raised the specter of a global pandemic triggered by accident. What if the virus in the test kit escaped? What if a bench scientist got the bug? The possibility of a mishap seemed plausible; it highlighted the threat of dangerous microbes that laboratories and culture collections were overlooking.

Confronted with the possibility of a pandemic triggered by accident, health authorities decided to nip it in the bud, and a systematic effort to destroy all panels containing the virus followed. In the United States, the CDC ordered that all laboratory workers destroyed the panels immediately. Yet it was the analysis of the contaminated patient specimen that caused this CDC response, not the test kit itself, which contained samples of the H2N2 virus. Indeed, the H2N2 virus stirred concerns among health officials precisely because it had been detected in a *patient specimen* rather than in a *testing sample*. The contamination of the specimen thus played a crucial role, generating a sense of urgency and encouraging officials to deal with the issue in advance. Ironically, the mistake happened in the context of a program designed to evaluate the ability of laboratories to identify microbes *accurately*.

The mistake revealed a possibility, a possibility that never became reality. But the scenario was plausible; it could have happened. Thus, false alarms constitute a productive force fundamental for the identification of potentially hazardous procedures. In the world of preparedness, the false is positive: it reveals vulnerabilities and demonstrates how real the threat is. It triggers a powerful effect in the absence of a cause, allowing actors and institutions to keep people's awareness fresh and highlight the permanent possibility of a public health emergency.

In the world that has come into being in the shadow of the predicted pandemic, false alarms are the rule and constant warnings are given about the looming threat. But the fact that this form of preparedness is causing too many false signals can also be seen as a sign of its sensitivity: It actually constitutes a crucial part of its functionality. The false alarm is a consequence of the exceptional vigilance that is considered necessary to prepare for the inevitable pandemic. The false, in other words, is far from an aberration; it is a normal incident, the consequence of the caution that has become indispensable.

The CDC's systematic attempt to track down the "deadly samples" and destroy all proficiency-testing kits was accompanied by an avalanche of frantic media commentaries invoking the specter of a "killer flu virus" delivered to "thousands of labs all over the world," including Lebanon and Saudi Arabia.[11] The microbe's fate gripped the media for weeks. In newspaper articles, journalists exposed the shipment of the test kits as a shocking incident threatening the health and security of Americans. Commentators emphasized that the virus offered a unique opportunity for terrorist attacks: "Given all the concerns about biological terrorism since 9/11, how is it possible that such a deadly pathogen could be in the public domain, with no restrictions on its use?" a New York Times article wondered.[12] Medical historian Howard Markel was deeply troubled: "Why on earth . . . would such dangerous stuff be sent around anyway? Why isn't it kept under the tightest lock and seal?"[13] Michael Osterholm concurred: "We can't have this happen. Who needs terrorists— or Mother Nature—when through our own stupidity, we do things like this?"[14] As mentioned earlier, officials at the CDC took these concerns seriously and released a health alert that required the immediate destruction of all samples. Yet panels that had been shipped to Lebanon could not be located right away. In response, bloggers wondered anxiously whether it might be possible for terrorist groups to gain access to the missing panels and use the samples for nefarious purposes.

At a press briefing, CDC director Julie Gerberding announced that steps would be taken to prevent such incidents in the future and "determine whether or not these kinds of pandemic potential viruses should be handled like other select agents that could be agents of bioterrorism."[15] Driven by a growing sense of urgency, officials deemed the distribution of the "deadly samples" a serious violation of standard biological safety principles, even though the virus shipment had caused no disease in people. But what, in fact, are biological safety principles? How is safety practiced in the laboratory?

In the United States, responsibility for biological safety is divided among a number of federal agencies, ranging from the CDC to the National Institutes of Health (NIH), the Department of Homeland Security, the Department of Agriculture, the Environmental Protection Agency, and the Food and Drug Administration (FDA). A large number of safety protocols issued by various government agencies, international organizations, and institutional review boards are currently available, but the key guidelines regularly consulted by public and private labs alike are formulated in a manual titled *Biosafety in Microbiological and Biomedical Laboratories* (BMBL), published and regularly updated by the CDC and the NIH.[16]

The BMBL manual describes microbiological practices, safety equipment, and facility safeguards recommended for work with particular pathogenic agents. These recommendations, it is important to emphasize, are advisory and voluntary, but microbiologists apply them on a daily basis. BMBL fashions itself as a professional code of practice "that all members of a laboratory community will together embrace to safeguard themselves and their colleagues, and to protect the public health and environment."[17] According to the manual, the key principle of biosafety is "containment." Its purpose is "to reduce or eliminate exposure of laboratory workers, other persons, and the outside environment to potentially hazardous agents."[18] Containment thus responds to the inevitable risk that is associated with the handling of infectious matter. Because the BMBL is a professional code of practice, the biosafety procedures it formulates pertain not to the domain of sovereign law but to the domain of professional self-regulation. Safety has a particular purpose: protection; it has a particular principle: containment; it has a particular place: the laboratory; and it is concerned with a particular kind of subject: the laboratory worker.

The CDC responded to the mishap by reclassifying the H2N2 virus from a biosafety level II to a biosafety level III pathogen. Handling a biosafety level III pathogen requires a combination of laboratory practices, safety equipment, and facility design providing a higher level of protection to scientists, lab technicians, and the public. To minimize moments of exposure and reduce the potential for accidental infection, boundaries are drawn to keep things separate and contained. The four different levels of biosafety outlined by the BMBL manual refer to four distinctive combinations of practices, devices, and facilities designed to ensure that things are enclosed and remain enclosed within other things. With its special doors and sealed windows, its air treatment and waste management systems, the facility of the laboratory functions as the most encompassing container. Labs contain a series of additional containers, among them safety cabinets, which contain centrifuges, which contain test tubes, which contain cell cultures, which contain pathogenic agents. Gloves keep human skin separate from infected matter, and face masks protect people from inhaling dangerous aerosols. Biological safety thus entails a complex assemblage of architectural structures, artifact design, and embodied practices aimed at enclosing things practically and materially within other things.

The purpose of containment therefore is to *prevent* infection. Yet there is also another form of containment that is distinctive for microbe farming, and it *presumes* infection. Viruses are parasites, which depend on the genetic machinery of host cells to reproduce their own kind. Viruses infect cells and thus primarily exist as things contained within other things. In the natural environment, it is mainly human or animal cells that contain influenza viruses. In the laboratory, chicken eggs make it possible for the viruses to replicate and reproduce. This form of containment is thus predicated on infection. Significantly, the entities that are contained are not separate from their containers; they adapt to them. What are the implications of this lack of separation for safety practices?

As we have seen in earlier chapters, the chicken eggs in which viruses are grown are hatched industrially under special safety precautions in high-tech facilities, and each contains a living chicken embryo. Fertilized chicken eggs are ubiquitous in influenza research because they serve a very practical purpose. Eggs serve as living factories, tiny bioreactors so to speak, that give life to things that have no life. Fertilized chicken eggs are used as the primary medium to isolate and grow influenza viruses, which infect the cells of the chicken embryo and replicate. Fertilized chicken eggs had been used as early as 1920 for the cultivation of the fowl plague virus (which was subsequently recognized to be an avian influenza virus). When Sir Frank Macfarlane Burnet developed and refined his inoculation technique in the 1930s, using chicken eggs became the standard procedure, replacing the much more tedious, time-consuming, and hazardous method of ferret infection. Today, the isolation of influenza viruses in the fertilized chicken egg is still considered the "gold standard." Microbiologists value these eggs because they are small, cheap, and easily available. The CDC requires a sizable number of eggs for its surveillance program; it orders a total of 300 dozen eggs every week.

In their journey from fertilized chicken egg to fertilized chicken egg, influenza viruses adapt to their new animal host. As a consequence of this process, almost all influenza viruses that are preserved in the laboratory have been adapted to chicken eggs, and they are thus unlikely to cause disease in humans. Although *contaminations* of biological research matter frequently occur in the laboratory, *infections* with influenza viruses are extremely rare in the research context. For the microbe farmers with whom I worked, the H2N2 virus distributed to laboratories across the world was certainly not a deadly sample or killer virus. In their view, the panic over a possible pandemic triggered by the bug in the test tube was an overreaction. Paradoxically, the H2N2 virus, which seemed to require containment, was already contained.

Microbiologists agreed that the government's concern about the H2N2 virus was unwarranted. As I learned from microbe farmers, the way that influenza viruses reproduce and replicate in laboratories automatically reduces their ability to infect humans. Laboratory strains are grown in fertilized chicken eggs, a practice that makes it possible for bench scientists to produce enough viral substance for research projects. In the process, these laboratory strains, derived from humans, adapt to their hosts, the chicken eggs. Such adaptation causes them to lose their former capacity to infect humans. The promotion of one form of infection hence prevents another form of infection. Consequently, the danger posed by the 2004 virus shipment seemed to be minimal. It was a strain that had been grown in a laboratory to be used in other laboratories for testing purposes. According to microbe farmers, the concerns that journalists, politicians, and government officials expressed were exaggerated. "It's not easy to take a virus out of the freezer and put it back into humans," said Robert Webster when we met to discuss his work. "When you adapt a flu virus to an egg it's no longer human."

If labs can be said to contain viruses, then viruses can also contain labs. Once made to reproduce and replicate in the artificial environment of the laboratory, influenza viruses embody the conditions of their existence. The H2N2 strain distributed as a proficiency-testing sample in 2004 was not a primary isolate, but a reference strain. It had spent a half-century in a laboratory passing numerous times through fertilized chicken eggs to produce large amounts of the virus so that it could be delivered to diagnostic laboratories participating in the proficiency-testing program. Adapted to fertilized chicken eggs, the strain was growing well. The fact that it was growing well was also among the reasons why Meridian Bioscience relied on it for production of the proficiency-testing kit. The strain was suitable for industrial mass production, and it came with the promise of efficient growth and easy profit. Interacting with its new animal environment, the strain had gradually adjusted to its new container and changed its biological features. Paradoxically, the virus that was said to be in urgent need of containment was contained already. Nevertheless, the situation changed abruptly in 2005, and the H2N2 influenza virus was set apart from other influenza viruses by the U.S. government. The

FIGURE 16. The laboratory freezer. Virus samples stored in boxes in a laboratory freezer at −70 °C. Such microbial archives contain thousands of strains collected continuously over decades by generations of researchers. Photograph by the author.

contamination and misidentification turned the microbial creature, stored in the microbe farmers' freezer, into a dangerous pathogenic agent that was posing a serious threat to the public's health.

LAB REPORT

Because of the peculiar conditions of experimental research, most viruses investigated in the laboratory have lost their ability to cause disease in humans. As a result, accidental *infection* is unlikely to occur. Accidental *contami-*

nation, by contrast, is a frequent occurrence that often disrupts the research of workaday microbe farmers. In 2008, Gina Conenello, a graduate student in the Palese lab, tried to synthesize two viruses by means of reverse genetics. The "rescue," as she called the experimental procedure, took two days.

Conenello began the rescue by grabbing a bucket with eight plasmids and moving to a concrete, windowless room located at the end of a corridor. She did the experiment in a biosafety cabinet not only to protect herself but also to prevent any possible contamination of the plasmids during the rescue. Using a powerful 70 percent ethanol disinfectant, Conenello carefully cleaned all the tubes, dishes, and flasks before placing them in the safety cabinet. She turned on the hood, sterilized the test tubes again, and began to synthesize the two viruses. To avoid any contamination, Conenello frequently changed the tip of the pipette that she was using to transfer liquids from one tube to another. While doing the experiment, the following exchange with Samira Mubareka, a postdoc, unfolded:

"What are you doing, Gina? A rescue or something?"
"Yeah. Hm. I don't think it's going to work."
"Are you doing PR/8?"
"Yeah."
"And it's not working?"
"It's not."
"It will work, damn it!"
"It will! It will! It's just I have bad hands."
"You shouldn't say that! I've got mine working after I added a lot more
    plasmids."

Eventually, Conenello realized that her effort to rescue the two viruses had failed. The liquid, which was covering the cell cultures with the two viruses, had turned yellow—the sure sign of a bacterial contamination. A few days after she aborted the experiment, I asked Conenello about the problem of contamination that kept disrupting research that was done in the laboratory. "It depends, I guess, on how clean you are," she said. "Different people have different amounts of bacterial contamination and things like that. So it depends on the lab and the person doing the experiments. I guess if someone is not careful with his plasmids, and they are not in the hood, then they are more likely to be contaminated than somebody who is much more careful with his plasmids." "We're really into cleaning," a biosafety officer once explained to me during a biosafety course that was mandatory for doctoral students. Indeed, bench scientists are constantly disinfecting their equipment.

As Conenello noted, "I usually don't have too many problems with contamination. I am pretty careful. The problem comes when you borrow plasmids from somebody else. You have no idea where they come from; you don't know how that person handled them." But even plasmids can be cleaned. "It's actually pretty easy to get rid of the contamination in the plasmids; you just re-precipitate the DNA, which involves ethanol precipitation. And ethanol will kill any contaminants." Contamination can, of course, also happen during the experiment. "So if you touched with a pipette something and then put it into the cells, and whatever that was, wasn't clean, then that would definitely very easily contaminate the cells. You try to minimize things like that. And obviously if you saw yourself hit something you should really throw that out, instead of continuing to use it. So those are all things that you learn." But why are microbe farmers not using antibiotics to prevent contaminations? Conenello explained,

So there are a couple of things. First when you do a transfection, you're affecting the cell membrane of the cell. If you tried to add antibiotics you would kill the cell. So transfections have to be done without antibiotics. The other thing is: If you grow up the virus in a media that had antibiotics and then you would be giving the virus to a mouse you would be giving the mouse antibiotics as well as virus. So you want to minimize the extra stuff in the media. And the third thing is that sometimes what can happen is that instead of the antibiotics killing all the bacteria, it will keep the level of infection low so that the cells live but there's still a basic level of contamination and when you remove the antibiotics the bacteria grow up a lot and then all of the experiments that you've done with these cells can be thrown out because you had some background level of contamination that you didn't know about. So there are some places where they're not using antibiotics at all because they're worried about this kind of thing, which I think is completely valid. I try not to use antibiotics in my cell culture for that reason.

When contaminations occur, it is inevitable that microbe farmers repeat the experiment. For such work to be successful, it is important to identify the contamination's source. Conenello continued,

Generally it's easy to tell where the contamination came from. If it is something that you just made a mistake where you touch something, you usually remember those kinds of things, and that's also the reason why we have controls. So you would have something that had no DNA but transfection reagent, so if that was contaminated too, then you would know that your transfection reagent was a problem and probably not your plasmids. Another reason for all the controls that we do is to make sure that if something goes wrong you can figure out what it was. So that you can then go back and eliminate the contamination.

"It must be annoying, like recently when your rescue failed," I said. "Yeah, it's a little annoying," replied Conenello. "Because then you have to do everything all over again. And a lot of times you have to go back one step because you have to get rid of the contamination first. So if you have twelve plasmids it's probably best to simply re-precipitate all of them rather than figure out which one was contaminated. But it's kind of like something that happens and it happens to everybody so . . . it's part of your work. It's part of being in a lab."

In contrast to contaminations, which happen frequently in the lab despite the constant cleaning effort, it is rare for researchers to get accidental flu infections. "If something like that would happen," observed Conenello, "your lab would probably be shut down for inappropriate techniques. I mean, if you're infecting yourself, you're obviously doing something wrong. In order to infect yourself with the flu you would have to aerosolize the virus. And even if you would stab yourself that's not really going to work, right, because the flu has to get to your lungs." But this is very unlikely. "It's kind of hard to do that. The only way would be to aerosolize it. And that's why you have to be careful when you aerosolize it. I don't know of many cases of infection, I can't think of any cases here. Plus we all have to get flu shots. Some people work on mouse-adapted strains and with mouse-adapted strains an infection is very unlikely. And if something is really super-contagious, you have to work in a biosafety level III lab."

What was so annoying for workaday microbe farmers—the prospect of contamination—turned out to be valuable for health authorities. The *contamination* that occurred in the laboratory in Canada revealed a scenario that could have happened: *infection*. Health authorities perceived the H2N2 virus as a threat and requested that lab workers destroy the deadly samples to reduce the risk of a pandemic triggered by accident. Eventually, the virus became a select agent and was locked away. Although officials acknowledged that the virus posed a very low risk for the public's health because it was a laboratory strain adapted to chicken eggs, action was taken in the name of precaution.

Over the past decade, precaution has increasingly become an important principle for risk management in the United States and elsewhere. It has often been invoked in relation to issues concerning protection of the environment, as well as of human and animal health. Recourse to precaution is considered warranted when scientific information appears to be "insufficient," "inconclusive," or "uncertain." Precaution, in other words, is a political technology of risk management for situations in which risk assessment is inconclusive or even impossible and in which potential hazards might entail catastrophic consequences for health. In such a case, the principle of precaution requires authorities to consider the worst imaginable case as the most likely scenario. Precaution thus enables actors to commit a leap of faith and take a certain future for granted, even if there is no evidence that this future is likely to materialize.[19] Significantly, the crucial terms "insufficient," "inconclusive," and "uncertain" frequently crop up in expert and policy debates, but almost never in specific ways. It seems, however, that these terms, first and foremost, refer to the problem of an unknown future and uncertain probability calculations. In a context in which it is not possible to determine probabilities, "recognition of ignorance is the most appropriate approach," as two scholars recently concluded.[20]

Precaution amounts to a reaffirmation of agency and sovereignty in a world that is increasingly saturated with a complex array of scientific truth claims and ambiguous or unreliable test results. In cases in which scientific evaluations preclude a full and final calculation of probabilities or in which such an evaluation is impossible, the principle of precaution enables decision makers to proceed and intervene even if the risk in question has not yet been fully determined.[21] Faced with an unknown future and uncertain probabilities, the decision to proceed and intervene becomes an eminently political one, even if it does not appear as such. Not surprisingly, the principle has been discussed in relation to the pandemic threat. "In the face of major large-scale threats like those to human health from avian and pandemic influenza, there is little controversy around some role for precaution as a possible normative presumption in risk management," Andy Stirling and Ian Scoones note.[22]

Although public health officials argued that the H_2N_2 virus samples needed to be destroyed, they did not do so on the basis of a full risk assessment. Instead they rushed to this conclusion because of the urgency of the matter and the growing avalanche of accusations. Scientific information about the virus was available; nevertheless, it could not contain the perception of manmade danger that the media fueled. The bug had gripped the attention of people, the shipment of the samples was exposed as "stupidity," scientists were blamed for being "careless," and fears about terrorist attacks were spreading like wildfire. The pressure to do something was mounting day by day. The dramatic story about the dangerous virus preserved in the laboratory seemed to make an intervention necessary. Government officials insisted that it is always "better to be safe than sorry," as one public health professional put it to me. "We have to err on the side of caution," as CDC's director, Julie Gerberding, phrased it at a 2005 press conference, and as Nancy Cox, head of the CDC Influenza Branch, confirmed when I interviewed her in 2008. Time and again, officials told me that they had no choice; when there is uncertainty or disagreement, "it is only responsible to plan for the possibility that the optimists are wrong."[23] What the concept of precaution enables is a leap of faith, encouraging people to prepare for a catastrophe. In the world of preparedness, precaution has become a fertile ground for dire prophecy, allowing officials to proceed as if the most frightening scenario were about to come true.

Thus, precaution must be situated in relation to the more general problem of legal as well as moral and political responsibility and accountability. Significantly, responsibility and accountability appeared in this context in the form of an anticipation, an "anticipation of retrospection,"[24] which created a level of anxiety among officials. Precaution refers to a moment in the future at which an endpoint is given and a judgment is made retrospectively. This retrospective judgment is anticipated in the present. "Someday, after the next pandemic has come and gone," Osterholm suggested, "a commission much like the 9/11 Commission will be charged with determining how well government, business, and public health leaders prepared the world for the catastrophe when they had clear warning. What will be the verdict?"[25] Emerging on the horizon was thus not just the next pandemic but also the next commission. The commission's task was to assess each actor according to what he or she had done or failed to do.

Borrowing from Elizabeth Povinelli, we might say that the present is "interpreted from the point of view of a reflexive future horizon."[26] According to Povinelli, the future anterior constitutes a temporal structure characteristic of the late liberal government of bodies and populations. Events in the present are judged in relation to what will have been the outcome of these events "from the perspective of a future interpreter." The present is thus increasingly perceived from a point in time in which a future will have happened and in which a retrospective judgment will be made. Precautionary action makes it possible for actors to leap over the gap that has opened up between the present moment of decision and the future moment of judgment. The temporal incongruity between these two moments threatens the agency of public health actors and public health institutions. Precaution allows professionals in charge of the public's health to prepare for the next commission and to be ready for the day of judgment.

In the context of precautionary action, expecting the unexpected has increasingly mutated into presuming the worst and hoping for the best. Even though precaution is often referred to as a "principle," there is considerable disagreement among experts about what it actually means: Different versions exist and new definitions are proposed. The principle is entangled in larger contests over agency, sovereignty, responsibility, and accountability. It would be mistaken, therefore, to call precaution a political rationality; it may not even amount to a coherent principle. From an anthropological point of view, it seems more productive to follow Carol Greenhouse's lead and analyze the scene of caution as a site of contest where the "distribution of agency across social space" is at stake.[27] Significantly, precaution often equates intervention with safety and security.[28]

Considerations of precaution result not in less science, less knowledge, and less intervention, but in more. François Ewald and his colleagues propose analyzing precaution as a "giant machine for the production of knowledge; of knowledge in respect to what we know as well as of knowledge in respect to what we don't know."[29] Precaution, in other words, produces knowledge about the unknown. The aim of the machine is not to reduce the realm of the unknown, but to know more about it. In so doing, it inflates the force of the speculative fact and expands the power of scientifically inspired prophecy. Precaution responds to a temporal incongruity and enables intervention beyond all proof, encouraging people to have faith in the worst case, however unlikely it is. Such faith comes with a promise attached, the promise of protection. "If we are prepared for the worst, we are prepared for all that may come along," a public health specialist told me. "What we're trying to do is to model everything after the worst-case scenario, so that if it's not as bad, we have the plans. So we're ahead of the game."

The test-kit error and the media scare triggered not just one intervention, but a series of them. It spurred authorities to reconsider the rules under which laboratories could work with viruses. The American Type Culture Collection, a nonprofit biological resource center, removed H2N2 viruses from its catalogs of standard reference pathogens and introduced its own proficiency standard program to address safety and security issues. More testing became the solution for the testing error. But more testing concomitantly entailed the risk of false positives; that is, false alarms. Such false alarms are characteristic of the world of preparedness. False alarms reveal new sources of risk and affirm the reality of the threat—entangling experts, officials, and observers ever more in a perpetual screening of the surroundings for new types of threat.

The CDC and the NIH revised the recommendations concerning the handling of what they termed the "non-contemporary human influenza viruses." Among the most important revisions suggested was the decision to raise the recommended biosafety level for this special category of viruses.[30] As the 2005 Interim Recommendation phrased it, non-contemporary human influenza viruses "should be handled with increased caution."[31] Of course, all viruses stored in the freezer are bound to become "non-contemporary." They cease to evolve and become suspended in time, preserved at -70 degrees Celsius. The recommendation suggests that biosafety level III practices, procedures, and facilities are required for experimental work with this particular category of influenza viruses. The fact that influenza researchers had been working with their microbial archives for more than fifty years with no documented incident of human infection occurring seemed irrelevant. As a result of the 2005 incident and the response to the potential event, the H2N2 virus "got locked away," as microbiologist Robert Webster phrased it.

THE DAY BEFORE

From the perspective of microbe farmers, the government's intervention amounted to an overreaction, given the fundamental difference between contamination and infection. In contrast to contamination, infection requires not just one body, but two. For an infection to occur, the host must be susceptible to the virus, but the virus must also be able to interact with the host and its cells. Microbiologists are acutely aware that infections are much more complex and much more unlikely than contaminations, which constantly occur in everyday laboratory work.

The test-kit error caused great concern, as we have seen. But health officials suggested that the incident was positive because it revealed a serious lack of preparedness. The false alarm, triggered by the detection of the H2N2 virus in the patient specimen, allowed government officials to review procedures, revise recommendations, reinforce surveillance, and improve readiness. Officials considered the incident a valuable test of preparedness that allowed them to introduce new safety and security measures. But this ever-expanding language of the test led to another perception: the perception of reality *as itself a test*. A dialectic was set in motion in which "reality" was bound to become less and less "real" to eventually come into view *as just another test*. The response to the 2009 swine flu pandemic exemplifies this striking perception of reality as a test. For public health professionals, it was not only a pandemic; it was also, and perhaps primarily, a rehearsal—a rehearsal for "the big one."

A 2012 report published by the Association of Public Health Laboratories highlighted the crucial role of the diagnostic network in the pandemic response in 2009.[32] The rapid diagnostic test was the "*sine qua non* of every action in public health regarding the virus, from closing a neighborhood school to shutting down international flights. Effects near and far rippled from what the test could tell about the virus."[33] The pandemic declaration was perceived as a moment of truth for practitioners of preparedness. "Years, even decades, of preparation, training, and capabilities were compressed into those . . . weeks. Patterns and procedures that might have emerged over months in other crises were adopted, attempted, and adapted in a matter of days. Every chit was called in; nascent partnerships advanced overnight; missing pieces were revealed in stark relief under time pressure. Heroes, individual and collective, surprised even themselves by rising to the challenge."[34] The pandemic appeared retrospectively as the "greatest challenge and finest moment in laboratory science."[35]

The rapid diagnostic test allowed laboratory science to demonstrate its abilities. "The H1N1 pandemic really put our lab to the test," said Patricia Levins, a lab coordinator in Texas.[36] For her colleagues, the pandemic was "a great learning experience."[37] The worldwide outbreak of disease exposed scientists and health officials to a real emergency. Labs across the nation came under permanent pressure, testing thousands of specimens a week. A report released by the Homeland Security Policy Institute of George Washington University said the event offered "the first real-time test of the global and domestic preparedness activities that have moved forward over the past few years."[38] For public health professionals, it was a "unique opportunity" to assess a decade of intensive emergency planning. According to a Health and

Human Services report, the "real-world test of the 2009 H1N1 response provided valuable insight into the scope of previous planning and emphasized the need for continued planning."[39] As early as June 2009, soon after WHO officially declared the pandemic, the Trust for America's Health concluded that the disease allowed health professionals to conduct a "real-world test that showed the strengths and vulnerabilities in the abilities of the United States . . . to respond to a major infectious disease outbreak."[40] The pandemic had hardly begun, but reports were already making recommendations for the next one. In the middle of the action, agencies published after-action reports. For some observers, the pandemic was over the day it was announced.

Not surprisingly, the Trust's report highlighted the need to address "serious continued vulnerabilities in the nation's preparedness."[41] Health professionals perceived the pandemic as an occasion, offering a "valuable opportunity" to test models and "enact and refine an actual response to what was previously a hypothetical solution."[42] Experts nationwide were relieved to learn "that the many hours spent on pandemic flu exercises and community collaborations could be successfully transferred into a real-life application."[43] The test proved that investments in pandemic planning paid off; that it was essential for preparedness to be science-driven; that school closings had major ramifications; that the health care system was likely to be overwhelmed; that communication must be better coordinated; that information was liable to cause confusion; that international coordination was more complicated than expected.[44] The pandemic was itself a test, a demonstration.

To assess the state of preparedness, the U.S. government made trainings, exercises, and drills mandatory by law. In this vision of preparedness, the pandemic came to operate as the ultimate test, a "real-life," "real-world," "real-time" test. A vicious circle came into being between testing and the real. Ultimately, reality itself turned into a test, and the "essential difference between the test and what was assumed to be real" increasingly blurred.[45] Among the consequences of this blurring was difficulty in experiencing a pandemic as an event. The coming plague overshadowed the current plague. "Today is the day before," a TV spot released by the Federal Emergency Management Agency (FEMA) declared. "Prepare for tomorrow," it proposed. According to this perception, preparedness was concerned with what is to come.

It seems as if there can never be a genuine event in this vision of preparedness. Each emergency will appear as a test for tomorrow's emergency, offering

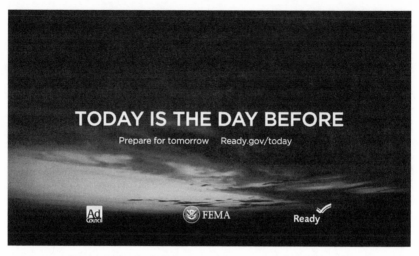

FIGURE 17. "Today is the day before. Prepare for tomorrow. Be informed. Make a plan. Build a kit. Get involved." TV spot released in 2012 by the Federal Emergency Management Agency.

unique opportunities to test strategies of interventions. "There are only trials," we might say with Bruno Latour in mind.[46] This perception of the pandemic as itself a test is no coincidence: It corresponds with the aim of officials to make "preparation a stronger priority than response."[47] In such a context, the pandemic itself is less important than the preparation for it, just as planning is assumed to be more important than the plan. The current pandemic is primarily a test, a proxy for the coming pandemic, which is the proper event—the event that seems *more real* precisely because it has *not yet occurred*. In this culture of constant testing, nothing ever seems to really happen. The event is blocked from becoming a proper event because it is constantly deferred into the future, where it remains available for prophetic appropriation. The pandemic lingers forever on the horizon, where it is about to happen. Thus, the perception of the present as a test, as a real test, makes it more difficult for observers to perceive the present as a time of fulfillment. Prophetic claims remain unfulfilled, and the foreseen and foretold are forever deferred into a time that is still to come. Pandemic influenza is always before us. It has the future as its nature.

Asked to comment on the "killer flu virus" that was distributed to "thousands of labs all over the world" in 2004, a lab director suggested that the scare was beneficial because it offered the unique possibility "to exercise testing capabilities and review safety and infection control processes."[48] The incident was an exercise. A test, a real test.

THE DAY AFTER

It was obviously a protracted pandemic, said Nicholas Cagliuso about the spread of swine flu in 2009. I had met Cagliuso for the first time in the summer of 2007 when he told me how he was working on the eighty-sixth floor of the World Trade Center on September 11 when the first plane hit. In the aftermath of the terrorist attacks, he switched careers and became coordinator of emergency preparedness for the New York-Presbyterian Healthcare System. When I met him again a few years later to ask him about his view of the 2009 swine flu pandemic, he was corporate director of emergency management at Mount Sinai Health System in New York City. In addition to this role as emergency manager, he was also director of admitting and hospitality for two of the seven hospitals that make up the Mount Sinai system. I asked Cagliuso about his experience of the pandemic. "All in all, it was a very good learning experience," he said. The outbreak of disease was important "because it was real." Cagliuso explained, "Because we really had patients who were actively ill, we had the worried-well, we had all sorts of challenges presenting, it was sort of progressive onset, and then a sort of gradual tapering." According to Cagliuso, the experience of the pandemic was valuable from an emergency management point of view because it completely changed daily operations and introduced "a new normal." This new normal lasted over an extended period of time:

> So for us a lot of it really revolved around a couple of things. We took a very active role in ensuring that we would use the facilities and the resources that we have to help vaccinate lay people. Because the notion was, look, if we could collaborate with the government who was getting the stockpiles of flu vaccine, we would make available our resources to help do that. So one of the things we had done at one of our facilities on Union Square, is that we were able to vaccinate 900 lay people in about four hours. We set up an incident command structure, basically, had people cued up outside on Union Square and coming in and had a true incident command structure, and we were really able to do a good public health service while at the same time informing people, like, look, if you're symptomatic, you don't need to come to the emergency department, and I think that went very, very well.

The pandemic offered a possibility for physicians and nurses to be actively involved in a public health service. This involvement lasted for only a day, but it was a good exercise, a valuable training for the future. What it offered was a proof of concept; it showed that the clinic was able to deliver nine hundred flu shots in four hours. "It was an exercise, except it was real, you know; we actually vaccinated people," said Cagliuso. "This was real because we were actually able to go out there and truly do a public health initiative, which was really great." It was a real test, not a simulated exercise.

Another challenge was the management of surges of patients to the emergency department:

> Because inevitably, after some news reports, we'd see an uptick in emergency department visits. The way we really coordinated that was twice or sometimes three times daily conference calls really to get a sense as to where we are, and then there was everything from staffing to gloves, gowns, masks, and personal protective equipment. And then spending a lot of the time on these calls distilling and working through the recommendations and the information that we would get from the various governmental agencies. So what was the CDC saying, versus the State Department of Health, versus the City Department of Health? And there we would really tap into our infectious disease clinical leadership and our emergency department leadership, again to distill it, to translate it, and share it with everybody. So those I think were our key experiences.

The pandemic, which came into view as a real test, revealed a series of shortcomings:

> Really one of the gaps that remains and that we need to continue to work on is informing and educating the public that the emergency department does not necessarily need to be the first place you come to for evaluation. Now clearly, if you were acutely ill, obviously, you never want to dissuade the public from doing that. But often times it was the ability for people to have them be evaluated either at an emergent care center or go to your primary care physician. What we found was that there was a lot of physicians themselves who were uncertain as to how to manage this and who were closing [their offices]. So they weren't even providing their core services. So what happened was that demand that would have been absorbed there was then shifted back to the emergency department. So we'd put in place a number of triage assessment areas at the emergency departments.

For Cagliuso, the pandemic was real because it changed daily hospital operations. "The way we operated was changed for those weeks and months.

And to me, independent from an epidemiological perspective, thinking like a health care operations person, it very much looked like a pandemic, because it really did affect the way we provided our services, day in and day out. It changed the way we operated. It met our criteria for pandemic. It was a different demand for our resources."

In our conversation, Cagliuso emphasized that real tests were much more effective than simulated scenarios:

Do I think there is value in training, and drills, and exercises? Absolutely! I think the problem that we have is getting people to buy in and to understand that the way you perform is based on the way that you practice. And often times if you read after-action reports and improvement programs that have been generated,... the commonality that runs through all those after-action reports is basic stuff: communication, coordination, funding, staffing, whatever it may be. So I can't say, and if you use 9/11 as a turning point, I can't say that we've really become leaps and bounds in transcending them. I think training, drills, and exercises are important, but I think until people start to buy into them and take them more seriously, it's really the actual incident that I think has moved us along further.

Just like the false positive that triggered a real response, the actual incident was more effective than the simulated exercise. Such an actual incident could be as simple as a storm. Referring to the bad weather that had been predicted for the day of our meeting in Cagliuso's office at Roosevelt Hospital on Fifty-Eighth Street, the emergency manager related,

We had a number of planning calls, and when you look outside there is not much to be concerned about, but we had a number of planning calls on Friday, yesterday afternoon, collected some situation reports, and then essentially at 5:30, 6:30 this morning when we saw what was really taking place we called all that off. Those tend to get people more engaged than if you and I let's say design an exercise in a month from now and, you know, sort of played out a fictitious scenario.

"And that's because it's fictitious?" I asked. "Yeah, I think what happens is, we're so enthralled in the daily operations that if it's a fire drill or an emergency management drill or exercise, it's like, I can't be bothered with this; I have twenty real things I need to manage right now." But even these real things, these daily issues, were not as effective as they could be:

The reality is, and we go back to these after-action reports and these improvement plans, if you look at the commonality, it's a lot of the [same] stuff over and over: communication, coordination, funding, staffing. So my take is: What have you done to transcend that (i.e., identify a gap and transcend it)? And I think there is a certain degree of both passive and active denial that takes place. In a passive way, it's sort of this notion that, a shrug of the shoulder, so an indifference. Well it is what it is, and this is all we have. I only have x nurses on this unit, or I only have so much funding, so many resources in this area. In an active way, it's, look, we can't go out there and actively say that we dropped the ball in areas a, b, and c.

After-action reports were retrospective reviews; they were confessions of vulnerability. Such confessions made some gaps in the plan and some failures of performance visible while leaving others invisible. In a 2009 article, Cagliuso and his colleagues wrote, "Experience with crafting after-action reports following drills, exercises, or actual incidents almost always includes substantial editing by involved parties to minimize gaps in the plan or failures of performance, and to create the shortest possible list of needed corrective actions."[49] Despite endless efforts, health care institutions were unable to address the broader structural problems that made these institutions so vulnerable in the first place. After-action reports identified the same issues over and over again. "So we have an incident," the emergency manager told me, "whether it's real or fictitious, and we identify the same issues, over and over again, but my question continues to be, well, what have we done to hold those in charge accountable for those chronic gaps. And I think we've done a very poor job. We've done a very, very poor job. And I think that's why we are where we are." Emergency managers perceived preparedness efforts as frustrating, time consuming, and inefficient: "Because you realize where the gaps are, and you realize some of the low-hanging fruit fixes, but because of myriad reasons that are often times outside of your control, you can't necessarily get to that next level. So that's I think where a lot of the frustration as a key sentiment comes through." In the United States, health care institutions were in a critical condition:

> Some time ago, it was a statewide commission that essentially said that New York is over-bedded. There are too many hospital beds. The problem with that is right now we have patients cueing up in emergency departments. There are several patients waiting for an in-patient bed. We have beds, but the problem is that they are not staffed. The conundrum is, ok, you have patients having a poor patient experience because they're cued up in the emergency department, but you technically have beds, but they're not staffed beds; they're physical beds, they're not staffed beds. So you then evolve that into an emergency man-

agement mindset, which says you have a sudden acute incident, whether it's natural, technological, or intentional, where we need to surge on the inpatient side and your capacity now on the inpatient side is diminished. It used to be very much, well, if you have disaster activation, one of the first things you would try to do is rapid patient discharge. You get the physicians to rapidly assess the inpatient units, and say okay, you know, John and Smith and this one can be rapidly discharged. That's all good and fine. But what about staffing the shuttered units so that you can provide additional capacity?

In addition, the staff turnover in New York City hospitals was extremely high. Senior managers preferred buying stuff, but there was nobody who could actually use it. I asked, "So you have a crisis almost every week?" "Almost every day!" Cagliuso replied. He continued,

Because what's happened is, you know, in trying to balance the costs of daily operations, you've put yourself into a position that can be very concerning. So, you know, what we've begun to do is to use hallway beds. So essentially rather than having patients cue up in the emergency departments, we will put up to two patients per unit in hallways outside of physical rooms. From a patient's satisfaction, a patient's experience point of view, most patients would prefer to be in a hallway on an inpatient unit than in, you know, the sort of chaos of an emergency department. So we're constantly in this sort of ebb and flow; so yes, day in and day out, there are often operational challenges that sort of tease whether or not we should activate an incident command structure to manage them.

ETERNAL EXPOSURE

In trainings, exercises and drills, which became mandatory for health care providers in the United States in 2006, eruptions of infectious disease appeared as a trial. In staged performances of preparedness, actors and institutions were supposed to demonstrate their capacities, and their limits, to respond to catastrophic outbreaks of disease. The purpose of these performances was to enhance preparedness and "generate knowledge about vulnerabilities in response capabilities."[50] Official statements promoted emergency preparedness as a permanent project, a project that required the sense of interruption to go on without interruption. In the words of emergency manager Jean Paul Roggiero, "There has to be a continuum." Preparedness must go on; it must continue. He told me, "You have to test the plan, you have to rewrite the plan, make revisions, . . . We stress the fact that, OK, you have a plan now, but it won't be as effective if you don't continue doing the work. Just putting it in a binder, putting it up on a shelf, won't solve the problem. Because six months from now, how many of your employees will remember where that shelf is? You have to actually test employees, train them, quiz them. You need constant, constant exposure."

Officials perceived exercises as proxy measures to assess, maintain, and improve the nation's state of readiness. The government relied on constant testing. However, after-action reports and improvement plans both revealed and concealed failures of performance, and they often resulted in the lowest possible number of proposed measures.[51] Hospitals encountered critical situations in daily operations, and emergency managers were aware that they would not be able to address these chronic gaps. These managers were doing more and more preparedness each year, and yet there was a crisis almost every day. In health care institutions, normal and exceptional circumstances were bleeding into each other on a regular basis. Crisis was the hospital's permanent condition as an institution, and vulnerabilities continued despite efforts to plan and prepare.

A particular kind of scenario was at the heart of preparedness efforts. "What I'm aiming to do is tell stories about real dangers we face. I won't give you a balanced view. I will intentionally ignore the bright side of these issues and focus on the question, How bad can it be," explained the editor of *Scientific American* in a 2012 bestseller on superviruses and the fate of the species.[52] Prophets of doom are masters in the art of exaggeration. They are intentionally one-sided.

"The worst case is the event that everybody loves planning for," a nurse and emergency coordinator told me. "We are fascinated with scary things." She went on, "I think we went off the deep end on bioterrorism. I think we've gone off the deep end on some parts of the influenza piece. I am much more concerned that we be able to handle more routine things well." The nurse was worried about ordinary things, regular nuts and bolts problems: "You can say if you plan for the worst, you'll handle the routine things well. But I'm not sure that's true. I think we need to think through and practice at handling sort of mid-range emergencies a lot better and then think about scaling up to the bigger one if it happens."

But the emphasis of preparedness remained on the worst-case scenario. Public health professionals designed new plans and tested new strategies of intervention for the catastrophic pandemic. Epidemiologists conducted surveys in local communities and approached people to identify their needs. They took advantage of the pandemic and tried to get populations better access to care. In Brooklyn, nurses went from house to house to vaccinate community members; they brought little portable seats on which people could sit to get their flu shots free of charge. "The nice thing about influenza is that every year there's a new vaccine, so every year we have the opportunity to revise and adjust the intervention. It's the perfect disease for preparedness," Danielle Ompad, a member of the Center for Urban Epidemiology at the New York Academy of Medicine explained to me one day in her office. For the performance of preparedness, influenza was the perfect disease. The periodic return of the mutant strain offered the certainty of a regular opportunity to test new forms of intervention. Each new season of the flu provided the possibility to develop new interventions and design new plans to put to the test. Seasonal flu was a real disease, an actual incident; it came to operate as a proxy for the catastrophic pandemic.

The circulation of the communicable disease allowed professionals to engage in a continuous process of threat communication. It also provided a test site for preparedness, making it possible for actors and institutions to both reveal and conceal their abilities to respond to public health emergencies. Over and over again, after-action reports and improvement plans documented the same set of issues: Problems with communication, coordination, funding, and staffing continued to plague America's health care system. After almost a decade of action, most gaps remained what they were: gaps in the system. Preparedness was in danger of becoming a continuum without progress.

SIX

The Great Deluge

INFLUENZA VACCINES TYPICALLY contain inactivated strains of the virus that have been replicated under controlled conditions in fertilized chicken eggs. These strains cause the immune system to produce protective antibodies against the pathogenic agent. However, because the virus is changing continuously, a new vaccine must be given each season. In the case of a pandemic, however, flu shots will not be available in advance, and the supply will grow only incrementally. Health officials hence face the difficult problem of how to allocate a scarce pharmaceutical resource. In 2005 the CDC launched a series of public engagement meetings to discuss priorities for the allocation of flu shots during a public health emergency. Central to these meetings, which were organized in a number of locations in the United States, was the question of how to dispense the scarce pharmaceutical resource in the event of a catastrophic pandemic. When health officials reformulated the fraught question in ethical terms, a new vaccination scheme emerged. Validated and authorized by a distinctive mode of "participatory governmentality," this new scheme focused not on the protection of vulnerable populations at risk for serious complications, but instead on the preservation of "essential services;" namely, "public safety" and the "functioning of society" during a public health emergency.

The new vaccination scheme was predominantly concerned with the optimal circulation of people, goods, and things during a state of rupture caused by the sudden spread of a dangerous virus. The crucial fact that the scheme arose out of a series of government-sponsored public engagement meetings, held in response to intensive debates over the legitimacy and accountability of public health policy more generally, is what interests me here. These meetings demonstrated how health authorities animate and mobilize publics to validate and authorize strategies of pharmaceutical prevention today. Indeed, the logic of publicity is increasingly embedded in a growing number of approaches employed by public health professionals.

Michael Warner argues that every reference to the public is a "necessarily imaginary reference." He emphasizes that, in fact, "we have no way of talking about the public without theorizing the contexts and strategies in which the public could be represented."[1] This chapter follows Warner's suggestion and explores contexts and strategies in which the public is called into being in the prophetic scene of pandemic influenza.

CHANGING PRIORITIES

In early 2005, two prominent expert advisory bodies to the federal government, the Advisory Committee on Immunization Practices (ACIP) and the National Vaccine Advisory Committee (NVAC), formed a joint working group to assist the Department of Health and Human Services (HHS) in its effort to develop a prioritization scheme for the allocation of influenza vaccine in the event of a pandemic. The joint working group mobilized technical experts, consulted with representatives from a number of government agencies and nongovernmental organizations (NGOs), and confirmed that it was the primary goal of the pharmaceutical intervention to reduce morbidity and mortality as much as possible. The recommendations suggested by the working group were adopted by both advisory committees unanimously on July 19, 2005, and were subsequently included in the HHS Pandemic Influenza Plan, an exhaustive official planning document released in November 2005.[2]

Pandemics are believed to occur at irregular intervals. The industrial mass production of a safe and effective vaccine for a pandemic takes considerable time; health officials estimate that the earliest batches would become available about twelve to sixteen weeks after the successful isolation and identification of the new virus. Because demand for a protective vaccine is likely to exceed supply, especially in the event of a catastrophic pandemic, health authorities are expected to allocate the scarce resource as effectively and as fairly as possible. Charged by the U.S. government to prepare for the next pandemic, health officials anticipated the future need to prioritize pandemic vaccine and tasked the ACIP and the NVAC to address the projected state of exception in advance. Faced with a tailor-made problem formulated in technical terms, the ACIP mobilized its expertise, consulted with stakeholders, and approached the hypothetical question by developing a provisional plan.[3]

The highest priority groups in the 2005 ACIP vaccination plan reflected for the most part the high-risk groups that the advisory committee had already recommended for vaccination during regular seasonal flu. According to this scheme, persons with high-risk conditions, household contacts of children younger than six months, household contacts of severely immunocompromised persons, pregnant women, and health care workers should receive the first shots in the case of a catastrophic eruption of pandemic influenza. These people, public health experts reasoned, either are themselves most at risk of death and disease or are in close contact with such persons. In addition—and in contrast to the recommendations for vaccination during regular seasonal influenza—key government decision makers and vaccine and antiviral manufacturers were included in the highest tier.

In late February 2007, I traveled to Atlanta to participate in an ACIP meeting as part of my fieldwork. After passing a tight security screening at the entrance of the CDC where the meeting was being held, I arrived just in time for the presentation of a new prioritization scheme. As I eventually realized, this new plan clearly was more appealing to some officials than the ACIP recommendations already included and published in the 2005 HHS Pandemic Influenza Plan. At the core of the new scheme, as Dr. Ben Schwartz of the National Vaccine Program Office (NVPO) explained, was not the protection of vulnerable populations at risk for serious complications, but rather the preservation of "essential services." The focus was on the "functioning of society" during a public health emergency. Although the ACIP recommendations attended to the needs of young children, pregnant women, immunocompromised persons, and other high-risk groups, Schwartz argued that it was necessary to bring these "valid concerns" with vulnerable populations into "balance" with the requirements of "homeland security" and "critical infrastructure protection."

The new vaccination plan was primarily concerned with the optimal circulation of persons, goods, and things in a state of rupture—a concern, as Foucault reminds us, that lies at the heart of the security apparatus.[4] Among ACIP members, a skeptical view, to say the least, prevailed. "This is the second time," as Dr. Ban Mishu Allos crisply remarked in the aftermath of Schwartz's presentation, that the federal government "is taking away a vaccine recommendation from the ACIP."[5] Although Allos's public comment made no immediate impact, it revealed that the air-conditioned room at the

CDC was teeming with power and politics. A CDC official told me, "The government thinks that what they got from the ACIP was not the best advice." Government officials from the George W. Bush administration accused the ACIP of having "a health lens." They called for revision of the prioritization plan and for looking at the question more broadly: "When the government said this is bigger than health, all of society is going to be affected, they created an intragovernmental committee that has representatives from the Department of Homeland Security, the Department of State, and the Department of Commerce. They said that the Department of Health is going to take the lead at implementation, but that now the recommendation is coming from all the government, not just the Department of Health." In this shift of emphasis, the creation of the intergovernmental committee and the organization of the public engagement meetings played an important role, potentially delegitimizing the concern of health experts with vulnerable populations at risk of death and disease. At a follow-up ACIP meeting in October 2007, Schwartz presented the most recent draft of the revised federal guidelines for the allocation of pandemic vaccine, which again focused on mitigating potential economic disruptions, rather than preventing negative health effects. On this occasion, however, ACIP members made no public comments in response to the presentation, presumably because of time constraints. Apparently, the predominant view within the ACIP was "to let things go," as one member of the advisory committee told me during a break.

The new guidelines with their distinctive orientation toward the functioning of the economy were officially released in July 2008. As Dr. Jeffrey Runge, assistant for health affairs and chief medical officer at the Department of Homeland Security, remarked, the new guidelines were developed "to ensure that our nation's critical infrastructure remains up and running."[6] In a news release, HHS secretary Michael Leavitt underscored that the vaccination plan represented "the result of a deliberative democratic process" in which, he claimed, all interested parties extensively participated. According to Leavitt, the document directly reflected "the values of our society and the ethical issues involved," representing "the best of shared responsibility and decision-making."[7]

But the process was not quite as transparent as the secretary suggested. It obscured how government officials from the Bush administration invoked the public to question a prioritization scheme that had been suggested by the advisory committee on immunization practices. Rather than celebrate this alleged instance of democratic decision making, we should heed Jenny

Reardon's advice when she argues that "energies are best spent not on energetic calls for democratization, but on the more subdued task of analyzing how democratization happens—what logics underlie it, what practices make it up."[8] Among these practices is public engagement, which was said to be essential because ethical values were at stake.

As Sarah Franklin and others have shown, ethical reasoning has become a central mode of public conversation about contemporary orders of health and disease.[9] Extending Warner's theorization of the public, Cohen suggests that this ethical conversation is not just "located *in* the public sphere but more fundamentally . . . [is] constitutive *of* it."[10] Ethical reasoning, in other words, is actively involved in the animation and mobilization of publics for the management of populations. How, then, is ethical reasoning engaged in the constitution of those publics that are increasingly required for the performance of participation? Exploring this question illuminates an emerging structure of pharmaceutical prevention in which the animation and mobilization of the *public* by ethical reasoning have become means of identifying and circumscribing the *population* as a target of regulation.[11] How is the juridical notion of the public—conceived of as a collection of legal subjects endowed with reason and the capacity to articulate personal preferences—reactivated and redeployed in this structure of pharmaceutical prevention?[12]

FACTS AND VALUES

On June 19, 2002, Dr. Roger Bernier testified before the U.S. House Committee on Government Reform in his role as associate director of science at the CDC. Bernier is a mild-mannered, soft-spoken man in his mid-sixties who, after graduate school, joined the CDC's famed Epidemic Intelligence Service, as did so many of his colleagues. His career began with early field assignments to the Venereal Disease Program in New York City and the Smallpox Eradication and Measles Control Program in Niger, West Africa. Assigned to the National Immunization Program as a staff epidemiologist, he was named chief of the Epidemiologic Research Section later on and then became the CDC's associate director of science. Bernier's professional work at the CDC has focused primarily on epidemiological studies of the safety and efficacy of vaccines.

In 2002, his testimony at a congressional hearing came in response to growing public concerns that thimerosal, a mercury-containing preservative in vaccines, might be responsible for autism, a condition characterized by impaired social interaction, communication difficulties, and repetitive behaviors. In his carefully worded presentation on Capitol Hill, Bernier meticulously described the CDC's ongoing vaccine-safety research activities. Thimerosal was a hotly contested, politically charged chemical compound, and Bernier's response was supposed to demonstrate that federal agencies were taking seriously the deeply rooted concerns regarding the safety of vaccines. To determine the potential role of thimerosal in causing autism and other neurodevelopmental disorders, the CDC had initiated a case-control thimerosal/autism study as well as an extensive thimerosal follow-up study. Further research and more reliable scientific evidence, Bernier confidently emphasized, were in the offing. At the conclusion of the congressional hearing, an autism activist approached Bernier and told him that CDC's studies were "dead on arrival" and deserved no serious consideration.

Bernier told me this anecdote in 2007, when we met in the CDC's newly designed library following an ACIP meeting. It seemed that no scientific evidence—however clear, however hard, however tried and tested—could allay the public's concern about a connection between vaccines and autism. What was necessary, Bernier realized, was not a new case-control study published in a prestigious journal shelved in the CDC's modern library, but a different approach altogether. "My conclusion was," Bernier reasoned, "that this was a trust problem. More research was not going to solve this problem. There was a relationship problem." Shortly after his revealing encounter with the autism activist on Capitol Hill, Bernier asked to go on a special assignment to explore more systematically the germ of an idea that had caught his interest: public engagement. The call to enhance public engagement or to foster public deliberation or to conduct public consultation in policy matters was not a new development.[13] In fact, the CDC had organized a series of public engagement and stakeholder meetings in the previous decade in relation to a variety of public health issues. Bernier, at any rate, became an enthusiastic promoter of the promising idea at the federal agency.

As Bernier explained to me, he considered resolution of the contentious debate around thimerosal to be hopeless. There was nothing one could do to resolve the fundamental disagreement. For a public engagement project to be successful it had to be launched at the outset of an emerging debate before the critical dialogue turned into a polemic of accusations and became an irresolvable dispute. Furthermore, as Bernier explained, "When there is an open conflict, you really don't want to bring in the man on the street who is not involved in the conflict." Although the idea of public engagement was developed in response to controversial public matters, it was, in fact, essential for its success that it address *noncontroversial* or *not-yet-controversial* matters in public policy.

In early 2005, Bernier found himself searching for a "potential conflict" on which to test his newly developed model of engaging the public on a vaccine-related policy decision. The ACIP deliberations, in which he was involved as an expert, immediately piqued his interest, and in July 2005 Bernier and Dr. Edgar Marcuse, a professor at the University of Washington and associate medical director at Children's Hospital in Seattle, launched what they called the Public Engagement Pilot Project on Pandemic Influenza.[14] This experimental project was funded and supported by a number of organizations, among them the CDC and the Institute of Medicine of the National Academies of Science. They selected this issue for public engagement primarily because the possibility of a pandemic offered a unique opportunity to test the new model of public engagement before introducing it more widely. The prioritization of pandemic vaccine was an intriguing public health policy question that was then being intensively discussed among experts but had not yet become a contentious public matter. The problem of prioritization also seemed a perfect test case because it involved "a consideration of both values as well as science," Bernier told me. It allowed officials "to come up with a pollable question."

OF INCLUSION AND EXCLUSION

Given the growing importance of audit practices in late liberal forms of government, it is not surprising that the Public Engagement Pilot Project on Pandemic Influenza launched by Bernier and Marcuse was extensively documented and meticulously evaluated.[15] An outside group of academic researchers was charged with reviewing it carefully, thereby rendering the success of the experimental endeavor visible in the institutionally recognized form of an independent evaluation. A final evaluation document titled *Citizen Voices on Pandemic Flu Choices* was published in December 2005.[16] According to this report, the project was based on the following three premises:

1. That the formulation of vaccine policies ... requires policy-makers to understand the range of society's values on the issues.

2. That the process which will best reflect society's values is a public engagement process.

3. That an inclusive public process . . . will produce sounder, more supportable decisions.[17]

The pilot project involved both stakeholder and public engagement meetings. Approximately fifty stakeholders (representatives from various government agencies, NGOs, and private companies) met twice to frame the issues, which were submitted to one-day public engagement meetings convened in Atlanta, Boston, Omaha, and Portland. A total of 250 U.S. citizens participated in these four meetings held in urban centers representing the South, Northeast, Midwest, and West.

The recruitment of participants for such consultations, as a local organizer of one of the public engagement meetings emphasized, was key to their success. She suggested that it is not simply the "public" but the *right* public that must be gathered into the fold of public health. The public that these public health specialists wished to engage was not just a random pool of citizens, but a selected group of people representing society at large. The local organizer told me,

> The hardest part was making sure that we got a good cross-section of the population. That was the hardest thing to do. We did pretty good with the minorities. The only thing that I feel we didn't have was we didn't have a good representation of college-age people. That was not good. That was a fault. Because I think they would have brought a different slant on things. So we didn't have enough representation on that. Definitely enough representation for middle age and for the senior population. We had a good population of Hispanics. We had a good population of African Americans.

This selected group of participants was supposed to form a collective body that included, involved, and transcended each individual because what is at stake in public engagement is not just individual preferences, as health officials maintain, but "society's values." Establishing this representative collective body involved a process of pre-selection that entailed both *inclusions* and *exclusions*. As the local organizer explained to me,

> We were very selective of who we took. We wouldn't take anybody with [an] emergency management background. We wouldn't take anybody with a big knowledge on health care. I didn't want anybody that came in a little bit tainted, that knew already a lot about pandemic flu. So we were pretty good

at screening. And then originally we got a lot of people in that we thought were too qualified. We called them up and asked them not to participate. Everybody was very gracious and agreed. We said, you know, what we really want is a true picture of people who don't really have a lot of knowledge about pandemic flu.

The normative principle of representation, the goal of generating a "true picture of people" not already familiar with the problem of pandemic influenza, made it necessary for participation to include a process of deliberate exclusion. The recruitment and selection of participants were guided by a particular set of ideas that reflected the kind of "public" that the organizers wished to engage in the first place. The public, it seems, can only validate and authorize a public health policy of pharmaceutical prevention if it manifests itself in the appropriate form. Here, I am borrowing an argument about efficacy proposed by Marilyn Strathern in her study of Melanesian sociality. Strathern suggests that persons, things, and actions must assume a recognizable form to elicit a particular effect.[18] She shows in great detail how the Hageners of the Papua New Guinean Highlands engage in a variety of processes aimed at making the appropriate form appear at particular moments of social life. The public, we might say here with Strathern's argument in mind, must take the right shape to validate and authorize public health policy. It is only able to perform "participation" and produce a persuasive resolution if it assumes the appropriate form and appears in the right shape.

At one of these meetings, I talked to an organizer who told me, "My ego is out of the door. We want to hear the people. It's about putting the public back into public health." And yet, it turned out to be a very particular kind of public that these promoters of public engagement were putting back into public health.

At the heart of the constitution of the right public was the crucial distinction between facts and values. As Bernier suggested, there are empirical facts just as there are ethical values, and the vexed question is how to conjoin them. In this model of public engagement, scientific experts are responsible for the determination of facts while ordinary citizens deliberate their normative implications. Experts, accordingly, were not considered a part of the "public;" they were outside of the reference. In fact, organizers deliberately excluded experts from the process. Of course, it was a particular type of experts that they singled out: not economists or political scientists, but those with a "health lens;" that is, health experts. The precarious distinction between facts and values thus determined the constitution of the public and rendered policy making amendable to participation in the first place. The price paid for the internalization of the public was the externalization of ethics, conceived of as a sphere of norms situated outside the domain of the merely technical. In the very attempt to overcome the separation between facts and values, the distinction was thus reproduced and reinvented through the imagined reference of the public. What, then, happens to such an externalized ethics when it is called on to do the work of bringing the public into being? What kind of ethics is most appropriate for the constitution of the public? Is there perhaps an "appropriate ethics" just as there is an "appropriate public"?

THE VERDICT

A few health experts were in fact present at the public engagement meetings. When the meetings began, they were asked to present "facts" about the epidemiological features of influenza, the virus, the disease, current vaccination policy, and past and future pandemics. Based on my own involvement in such meetings, these expert presentations are typically very brief, and participants often have a hard time understanding the scientific information. Typically, they are concerned about the safety of vaccines, and they often come with questions about the side effects of drugs. "This is the first time I heard about the flu," one participant professed. "Where are these viruses coming from and what are the symptoms that tell me I should go see a doctor?" The expert responded, "There is no pandemic now."

When I discussed the problem of vaccine prioritization with a workshop participant, she responded, "Everybody is at risk. But the same solution does not apply to everybody. Specific people have specific needs." How, then, would it be possible to come up with a scheme that would account for these specific needs? Subsequent to the presentation of the scientific information, participants were asked to complete several "ethics exercises" in order to "grasp the nature of values dilemmas and the challenges incumbent in policy decisions involving competing values and no obvious right choice."[19]

If it is true that the internalization of the public concomitantly implied the externalization of ethics, what happens to the ethical when it is called on to bring a public into being? What kind of ethics most eloquently articulated the collective body that participants were supposed to constitute? What kind of ethics was able to accommodate the idea that specific people have specific needs? According to Bernier, participants were told at the public engagement meetings that their task was to rank in order of priority the following potential goals for a future pandemic influenza vaccination program:

1. Save those most at risk.
2. Put children and young people first.
3. Limit the larger effects on society.
4. Use a lottery system.
5. Use the principle of "first come, first served."

After a round of open deliberation in small groups, participants were asked to solve a very complex and difficult public health matter by placing dots next to the three goals they thought were of highest priority. According to the local organizer of one of these public engagement meetings, the purpose was to "get a picture of how society feels about vaccine prioritization." The participants were supposed to act as a collective body and express "society's values." Hence, the importance of public *deliberation*, which allowed participants to engage in a process of mutual *persuasion* and to gradually overcome particular concerns in the name of collective interests. As it turned out, the simulation of a social verdict, to use Strathern's apposite term here, resulted in a priority list that consistently ranked first the "limiting of the larger effects on society."[20]

As an ethical value of sorts, the goal of "limiting the larger effects on society" greatly appealed to the participants in all public engagement meetings. What might perhaps explain this appeal was that it was an ethical value explicitly articulating a collective interest, rather than an individual concern. The very formulation "limiting the larger effects on society" indicated that a public health intervention of pharmaceutical prevention organized around this normative principle would benefit neither random individuals nor special groups, but society as a whole. Charged with constituting a collective body, the participants thus selected an ethical value that most clearly expressed a collective interest, one that would benefit everyone. In this way, participants achieved precisely what they were supposed to accomplish: establish a collective body and transform the particular concerns of each into the common interest of everyone. Charged with representing society and expressing its values, the public selected a value that represented society. This choice thus allowed participants to manifest themselves in a shape appropriate to the purpose of public engagement. But what exactly is society? What exactly might its protection entail? And what kind of emergency was at stake?

THE OTHER EMERGENCY

According to the organizers, participants in public engagement meetings were primarily concerned with "assuring public safety" and "keeping society running." But these terms came from the organizers themselves, who proposed that "essential services" and "critical infrastructure" required some special form of protection so as to maintain "social order" and assure the "functioning of society."[21] Policemen, firemen, emergency responders, decision makers, utility workers, food distributors, and the military were deemed central actors who perform vital roles in dramatic times. As we have seen, the ACIP recommendations also put public health workers on top of the list but not because of the panic that nurses and doctors might not show up for work due to fear of infection, but, more importantly, because they might inadvertently infect patients at risk of serious complications.

To understand better this overwhelming concern with public safety and the functioning of society within a selected group of American citizens who represented the public, we must examine in more detail the distinctive conceptualization of the emergency that came to matter in the meetings. The emergency that seemed to operate as a source of collective identification took a historically distinctive form—one that turned out to be not only very particular but also very effective.

The first public engagement meeting was held in Atlanta on August 27, 2005. The following meetings in Boston, Omaha, and Portland were convened in September and October. On August 23, Hurricane Katrina formed over the Bahamas, crossed Florida, and gained strength over the Gulf of Mexico; on August 29 it made landfall in Louisiana and Mississippi. In the days and weeks that followed the catastrophic "natural" disaster wrought by the hurricane, the loss of lives, the suffering of people, the destruction of homes, and the fatal consequences of a failed emergency response took center stage in the nation's conversation. Entire populations and communities had been left on their own in the midst of a devastating disaster. In addition, the U.S. news media kept disseminating troubling images of anarchy, crime, and lawlessness crystallizing in the racialized figure of the "looter." These images of death, destruction, disability, anxiety, vulnerability, and insecurity produced a sense of total breakdown that seemed to threaten the most basic foundations of society. The emergency response "coordinated" by the government failed miserably both before and after the catastrophic event. Nancy Scheper-Hughes wrote in a 2005 editorial that "it is difficult to say which is worse—the killer hurricane or the national response to it."[22] "Look at New Orleans," a public health professional reminded me. "That was embarrassing, shameful."

At the public engagement meetings, the killer hurricane loomed large. Organizer Anna De Blois linked the pandemic with the storm. She asked, "What if the big one hits, like Katrina? What if there is no electricity? What if things slow down? What if the lights go out, if the water stops flowing, if there is no food? We are all at risk." This organizer's focus on water, food, electricity, and transportation was clearly an immediate reflection of the Katrina disaster. Here a recollection of the past was bleeding into an anticipation of the future. "We talked about keeping your lights on, what about keeping your phone service on, what about water? I mean the critical infrastructure that nobody really thought about. And when we brought it up, it was like, 'Oh wow we didn't really think about that.'" Given this emphasis on an experience that seemed prophetic, it is perhaps less surprising that the citizens who participated in the public engagement meetings right after Hurricane Katrina's landfall seemed inclined to rate the functioning of society and the protection of people as a key value.

Perhaps the citizen voices that were emphatically invoked but insufficiently engaged by the pilot project were trying to say much more in response to the question about pandemic vaccine prioritization. A focus less on its decontextualized meaning might perhaps reveal that these voices were responding, in however ambiguous terms, not only to an emergency of the future but also to a crisis in the past. As a matter of fact, it might well be true that participants made their ratings not only in anticipation of what might come but also in reaction to what had just been. It seems that these voices were haunted by the specter of Hurricane Katrina. Perhaps they were calling for better federal leadership in disaster management and public health provisioning. Perhaps they were urging the government to take responsibility, improve capacities, and care for people in times of crisis. Perhaps these citizens were concerned with the reliability of an emergency response lacking in adequate equipment because of inadequate federal support. Perhaps they were trying to create pressure to get the government to think about fundamental issues. What-ever the multiple and ambiguous meanings of what was articulated at these meetings in the shadow of Katrina, and whatever the subliminal influence of troubling images of a threatened order and the sudden realization of the fatal consequences of a poor emergency response, no documented effort was made to understand what participants were trying to say. The formal act of placing three dots on posters not only managed to cut off the deliberation midstream but also offered the false hope of forever determining the mean-ing of the perspectives that were brought to bear on the issue, as if one could freely choose and permanently settle the true meaning of one's words at a mo-ment's notice.

At the core of the pilot project was the paradox that it actively tried to take into consideration the social world that people were said to come from. There was an honest and genuine effort to mirror the geographical parts of the coun-try and to include representatives from various communities. However, the deep concern to include participants from all social backgrounds with a broad range of perspectives contrasted sharply with the insufficient effort to com-prehend these backgrounds and perspectives in the context of their articula-tion; that is, in the face of real disaster. Paradoxically, the project erased the subject of "participation" in the very moment of its production. It is undeni-able, of course, that every model of public engagement depends on limited funding and is shaped, at least to some degree, by the practical exigencies of bureaucratic organizations. But it is nonetheless troubling that the report, with its detailed analysis running more than ninety-five pages, fails to men-tion the hurricane even once, although it clearly was a matter of great concern during all discussions. In the report, Hurricane Katrina is completely ab-sent. This symbolic neglect, and maybe even denial, is perhaps no coinci-dence and may be related to the narrow design of this particular type of pub-lic engagement process and the crucial aim of the pilot project to demonstrate the efficacy and feasibility of "participatory governmentality" more generally. Instead of exploring the historical context and the social worlds of the people who participated in the meetings, the pilot project focused on the presum-ably less ambiguous task of counting the number of dots that had been placed on posters at the end of the day in response to a pollable question. The as-sumption that people always come from somewhere rather than nowhere both did and did not count. The fact that "limiting the larger effects on society" might have a particular meaning and a particular appeal in the context of Katrina was not examined.

According to the organizers, participants were primarily concerned with the protection of society. Yet when it comes to the meaning of "society" and its "protection" in a state of "emergency," the problem becomes more complex and intricate, especially when that society is asked to imagine an emergency in the future while it is confronted with a disaster in the past. What exactly might society mean? And what exactly might protection entail? And what kind of emergency is at stake? For homeland security officials it was clear what the citizen voices were trying to say when they invoked the protection of society. What the public apparently was asking for was "critical infrastructure protection." The public's concern, as it was framed in the public engagement meetings, was translated by government officials into a technical concept of "security" that had been signed into law after the terrorist attacks of September 11, 2001, and the ensuing dissemination of four anthrax letters. Although the concept primarily referred to information systems at the time, it was enlarged to include the sectors of telecommunications, energy, financial services, manufacturing, water, transportation, health care, and emergency services after Hurricane Katrina. The possible disruption of this nationally conceived infrastructure in a state of emergency became a foundational problem for homeland security and the idea of preparedness.[23] A new epistemological field of representation and intervention was carved out and populated with truth claims, methods for producing those truth claims, and a mix of experts, each representing a particular node of the infrastructural network keeping society—defined primarily in economic terms of seamless circulation—running.

In May 2006, Homeland Security secretary Michael Chertoff requested that the National Infrastructure Advisory Council (NIAC) formulate specific recommendations for the prioritization of pandemic countermeasures for essential workers in the critical infrastructure and key resource sectors.[24] Specifically, the NIAC was asked to identify and define critical services, to establish criteria and principles for critical service prioritization, and to determine critical employee groups in each service area. In its final report, employees assigned exactly 12,389,077 people to the first tier—a parody of precision verging on the surreal.[25] These people were part of the critical infrastructure, which included the sectors of banking and finance, chemical and commercial facilities, communications, electricity, emergency services, food and agriculture, health care, information technology, nuclear, oil and natural gas, postal and shipping, transportation, and water and wastewater. Paradoxically, in this account of technical networks, employees appeared as autonomous actors detached from social networks, ready to be vaccinated while their unprotected families remained at risk.

Having determined, based on speculative projection, not historical evidence, that the protection of critical infrastructure would indeed be a significant problem during an eruption of pandemic influenza, government officials began searching for a suitable way to change the official, already published ACIP vaccination scheme, which was accused of having a "health bias," of being too much concerned with matters of health rather than economic well-being, as one expert phrased it in a discussion with me. The Public Engagement Pilot Project and the translation of its ambiguous results into the technical concept of critical infrastructure protection allowed government officials to revise the prioritization scheme. Yet the experimental character of the pilot project threatened its legitimacy. To justify the change, the National Vaccine Office agreed to launch a second cycle of public engagement meetings, which it deliberately avoided casting as a "pilot project." These meetings were convened in 2007 in Nassau County, New York, and Las Cruces, New Mexico, and were organized not by Bernier but by Schwartz. The public that was mobilized for these new meetings was supposed to respond once again to the same question that the pilot project had already posed.

Although the prioritization scheme that came out of the public engagement meetings appears to be more representative than the ACIP guidance, it is not necessarily more ethical. From an anthropological point of view, the difference lies primarily in the fact that in one case ethics was made explicit. This process of generating a moral paper trail documenting the fact that ethical concerns have been taken into account in the making of public policy is a distinctive feature of the "new bureaucracies of virtue," to borrow Marie Andrée Jacob and Annelise Riles's apt phrase.[26] By rendering the normative dimension of public health policy explicit and by actively involving the "public" in the decision, an "ethical prophylaxis," to use Franklin's term, was built into the new vaccination plan.[27] A form of democracy was performed in which representation and calculation seemed to stand in for deliberation and contestation. However, the public engagement meetings with their foundational language of *ethics* rendered the *politics* of the problem invisible. Participants were not aware of the disagreements between health experts and security experts; they were not informed about the struggles waging between and within U.S. government agencies.

When Ben Schwartz presented the draft of the new federal guidance on vaccination prioritization, he underscored that, in contrast to the ACIP plan, the new recommendations, concerned primarily with "critical infrastructure protection," were based on a much more "complex," and thus presumably more "realistic," scenario of pandemic influenza. The new guidance, Schwartz declared, considered not one but three possible scenarios of pandemic influenza. As Julie Gerberding, director of the CDC, explained at a press conference, one "very important and . . . new concept that we introduced . . . is the concept that not all pandemics are equally severe."[28] Given this view of pandemic influenza, the vaccination plan was specified for cases of severe, moderate, and less severe pandemics. This new classification of pandemic influenza was based on a severity index that the CDC had recently developed. The key principle used to measure pandemic severity is mortality or, to be more precise, the case-fatality ratio, which is the percentage of deaths out of the total of reported cases of disease. Government officials initially developed the Pandemic Severity Index for *nonpharmaceutical* interventions, and planners deliberately designed it to mimic the Saffir-Simpson Hurricane Scale. This reference to the hurricane in preparedness planning was explicit and deliberate. As Gerberding noted, with recent memories of Hurricane Katrina "we have embedded in our minds some understanding of the difference in severity."[29] She added,

> A pandemic that does not move very fast from person to person, or does not have a very high fatality rate would likely be a fairly mild pandemic. . . . And the kinds of interventions that we might recommend in that setting wouldn't be the full court press that we would use if we were dealing with something more serious. On the other hand, we know in 1918 for example, we had a pandemic that not only moved with extraordinary speed from person to person and around the world but it also had an unusually high mortality rate. We would categorize that as a category 5 pandemic.[30]

Use of this severity index would thus benefit the planning process. Dan Jernigan, a CDC official, explained, "By providing a scale you can say at category 4

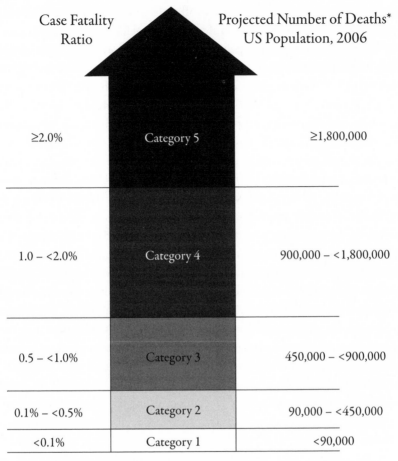

Case Fatality Ratio		Projected Number of Deaths* US Population, 2006
≥2.0%	Category 5	≥1,800,000
1.0 – <2.0%	Category 4	900,000 – <1,800,000
0.5 – <1.0%	Category 3	450,000 – <900,000
0.1% – <0.5%	Category 2	90,000 – <450,000
<0.1%	Category 1	<90,000

*Assumes 30% illness rate
and unmitigated pandemic
without interventions

GRAPH 1. The pandemic mutates into a hurricane. Pandemic Severity Index released by U.S. government officials in February 2007. The Severity Index mimics the Saffir Simpson Hurricane Scale.

or 5, we should do x, y, and z. The pandemic severity index makes it easier to plan."

For some of my interlocutors in the public health community, the hurricane analogy seemed inappropriate, given the failure of the federal government to provide emergency relief after Hurricane Katrina struck. Furthermore, when I asked health professionals at the New York City health department about the Pandemic Severity Index, as officials termed it, they suggested that it might not even constitute a useful planning tool for vaccine prioritization. As Gerberding pointed out, pandemics can vary enormously. They can be indistinguishable from regular seasonal influenza in terms of morbidity and mortality.[31] When comparing different pandemics with each other *in retrospect*, it is indeed possible to distinguish between a severe, a moderate, and a less severe pandemic. But is it possible to envision a pandemic as it happens? The devastating pandemic of 1918 came in three waves. The first was moderate, the second severe, and the third moderate again. Furthermore, there can be significant geographical differences in terms of morbidity and mortality. At what point, then, can officials qualify a pandemic as severe when it may be moderate at first, severe four months later, and less severe another four months after that? How would a vaccine be distributed over the course of a year when the *same* pandemic may be severe, moderate, and less severe? And what happens when the case-fatality ratio turns out to be higher in Florida than in Kansas or when it is elevated among low-income people? Morbidity and mortality are not evenly distributed across the population. In contrast to a hurricane, a pandemic comes in a series of waves that may or may not vary in severity. So what does it mean to prioritize protective vaccine according to distinct categories of pandemic influenza modeled on a concept of hurricanes? Analogies, of course, always have their faults, but in "post-Katrina, pre-pandemic America" the hurricane analogy seemed to make cultural sense, not only among ordinary citizens but also among government officials.[32]

A few months after Hurricane Katrina's landfall, Michael Osterholm underscored in testimony on Capitol Hill that "we must never forget that influenza pandemics are like … hurricanes; they occur."[33] For the CDC, Hurricane Katrina was a "lesson like no other."[34] According to Gerberding, "what CDC learned in its response to Hurricane Katrina … is to prepare for the world's worst potential infectious-disease emergency: pandemic influenza."[35] Public health professionals suggested that the hurricane would "benefit preparation for a deadly global virus."[36] Of course, a violent storm "may seem very different from a microscopic virus," Gerberding admitted, "but to CDC's professionals, that storm provided a 'road map' through which the agency can gauge and improve its performance and achieve its urgent mission during the next emergency."[37] The failed emergency response to Hurricane Katrina was recast as a road map for improvement. In a preparedness update published in 2006, Secretary Leavitt noted that there are also important differences between a hurricane and a pandemic: "A pandemic is not like a hurricane ... where resources and help can be shifted from one area to another. Should it occur, every community will need to rely on its own planning and its own resources as it fights the outbreak."[38] A pandemic, Leavitt emphasized, would affect the entire country. It was a total threat, affecting everyone. And so everyone would need to prepare.

Hurricane Katrina loomed large in debates about pandemic preparedness in the United States. But these debates with their orientation toward the future made it difficult to accomplish the daunting task of inheriting the past in the present. The hurricane analogy signaled both the need to inherit the past in the present and the inability to do so. It revealed the making of a uniform public exposed to a total threat, a threat that was said to affect everyone. What the analogy sanitized in post-Katrina, pre-pandemic America was the differential vulnerability of people; that is, the uneven and unequal exposure of sections of the population to the consequences of contagion.

When I mentioned the prioritization scheme, a New York City public health official asked me, "Why are old people and children marginalized?" They are the most vulnerable, they are the least protected. "Society doesn't value kids and seniors a lot."

Epilogue

Looking out toward the future, prophecy is fulfilled in the continuity of the expectation.

ANDRÉ NEHER

HOW MUCH TIME will it take to bring this book to an end? The problem is that just when you think the story has ended, it begins all over again. The virus had vanished, but no, here it is again, in a new shape, and seemingly more powerful than ever. A new strain appears in China, infecting people sporadically. Scientists examine the pathogenic agent and ponder the future. Officials declare a public health emergency, spurring speculations about the imminence of a catastrophic event. Journalists track the mutant strain, relying on a pool of people, places, and plots that are already well known. And the prophets rise again, and they spread the word, and they urge people to prepare for the inevitable.

The scene is prophetic. It is prophetic because scientists look out toward the future, claiming to see what others cannot see. It is prophetic because they speak without rest, and they speak with certainty and authority. The scene is prophetic because government officials refuse any delay, arguing that the day is near, closer than you think. The scene is prophetic because public health professionals assert that it is essential for preparedness to have faith in the coming plague. The scene is prophetic because newspapers and magazines invoke the future to disambiguate what remains ambiguous about the present. The scene is prophetic because almost everything that occurs seems to glow like a sign, foreshadowing what has been foreseen and foretold. The scene is prophetic because the past prefigures the future and the future fulfills the past. The scene is prophetic because people are concerned about the prophets and what they see and what they say and what they do.

In March 2013, the flu season was coming to an end and worries about a pandemic were easing when news agencies reported that two Shanghai residents had died after contracting a strain that had not been previously seen in humans. Laboratory tests confirmed that both men were infected with an avian influenza virus identified as H7N9. Over the next six weeks, more people contracted the bug and succumbed to the infection. The World Health Organization considered the rising number of cases a cause for concern and released a series of alarming statements about the circulation of the new agent. Chinese officials raised the level of alert, ordered the culling of birds, and closed poultry markets to curb the spread of the virus. In the United States, the CDC announced that microbiologists were growing the bug in the test tube in order to develop a vaccine to protect the population in the case of a pandemic. "This is definitely one of the most lethal influenza viruses that we have seen so far," WHO's Keiji Fukuda declared. It was imperative to stay on a "high level of alert."[1] Scientists, health officials, and the media speculated about the number of people who might fall ill and die. Microbe farmers examined the virus in the laboratory, sequenced all genes, and published the genetic information on a public database. Preliminary studies of the virus suggested that it was gradually adapting to humans. The deadly germ was spreading rapidly like a fire and seemed to pick up mutations along the way. "It's not an atmosphere of alarm, but an atmosphere of concern," said Dr. Malik Peiris, a microbiologist at the University of Hong Kong.[2] Health officials worldwide followed the news coming out of China very closely and speculated about the significance of the situation. The WHO assembled a team of experts to investigate the disease, isolate patients, and intensify surveillance.

Meanwhile, Ron Fouchier and Yoshihiro Kawaoka revealed their plans to manipulate the new virus in the laboratory in an attempt to understand how it might change and cause a pandemic. The two microbiologists suggested that it was essential to make the microbe more virulent in scientific experiments because doing so would support efforts to produce frontline drugs to protect the population. The research would also allow health officials to watch out for dangerous mutations that could make the virus more transmissible among humans and spark a global pandemic. Crafting a contagious virus under controlled conditions would make it easier for governments to deal with a catastrophic outbreak of disease when it occurs, the researchers argued. The U.S. government announced that a panel of experts would review all experiments and supervise scientists to prevent anticipatory research from generating what it anticipated.

In a 2013 article published in the *New York Times*, Michael Osterholm predicted that the next contagion was "closer than you think."[3] He, too, was worried about the new virus that was spreading in China, where it was causing sporadic illness. The plague was coming; the time was near. But Osterholm also emphasized a "more widespread ailment that has gotten little attention." The public health professional termed this condition "contagion exhaustion." Terrible news about terrible events that failed to occur had caused the public to "dismiss warnings about the latest bugs as 'crying wolf.'" Such a dismissal could be deadly in a cosmology of mutant strains. The struggle against doubt and disbelief was vital; faced with disappointment, the prophet urged his audience to remain vigilant and prevent expectation from leading to gradual exhaustion. Osterholm argued that the failure of fulfillment should result not in the dissolution of belief but instead in its reinforcement. He referred to the most recent incident in China and called for persistent faith in the coming plague.

According to public health professionals, viruses are in a deadly battle against the human host. When humanity has little to no immunity against them, the battle will "largely [be] played by their rules and on their schedule." The most recent emergence of avian influenza may perhaps seem far away in China, "but tomorrow [it] could be at America's doorstep."[4] It was thus essential to struggle against a loss of faith and overcome pandemic fatigue. In the battle against the bug, it was vital for survival to listen to the message and take it to heart.

CDC officials were also worried about the fading interest in preparedness. "If the pandemic doesn't hit soon," an official told me, "public interest is going to wane, congressional interest is going to wane, and we will lose the momentum because we will probably end up losing a lot of the funding, and we will lose the visibility, and we will lose the priority and status that we have." She went on, "We tend to be complacent, we go back, we put our guards down. Unfortunately, I think this country has to go through a series of events in order to be at the level that it should be in order to respond and effectively recover."

"Each different emergence of disease . . . is a story of its own. We're very early on. . . . We have to watch very carefully and see how the H7N9 story unfolds," a government official cautioned.[5] The virus was writing the rules, without rhyme or reason, and public health professionals were on the lookout for suspicious fevers and other symptoms. "Almost everything you can imagine is possible. And then what's likely to happen are the things which you can't imagine," a health expert said.[6] The world was again on the verge of an event, but the signs were obscure. Osterholm pondered: "Mother nature is trying to tell us something here. But I don't think any of us has a clue."[7]

At the core of these concerns about the coming plague are anxieties that have taken a historically distinctive shape. But these anxieties are not just anxieties about dangerous viruses. They are anxieties about a borderless world and a shrinking planet, in which microbes are said to know no borders. They are anxieties about industrialization, urbanization, deforestation, and an unprecedented destruction of the environment. They are anxieties about global climate change and the secret journey of tropical species into the temperate zones of the North and the South. They are anxieties about mysterious microbes breeding in remote jungle villages. They are anxieties about migrant and refugee populations in rural China. They are anxieties about obscure places where people are living in close proximity to their backyard ducks and rooftop poultry. They are anxieties about resistant viruses that are proliferating in nature's laboratory. Fatal strains of deadly disease are carried across international borders; the next pandemic seems no more than a plane ride away.

These are the nightmares of modernity, specters of a biological catastrophe that have contributed to the sedimentation of a geography of blame in which bugs are given a natural place in the dusty neighborhoods of developing nations. In this geography of blame, traditional ecologies, economies, and societies figure as "natural reservoirs" of deadly viruses. The political desire to police populations has expanded "across the animal kingdom in order to govern the 'global biological' as a single, integrated system containing emergent risks."[8] Interspecies contact zones are the hot zones that require the intensive surveillance promised by sophisticated biowatch programs. Modern trade and travel have rendered territorial borders permeable, and health authorities are increasingly worried that biological life is getting out of control in the global village of global capitalism. Accelerating processes of transnational mobility, including forced migration and displacement, have produced a new proximity between the advanced nations of the West and the primordial life of the Rest. The logic of containment suggests that the struggle against disease must be taken "over there," before it "reaches here."[9] Floating populations of migrants and refugees in southern China—"crowded into tenement housing, racialized as backward, largely without health care or public health services"—are quarantined preventively when international organizations are declaring public health emergencies.[10] Thus, today's fears about the pandemic threat highlight, in Jean Comaroff's terms, the geopolitical insecurities of "unrecognizable aliens capable of disrupting existing immunities, penetrating once-secure boundaries at a time of deregulated exchange."[11]

By the end of April, the H7N9 virus had infected 132 people and killed 37. But then it vanished as suddenly as it had appeared on the world stage. Chinese health officials detected no new cases of infection and wondered where the mysterious microbe had gone. Where was it hiding? Would it return again? Officials emphasized that the world could not afford to relax and let down its guard. The virus might return in winter season and become much more contagious. Based on previous experiences with the emergence of avian viruses, that possibility could not be ruled out. Early signs of imminent return could be subtle and imperceptible. It was important to pay attention to the most puzzling epidemic intelligence reports coming from the most remote places on the planet. The spread of H7N9 was another reminder that we must continue to prepare for the next pandemic. The episode demonstrated how dangerous is the situation with the virus. We cannot let our guard down. We must be ready. Nature's laboratory never sleeps.

Scientists were again under the influence of influenza, affirming the truth of scary viruses and the eternal nature of the threat. They were growing bugs and testing bodies in the laboratory; they were planning to perform experiments of concern, experiments that circulated as evidence of how worried they were. They devised dangerous trials, which were testimonies of their faith. Pharmaceutical companies were in the business of developing protective vaccines and manufacturing tests for the rapid detection of the disease. Experts made pronouncements about the future course of events, suggesting that humanity was on the edge of an event that was just about to happen.

But then the virus vanished.

And a new one appeared.

On March 22, 2014, the WHO declared that Ebola was spreading in West Africa where the virus had been killing people in the region for three months. In contrast to pervious outbreaks, the epidemic was not limited to rural villages. By the end of the year, it had killed approximately eight thousand people and had become the largest epidemic of Ebola in recent history. As observers underscored, the international media coverage rehearsed a moral discourse of blame, presenting the region as "helpless and hopeless, a tragic victim of illogical beliefs and dangerous cultural practices."[12] Medical anthropologist and physician Vinh-Kim Nguyen emphasized that "Ebola happened despite, and indeed as a result of, over a decade of pandemic preparedness efforts costing billions. These efforts not only failed, they produced this Ebola epidemic." Nguyen noted that a tremendous amount of funding had been devoted to preparedness over the past decade, "a nebulous construct that highlighted surveillance and simulation as key to readiness for bioterrorism and other epidemic threats." In West Africa, Ebola killed health care workers who were exposed to the virus due to a lack of infection control and personal protection equipment. "Health care facilities, already the weak link in the chain, have become the fault line along which Ebola tracks." Ebola happened because "all those efforts devoted to pandemic preparedness did not involve investing in health systems at the frontline of epidemics: hospitals."[13]

In the United States, it seemed almost impossible to talk about Ebola without simultaneously talking about the flu. "Ebola is bad, but the flu is worse," declared Kendall Hoyt, a professor of medicine at Dartmouth College.[14] "As we stare with horror at the ravages of Ebola, it is easy to overlook an old familiar foe: the flu." Influenza will claim more American lives than Ebola ever will, the professor predicted; we "simply cannot afford to be complacent about flu preparedness." The message was clear: Citizens were worrying about the wrong disease. In a weekly address, President Obama called on Americans to remain calm about Ebola. "We have to keep this in perspective," said Obama. "Every year, thousands of Americans die from the flu."

Michael Specter concurred in an article with a telling title, "After Ebola," published in the *New Yorker* in August 2014. At a time when the Ebola epidemic was hardly over, the journalist looked out toward the future. "Ebola won't kill us all, but something else might," Specter suggested.[15] Viruses are caught in a process of constant change. "That is why avian influenza has provoked so much anxiety; it has not yet mutated into an infection that can spread easily." The virus could evolve today and trigger a pandemic tomorrow. Thus, it was crucial for citizens to consider what might take place after Ebola. And that could only be the flu, the paradigmatic threat of the future, the condition that has the future as its defining nature. In the scene of pandemic prophecy, influenza comes to consciousness through the logic of deferral. It is a form of disease that refuses closure because it is always displaced into the future.

At the core of the cosmology of mutant strains is a fundamental faith, the faith that disease lies in the future. As pressing as the present may be, this form of faith is aspirational; it always hastens beyond the here and now; and in so doing, it takes the present away. The rush, the haste, the speed is essential, because nature is always one step ahead and the virus always carries with it the potential for an event. The prophet is impatient. The prophet is determined. The prophet sees and tells: "This is how it is . . ." The prophet speaks the language of sovereignty, the language of command that forces us to be attentive, look out toward the future, and prepare for the coming plague.

NOTE ON THE COVER IMAGE

The book's cover image is part of a small series of photographs documenting the Coimbra University Hospital in Portugal. "I want people to imagine what could have happened, what is happening, and what will be happening," said Portuguese photographer Inês d'Orey at the opening of an exhibition. A characteristic feature of her photographic examination of the contemporary conditions of existence is the illumination of abandoned places, interiors absent of any human presence: theatres, lobbies, living rooms, lecture halls, swimming pools. But these spaces without places, these deserts of the social that she continues to display, are never completely empty; on the contrary, they always contain traces of a former presence. These traces drawn in the sand inspire the imagination of her audience; the desert becomes pregnant with potential, suggesting stories that could have happened. What the photographer presents in her work are platforms for plots, stages for possible stories. These stories are never clear, to be sure, and the carefully choreographed scene always remains suspended between being and becoming. Something might have happened, or is happening, or will be happening, but we don't know what it is. This is eventfulness without events. Inês d'Orey is a photographer of the perhaps.

NOTES

INTRODUCTION

1. Avian Flu: Addressing the Global Threat. Hearing before the Committee on International Relations. House of Representatives. Washington, DC.

2. Ibid.

3. Ibid.

4. Michael T. Osterholm, "Preparing for the Next Pandemic," *Foreign Affairs* 84, no. 4 (2005), p. 32.

5. Ibid., p. 32.

6. Ibid., p. 35.

7. "Geography of blame" is Paul Farmer's term. He developed it in his early work on the AIDS epidemic in Haiti. Paul Farmer, *AIDS and Accusation: Haiti and the Geography of Blame* (Berkeley: University of California Press, 1992). On constructions of the body as nation and the nation as body in contemporary immunological discourse, see Emily Martin's classic essay: "Toward an Anthropology of Immunology. The Body as Nation State," *Medical Anthropology Quarterly* 4, no. 4 (1990).

8. Michael Specter, "Nature's Bioterrorist: Is There Any Way to Prevent a Deadly Avian-Flu Pandemic?" *The New Yorker*, February 28, 2005, p. 50. On the politics of scale in emerging infectious disease discourse, see the articles by Nicholas King: "The Scale Politics of Emerging Diseases," *Osiris* 19 (2004) and "Security, Disease, Commerce: Ideologies of Postcolonial Global Health," *Social Studies of Science* 32, no. 5–6 (2002).

9. "If . . . a virus remains inert and without locomotion, why should we privilege it with agency?" A. David Napier, "Nonself Help: How Immunology Might Reframe the Enlightenment," *Cultural Anthropology* 27, no. 1 (2012), p. 127. In chapter 1, I take up Napier's question and discuss it in relation to the ambiguous status of the virus in the order of nature.

10. Apoorva Mandavilli, "Profile Robert Webster," *Nature Medicine* 9, no. 12 (2003).

11. Thanks to Jim Faubion for his insight.

12. Celia Lowe, "Viral Clouds: Becoming H5N1 in Indonesia," *Cultural Anthropology* 25, no. 4 (2010), p. 626.

13. Nicholas B. King, "The Influence of Anxiety: September 11, Bioterrorism and American Public Health," *Journal of the History of Medicine and Allied Sciences* 58 (2003), p. 435.

14. Mike Davis, *The Monster at Our Door: The Global Threat of Avian Flu* (New York: New Press, 2005), p. 7.

15. Richard Preston, *The Hot Zone* (New York: Random House, 1994), p. 310.

16. Ibid.

17. On prophecy, see Jane Guyer's important and inspiring essay, "Prophecy and the Near Future. Thoughts on Macroeconomic, Evangelical, and Punctuated Time," *American Ethnologist* 34, no. 3 (2007). For a classic account, see E. E. Evans-Pritchard, *Witchcraft, Oracles and Magic among the Azande* (Oxford: Oxford University Press, 1937). See as well *Nuer Religion* (Oxford: Clarendon Press, 1956); Bengt G. M. Sundkler, *Bantu Prophets in South Africa* (London: Lutterworth Press, 1948); Edwin Ardner, *The Voice of Prophecy and Other Essays* (Oxford: Basil Blackwell, 1989); and Paul Spencer, *Time, Space, and the Unknown: Massai Configurations of Power and Providence* (London: Routledge, 2003). On prophetic speech, see Claus Westermann, *Basic Forms of Prophetic Speech* (Cambridge: Lutterworth Press, 1991).

18. For a historical account of prophecy belief in American culture, see among others Paul Boyer, *When Time Shall Be No More: Prophecy Belief in Modern American Culture* (Cambridge, MA: Harvard University Press, 1992); Stephen D. O'Leary, *Arguing the Apocalypse: A Theory of Millennial Rhetoric* (Oxford: Oxford University Press, 1994); Susan Friend Harding, *The Book of Jerry Falwell: Fundamentalist Language and Politics* (Princeton: Princeton University Press, 2000); James D. Faubion, *The Shadows and Lights of Waco: Millennialism Today* (Princeton: Princeton University Press, 2001); and Warren W. Wagar, *Terminal Visions: The Literature of Last Things* (Bloomington: Indiana University Press, 1982).

19. Kathleen Stewart and Susan Friend Harding, "Bad Endings: American Apocalypsis," *Annual Review of Anthropology* 28 (1999), p. 286. See as well Frank Kermode, *The Sense of an Ending: Studies in the Theory of Fiction* (Oxford: Oxford University Press, 2000).

20. Stewart and Harding, "Bad Endings," p. 286.

21. Joseph Masco, "'Survival Is Your Business': Engineering Ruins and Affect in Nuclear America," *Cultural Anthropology* 23, no. 2 (2008). For an excellent anthropological account of the nuclear state in post–Cold War America, see *The Nuclear Borderlands: The Manhattan Project in Post–Cold War New Mexico* (Princeton: Princeton University Press, 2006).

22. Joseph Masco, "Atomic Health, or How the Bomb Altered American Notions of Death," in *Against Health: How Health Became the New Morality*, ed. Jonathan M. Metzl and Anna Kirkland (New York: New York University Press, 2010), p. 152.

23. Pandemic discourse is public discourse. And public discourse is projective discourse; it is projective discourse because it is actively involved in the production and

protection of the culture of circulation in which the communication of danger achieves communicative power. I suggest calling this culture of circulation the "public culture of danger." This notion is a modified term derived from Michel Foucault's work. In his lectures on *The Birth of Biopolitics* Foucault argues that subjects of liberal rule are systematically reminded, through multiple channels of communication, that life is under threat. A prominent example is crime fiction, a literary genre that arose over the course of the nineteenth century and that confronted a reading public with potential perils lurking in the shadows. Another example that Foucault mentions are concerns and campaigns around contagion and hygiene. Individuals are conditioned "to experience their situation, their life, their present and their future as containing danger." The feeling of fear, associated with the exposure to existential threat, is at the heart of the modern social contract and the formation of modern political communities. I use the notion of the public culture of danger to highlight the projective nature of the discourse that I explore. It is important to emphasize that the notion is not meant as a description of what "the public" really feels about the possibility of a pandemic. In fact, every reference to the public is always "a necessarily imaginary reference." But this reference can be incredibly productive, contributing to the constitution of what it claims to represent. Pandemic discourse invokes a particular kind of public, a public that is assumed to be in danger, a public that is thought to be complacent about the threat of disease. Thus, pandemic discourse entails particular characterizations of the public. Of course, people may or may not recognize themselves as part of that audience that is supposed to listen. But the fact that pandemic discourse continues to circulate, the fact that the possibility of a biological catastrophe has gained a substantial presence in public life, indicates that there is an audience, that there are people who perceive themselves as members of that public, people who respond to the address and engage in the discussion. Michel Foucault, *The Birth of Biopolitics: Lectures at the College de France, 1978–1979* (New York: Palgrave MacMillan, 2008).

24. James D. Faubion, "Comments," *Current Anthropology* 55, no. 3 (2014). See as well *The Shadows and Lights of Waco*, pp. 47–52. My thanks to Jim Faubion for his help with this section. On the utopian moment of plague visions, see Elana Gomel, "The Plague of Utopias: Pestilence and the Apocalyptic Body," *Twentieth Century Literature* 46, no. 4 (2000). Thanks to Christos Lynteris for drawing my attention to this article.

25. A paraphrase from Robert Lowth, cited in Ian Balfour, *The Rhetoric of Romantic Prophecy* (Stanford: Stanford University Press, 2002), p. 74. Balfour underscores that prophecy should not be reduced to prediction. The temporal orientation of the prophetic word is complex and contradictory.

26. Ibid.

27. Davis, *The Monster at Our Door*, p. 24. For accounts of the history of the 1918 pandemic, see John M. Barry, *The Great Influenza: The Epic Story of the Deadliest Plague in History* (New York: Penguin Books, 2004); Davis, *The Monster at Our Door*; Pete Davies, *The Devil's Flu* (New York: Henry Holt, 2000); and Gina Ko-

lata, *Flu: The Story of the Great Influenza Pandemic of 1918 and the Search for the Virus That Caused It* (New York: Simon & Schuster, 2005).

28. Alfred W. Crosby, *America's Forgotten Pandemic: The Influenza of 1918* (Cambridge: Cambridge University Press, 2003). The first edition, published in 1976, was titled *Epidemic and Peace*. See *Epidemic and Peace* (Westport: Greenwood Press, 1976). For another example, see David A. Davis, "The Forgotten Apocalypse: Katherine Anne Porter's 'Pale Horse, Pale Rider,' Traumatic Memory, and the Influenza Pandemic of 1918," *Southern Literary Journal* 43, no. 2 (2011).

29. Crosby, *America's Forgotten Pandemic*, p. xi.

30. As Benedict Anderson argues, the paradox to "'have already forgotten' tragedies of which one needs increasingly to be 'reminded'" is characteristic of the constitution of a collective identity in a conception of history as national memory. Benedict Anderson, *Imagined Communities: Reflections on the Origin and Spread of Nationalism* (London: Verso, 1983), p. 200.

31. On the citational use of the past, see Walter Benjamin, "Über den Begriff der Geschichte," in *Abhandlungen. Gesammelte Schriften, Band I (2)*, ed. Hermann Schweppenhäuser and Rolf Tiedemann (Frankfurt am Main: Suhrkamp Verlag, 1991). "It isn't that the past casts its light on what is present or that what is present casts its light on what is past; rather, an image is that in which the Then and the Now come together into a constellation like a flash of lightning."

32. For such a program, see Arthur M. Kleinman et al., "Avian and Pandemic Influenza. A Biosocial Approach," *Journal of Infectious Diseases* 197 (2008) and "Asian Flus in Ethnographic and Political Context. A Biosocial Approach," *Anthropology & Medicine* 15, no. 1 (2008).

33. On the productivity of temporal incongruity, see Hirokazu Miyazaki, "The Temporalities of the Market," *American Anthropologist* 105, no. 2 (2003).

34. For a similar approach, see the important work of Frédéric Keck, which explores imaginations of the pandemic threat in Hong Kong. Frédéric Keck, *Un Monde Grippé* (Paris: Flammarion, 2010). See as well Theresa MacPhail, *The Viral Network: A Pathography of the H1N1 Influenza Pandemic* (Ithaca: Cornell University Press, 2014).

35. Stacey L. Knobler et al., *The Threat of Pandemic Influenza: Are We Ready?* (Washington, DC: National Academies Press, 2005), p. 1.

36. Tim Gihring, "The Pandemic Prophecy," *Minnesota Monthly* (2006). See as well Michael T. Osterholm and John Schwartz, *Living Terrors: What America Needs to Know to Survive the Coming Bioterrorist Catastrophe* (New York: Dell Publishing, 2000).

37. Editorial. "Plan for Pandemic but Avoid Panic," *Financial Times*, 2009.

38. "The art of adequately informing the public of escalating threats without inducing unnecessary fear lies at the heart of effective pandemic responses." Andrew Lea, "Balancing Panic and Threat: What 'Contagion' Tells Us about Pandemics Today," *Harvard College Global Health Review*, October 20, 2011. This effort to manage the American population through the affective medium of fear has a long history

that is inextricably linked with the Cold War. "A central project of civil defense was . . . to produce fear but not terror, anxiety but not panic . . ." See Masco, "'Survival Is Your Business,'" p. 368. See as well Masco's book, *The Theater of Operations: National Security Affect from the Cold War to the War on Terror* (Durham, NC: Duke University Press, 2014).

39. The influenza virus has two important proteins that are found on the surface of the virus: the hemagglutinin (HA or H) and the neuraminidase (NA or N). The hemagglutinin is responsible for binding the virus to the cells of the host. The neuraminidase allows the virus to be released again from these cells. Microbiologists use the two surface proteins to classify influenza viruses. They currently distinguish between eighteen H subtypes and nine N subtypes. The first three H subtypes, H1, H2, and H3, are found in influenza viruses that have infected humans in the twentieth century.

40. Osterholm, "Preparing for the Next Pandemic," p. 35. The problem of prioritization is the topic of chapter 6.

41. Ibid.

42. William Branigin, Mike Allen, and John Mintz, "Tommy Thompson Resigns from HHS. Bush Asks Defense Secretary Rumsfeld to Stay," *Washington Post*, 2004.

43. Ibid.

44. HHS. HHS Pandemic Influenza Plan (Washington, DC: Department of Health and Human Services, 2005), p. 1.

45. Ibid.

46. Redlener, Irwin, *Americans at Risk: Why We Are Not Prepared for Megadisasters and What We Can Do* (New York: Random House, 2006), p. xxvi.

47. HHS Pandemic Influenza Plan, p. 1.

48. Redlener, *Americans at Risk*, p. xxv.

49. Eliot J. Lazar, Nicholas Cagliuso, and Kristine M. Gebbie, "Are We Ready and How Do We Know? The Urgent Need for Performance Metrics in Hospital Emergency Management," *Disaster Medicine* 3, no. 1 (2009).

50. Osterholm, "Preparing for the Next Pandemic."

51. Ibid., p. 30.

52. Redlener, *Americans at Risk*, p. 180.

53. James Wesley Rawles, *How to Survive the End of the World as We Know It* (London: Penguin Books, 2009).

54. Michael T. Osterholm, "Unprepared for a Pandemic," *Foreign Affairs* 86, no. 2 (2007), p. 57.

55. David Rosner and Gerald Markowitz, *Are We Ready? Public Health since 9/11* (Berkeley: University of California Press, 2006). In New York City, Rudolph Giuliani reorganized the Office of Emergency Management when he became mayor in 1994. An emergency manager told me, "When Giuliani became Mayor, the New York City Office of Emergency Management was still part of the police department. And it was a backwater office; it wasn't very important. My best guess is that less than a dozen worked in the office. What happened when Giuliani became mayor, he

wanted to be seen as the public safety mayor. And there was a problem that evolved over time with the police commissioners potentially outshining him, so in order for him to have direct connection and being seen as the head law enforcement officer—For that and for other reasons, he moved the office of emergency management from being in the police department to being a mayoral agency, reporting directly to the mayor. The other big reason was because in New York City the police and the fire departments had traditionally battled each other for control at scenes. So when there was an argument over who is going to be in charge, the office of emergency management had responders whose job it was to say what the mayor wanted. So in that regard that was a very different responsibility for an office of emergency management. Because it reported directly to the mayor they had a lot of actual and a lot of perceived authority."

56. For the contrastive concept of slow death, see Lauren Berlant, "Slow Death (Sovereignty, Obesity, Lateral Agency)," *Critical Inquiry* 33, no. 4 (2007). "The phrase slow death refers to the physical wearing out of a population and the deterioration of people in that population that is very nearly a defining condition of their experience and historical existence. . . . Slow death occupies the temporalities of the endemic" (pp. 754 and 756).

57. New York City Department of Health and Mental Hygiene, *A Plan to Stabilize and Strengthen New York's Health Care System: Final Report of the Commission on Health Care Facilities in the 21st Century* (New York: New York City Department of Health and Mental Hygiene, 2006).

58. Ibid., pp. 4 and 48.

59. Lauren Berlant, *Cruel Optimism* (Durham, NC: Duke University Press, 2011), p. 7.

60. Osterholm, "Preparing for the Next Pandemic," p. 36.

61. The projectification of the pandemic threat reflects a more general trend characteristic of contemporary transformations of capitalism in late liberalism. As Luc Boltanski and Eve Chiapello suggested, the "project" has increasingly become a hegemonic form of management in the corporate world. Over the past two decades, the idea of the project has spread beyond the traditional domains of construction, engineering, and research; it is now at the core of corporations and their mode of operation. These corporations have increasingly moved from functional organization to project management. To be engaged in some sort of project has become the new norm of late liberal existence. "What matters is to develop an activity—that is to say, never to be short of a project, bereft of an idea, always to have something in mind, in the pipeline, with other people whom one meets out of a desire to do something." Typically, this activity takes the shape of a temporary project. "When they engage in a project, everyone concerned knows that the undertaking to which they are about to contribute is destined to last for a limited period of time." The project is transient, but the process of projectification is permanent: The "awareness that the project will come to an end" is always accompanied "by the hope that a new project will follow." Luc Boltanski and Eve Chiapello, *The New Spirit of Capitalism* (London: Verso, 2007), pp. 110ff.

62. Melinda Cooper, "Pre-Empting Emergence: The Biological Turn in the War on Terror," *Theory, Culture & Society* 23, no. 4 (2006), p. 113. For an account of recent constructions of biological threat and biological vulnerability, see Carlo Caduff, "On the Verge of Death: Visions of Biological Vulnerability," *Annual Review of Anthropology* 43 (2014). For investigations of preparedness in the governmentality tradition, see Limor Samimian-Darash, "Governing Future Potential Biothreats: Toward an Anthropology of Uncertainty," *Current Anthropology* 54, no. 1 (2013), pp. 1–22; Samimian-Darash, "Governing through Time: Preparing for Future Threats to Health and Security," *Sociology of Health and Illness* 33, no. 6 (2011), pp. 930–45; Samimian-Darash, "A Pre-Event Configuration for Biological Threats: Preparedness and the Constitution of Biosecurity Events." *American Ethnologist* 36, no. 3 (2009), pp. 478–91.

63. Rosner and Markowitz, *Are We Ready?* p. 57.

64. For the controversy around the drug, see Peter Doshi, "Neuraminidase Inhibitors: The Story behind the Cochrane Review," *British Medical Journal* 339 (2009). Helen Epstein, "Flu Warning: Beware the Drug Companies!" *New York Review of Books* 58, no. 8 (2011).

65. "Bioterror in Context. Interview with William R. Clark." Pacific Standard, May 19, 2008. http://www.psmag.com/culture-society/bioterror-in-context-4548. Accessed October 19, 2012.

66. Richard J. Webby and Robert G. Webster, "Are We Ready for Pandemic Influenza," *Science* 302 (2003), p. 1522. See as well Specter, "Nature's Bioterrorist."

67. Michael Coston, "Avian Flu Diary." http://afludiary.blogspot.ch/2013/04/h5n1-meanwhile-in-vietnam.html Accessed 2 January 2015.

68. COBRA is the Chemical, Ordnance, Biological and Radiological training facility of the Centre for Domestic Preparedness in Anniston.

69. Masco, *The Theater of Operations*. See as well Caduff, "On the Verge of Death." For Ulrich Beck's classic work on "risk society," see Beck, *Risk Society: Towards a New Modernity* (London: Sage, 1992); Beck, "Risk Society Revisited: Theory, Politics and Research Programmes," in *Risk Society and Beyond: Critical Issues for Social Theory*, ed. Barbara Adam, Ulrich Beck, and Joost Van Loon, 211–29 (London: Sage, 2000); Beck, "World Risk Society as Cosmopolitan Society: Ecological Questions in a Framework of Manufactured Uncertainties," *Theory, Culture & Society* 13, no. 4 (1996), pp. 1–32.

70. Niklas Luhmann, *Observations on Modernity*, trans. William Whobrey (Stanford: Stanford University Press, 1998).

71. Andrew Lakoff, "The Generic Biothreat, or, How We Became Unprepared," *Cultural Anthropology* 23, no. 3 (2008), p. 401.

72. Hirokazu Miyazaki, "Arbitraging Faith and Reason," *American Ethnologist* 34, no. 3 (2007), p. 431.

73. Maurice Blanchot, *The Book to Come* (Stanford: Stanford University Press, 2003), p. 79.

74. Michael T. Osterholm, "The Next Contagion: Closer than You Think," *New York Times*, May 9, 2013.

75. "Profane illumination" is Walter Benjamin's term.

76. John L. Austin, *How to Do Things with Words* (Cambridge, MA: Harvard University Press, 2001).

77. Ibid., p. 17. See as well Shoshana Felman, *The Scandal of the Speaking Body: Don Juan with J. L. Austin or Seduction in Two Languages* (Stanford: Stanford University Press, 2002), p. 57; and Alexei Yurchak, *Everything Was Forever, until It Was No More: The Last Soviet Generation* (Princeton: Princeton University Press, 2006), pp. 19–21.

78. Blanchot, *The Book to Come.*

79. Paul Rabinow calls such research "untimely anthropological work." See Paul Rabinow, *Marking Time: On the Anthropology of the Contemporary* (Princeton: Princeton University Press, 2008). Over the past years, scholars have studied the construction of the biological threat from a critical perspective, but this perspective appears to have lost its critical edge. Among the reasons is an overconfidence in a certain analytics of power and a related concern with "intelligibility." Scholars have shown in great detail how the threat was transformed into an object of knowledge through scientific discourses and practices. They have examined how experts problematized the future as a source of uncertainty and how these problematizations made interventions necessary in the name of preparedness. They have argued that anticipatory forms of action are now an important response to the prospect of catastrophic events. They have analyzed how styles of reasoning, strategies of intervention, and modes of subjectivity are assembled in emerging configurations of "public health security." This type of critical analysis has been incredibly instructive, but it has often reproduced the perspective of experts. Scholars have suggested that a "fundamental break" has occurred, that a "new regime" of "public health vigilance" has come into being, that a "new political rationality" has materialized, and that we are now living in a "world on alert." Yet the vision of a "global surveillance network" and "early warning system" described by experts in reports is often more virtual than real. The network is dispersed, the ties are thin, the surveillance erratic, and the meaning of the epidemiological information uncertain. The network is fragmented and fraught with inconsistencies. It is pictured as a seamless system of surveillance, but this is primarily the network's own mythology of coherence, logic, and rationality. A critical analysis that seeks to describe a "new regime" of "public health vigilance" as a coherent and consistent object thus runs the risk of reproducing a pretense. The trouble is that such forms of analysis tend to replicate the systematizing and totalizing worldviews that experts pronounce on television and elsewhere when they speak about the spread of a disease and the most effective way to manage it. In sum, there seems to be too much immanence in this form of analysis.

The coherence and consistence that this form of analysis projects prompts a fascinating question: Is the object of analysis coherent and consistent, or is it the analysis that is generating the coherence and consistence? For instance, to what extent is the notion of a "new regime" of "public health vigilance" itself a force in the making of structure and order? Is the notion constative or performative? Is the notion contributing to the construction of what it is describing? We might also wonder to what extent such a form of analysis is making it easier for projects of "public health vigilance" to impose themselves on populations in the global South. Public health vigilance is a curious and interesting techno-political project obsessed with catastrophic events. Yet, as Anna Tsing reminds us, there is no need for anthropologists to naturalize such projects "by assuming that the terms they offer us are true." We need to explore these projects outside their own terms. Tsing additionally suggests that we "investigate new developments without assuming either their universal extension or their fantastic ability to draw all world-making activities into their grasp." See Anna Tsing, "The Global Situation," *Cultural Anthropology* 15, no. 3 (2000). The critical vocabulary of "new forms of sovereign power" that have come into being and that have introduced a "continuous state of emergency" is problematic not least because it replaces one dramatic language with another. Such language evokes a sense of monumental change; it turns public health institutions into sovereign actors with sovereign power; it claims that older forms of governance have evaporated all of a sudden; it suggests that a new type of uncertainty has appeared; it presumes that power is effective in the world in which it operates; it makes expert discourse more uniform and homogeneous than it is; it obscures significant slippages in the mechanisms of power; it attributes an overarching logic and seemingly inexorable force to contemporary interventions into the conditions of life; and it assumes that the effects of such interventions are evident. Despite the critical reading practices that scholars pursue, such accounts tend to inadvertently rationalize and systematize, and thus stabilize and legitimize, the very modes of power that are under investigation.

80. Judith Butler argues that social studies of economics have illuminated the constructive nature of economic theory. This approach is important, but it has also limited the understanding of performativity, according to Butler. "My worry is that the cultural constructivist position thinks performativity works and that it imputes a certain sovereign agency to the operation of performativity." Butler underscores that economic theory can sometimes fail to produce what it anticipates. I extend this insight, arguing that pandemic prophecy fails, but that it fails not just sometimes, but always. However, in contrast to Butler, I suggest that the failure of pandemic prophecy to deliver its promise *does not necessarily establish the conditions of its undoing*. Failure does not necessarily enable resistance and resignification. Judith Butler, "Performative Agency," *Journal of Cultural Economy* 3, no. 2 (2010), p. 153.

81. Among the many journalistic accounts that are promoted in these terms, see Alan Sipress, *The Fatal Strain: On the Trail of Avian Flu and the Coming Pandemic* (New York: Penguin Books, 2009); Kolata, *Flu*; Davis, *The Monster at Our Door*.

82. Nathan Wolfe, *The Viral Storm: The Dawn of a New Pandemic Age* (New York: Henry Holt, 2011); Davis, *The Monster at Our Door*.

83. On the hermeneutics of suspicion, see Paul Ricoeur, *Freud and Philosophy: An Essay on Interpretation* (New Haven: Yale University Press, 1970). On the speaker's benefit, a related concept, see Michel Foucault, *The History of Sexuality: An Introduction* (New York: Vintage Books, 1990), p. 6.

84. Cori Hayden, "Rethinking Reductionism, or, the Transformative Work of Making the Same," *Anthropological Forum: A Journal of Social Anthropology and*

Comparative Sociology 22, no. 3 (2012). See as well "A Generic Solution? Pharmaceuticals and the Politics of the Similar in Mexico," *Current Anthropology* 48, no. 4 (2007).

85. Avital Ronell, *The Test Drive* (Urbana: University of Illinois Press, 2005), p. 14.

86. Ibid., p. 179.

87. Frank Macfarlane Burnet, *Virus as Organism: Evolutionary and Ecological Aspects of Some Human Virus Diseases* (Cambridge, MA: Harvard University Press, 1946), p. 102.

88. Avital Ronell, *Finitude's Score: Essays for the End of the Millennium* (Lincoln: University of Nebraska Press, 1994), p. xi.

89. André Neher, *The Prophetic Existence* (London: Thomas Yoseloff Ltd., 1969), p. 270.

90. Balfour, *The Rhetoric of Romantic Prophecy*, p. 130.

CHAPTER ONE

1. Georges Canguilhem, *The Normal and the Pathological* (New York: Zone Books, 1989), p. 35.

2. Ibid., p. 85.

3. On these early bacteriological attempts to find the cause of influenza and define the disease as a specific infection, see Michael Bresalier's articles: "Uses of a Pandemic: Forging the Identities of Influenza and Virus Research in Interwar Britain," *Social History of Medicine* 25, no. 2 (2011).

4. Hans Zinsser, "The Etiology and Epidemiology of Influenza," *Medicine* 1, no. 2 (1922), p. 244.

5. Thomas M. Rivers, "Viruses," *Science* 75, no. 1956 (1932), p. 655.

6. Ibid., p. 655.

7. Henry Hallett Dale, "Patrick Playfair Laidlaw. 1881–1940," *Obituary Notices of Fellows of the Royal Society* 3, no. 9 (1941), p. 599.

8. Thanks to Michael Bresalier for clarifying this point.

9. Ton van Helvoort, "A Bacteriological Paradigm in Influenza Research in the First Half of the Twentieth Century," *History and Philosophy of the Life Sciences* 15 (1993), p. 16.

10. At the heart of the microbiological revolution, as K. Codell Carter has shown, is a particular understanding of causality that portrays living organisms as *necessary* and *sufficient* causes of specific diseases. As Carter points out, it was not simply that heavenly bodies and earthly tremors were eventually replaced by living organisms cultivated in a few droplets of bovine broth. It was, rather, the concept of causality itself that was conceived of in a different way, now referring not to *predisposing* factors but to *necessary* and *sufficient* causes. The difficult task microbiologists set for themselves was to show that a pathogenic agent was able, by itself, to produce a certain pathological condition and that this condition could not exist without the

presence of the agent. Significantly, this new understanding of causality promoted by microbiologists in late nineteenth-century France and Germany, as Michael Worboys remarked in his study, initially almost completely failed to impress the medical establishment. K. Codell Carter, *The Rise of Causal Concepts of Disease: Case Histories* (Aldershot: Ashgate, 2003), p. 1; Michael Worboys, *Spreading Germs: Disease Theories and Medical Practice in Britain* (Cambridge: Cambridge University Press, 2000). See as well K. Codell Carter, "Koch's Postulates in Relation to the Work of Jacob Henle and Edwin Klebs," *Medical History* 29 (1985); "Edwin Klebs' Criteria for Disease Causality," *Medizinhistorisches Journal* 22 (1987); and "The Development of Pasteur's Concept of Disease Causation and the Emergence of Specific Causes in Nineteenth-Century Medicine," *Bulletin of the History of Medicine* 65, no. 4 (1991). The literature on Pasteur and Koch is large. See among others, François Dagognet, *Méthodes et Doctrine dans l'Oeuvre de Pasteur* (Paris: PUF, 1967) and *Pasteur sans la Légende* (Paris Synthelabo, 1994); Gerald L. Geison, *The Private Science of Louis Pasteur* (Princeton: Princeton University Press, 1995); Bruno Latour, *The Pasteurization of France*, trans. Alan Sheridan and John Law (Cambridge, MA: Harvard University Press, 1988); Thomas Dale Brock, *Robert Koch: A Life in Medicine and Bacteriology* (Madison: Science Tech Publishers, 1988); and Christoph Gradmann, *Krankheit im Labor: Robert Koch und die Medizinische Bakteriologie* (Göttingen: Wallstein Verlag, 2005). For a historical account of the emergence of bacteriology, see William Bulloch, *The History of Bacteriology* (London: Oxford University Press, 1960) and Andrew J. Mendelsohn, *Cultures of Bacteriology: Formation and Transformation of a Science in France and Germany, 1870–1914* (Unpublished Dissertation) (Princeton: Princeton University, 1996).

11. For biographical accounts, see D. A. J. Tyrrell, "Christopher Howard Andrewes. 7 June 1896–31 December 1987," *Biographical Memoirs of Fellows of the Royal Society* 37 (1991); Dale, "Patrick Playfair Laidlaw"; and D. G. Evans, "Wilson Smith. 1897–1965," *Biographical Memoirs of Fellows of the Royal Society* 12 (1966).

12. "Hope of 'Flu' Curb Seen in New Tests," *New York Times*, July 9, 1933. Wilson Smith, C. H. Andrewes, and P. P. Laidlaw, "A Virus Obtained from Influenza Patients," *The Lancet* (1933). The results were confirmed by Thomas Francis of the Rockefeller Institute in 1934. See Thomas Francis, "Transmission of Influenza by a Filterable Virus," *Science* 80, no. 2081 (1934).

13. On Koch's postulates as a historical artifact, see Christoph Gradmann, "Alles eine Frage der Methode: Zur Historizität der Kochschen Postulate 1840–2000," *Medizinhistorisches Journal* 43 (2008). See as well Carter, *The Rise of Causal Concepts of Disease*. As Koch argued, "First, it was necessary to determine whether the diseased organs contained elements that were not constituents of the body or composed of such constituents. If such alien structures could be demonstrated, it was necessary to determine whether they were organized and showed any sign of independent life. Such signs include motility—which is often confused with molecular motion—growth, propagation, and fructification. Moreover, it was necessary to consider the relation of such structures to their surroundings and to nearby tissues, their distribution in the body, their occurrence in various states of the disease, and

similar other conditions. Such considerations enable one to conclude, with more or less probability, that there is a causal connection between these structures and the disease itself. Facts gained in these ways can provide so much evidence that only the most extreme skeptic would still object that the microorganisms may not be the cause, but only a concomitant of the disease. Often this objection has a certain justice, and therefore, establishing the coincidence of the disease and the parasite is not a complete proof. One requires, in addition, a direct proof that the parasite is the actual cause. This can only be achieved by completely separating the parasites from the diseased organism and from all products of the disease to which one could ascribe a causal significance. The isolated parasites, if introduced into healthy animals, must then cause the disease with all its characteristics." Ibid, p. 136.

14. Smith, Andrewes, and Laidlaw, "A Virus Obtained from Influenza Patients." See as well C. H. Andrewes, P. P. Laidlaw, and Wilson Smith, "The Susceptibility of Mice to the Viruses of Human and Swine Influenza" (1934); P. P. Laidlaw, "Epidemic Influenza. A Virus Disease" (1935); and Wilson Smith and C. H. Stuart-Harris, "Influenza Infection of Man from the Ferret" (1936).

15. "Is Influenza Cheaper, After All?" *Sunday Herald*, January 7, 1951, p. 3.

16. Michael Bresalier, "Neutralizing Flu: 'Immunological Devices' and the Making of a Virus Disease," in *Crafting Immunity: Working Histories of Clinical Immunology*, ed. Kenton Kroker, Jennifer Keelan, and Pauline M. H. Mazumdar (Aldershot: Ashgate, 2008).

17. Claude Bernard, *Introduction to the Study of Experimental Medicine* (New York: Dover Publications, 1957), p. 146.

18. Ibid.

19. Georges Canguilhem, *Idéologie et Rationalité dans l'Histoire des Sciences de la Vie: Nouvelles Études d'Histoire et de Philosophie des Sciences* (Paris: J. Vrin, 2000), p. 63.

20. Ilana Löwy, "The Experimental Body," in *Medicine in the Twentieth Century*, ed. Roger Cooter and John Pickstone (Amsterdam: Harwood Academic Publishers, 2000), p. 436.

21. Ibid., p. 437. The use of animal models in experimental science has lately received more attention in scholarly work. See, among others, W. F. Bynum, " 'C'est Un Malade': Animal Models and Concepts of Human Disease," *Journal of the History of Medicine and Allied Sciences* 45 (1990); Georges Canguilhem, "Experimentation in Animal Biology," in *Knowledge of Life* (New York: Fordham University Press, 2008); Angela N. H. Creager, Elizabeth Lunbeck, and M. Norton Wise, eds., *Science without Laws: Model Systems, Cases, Exemplary Narratives* (Durham, NC: Duke University Press, 2007); Christoph Gradmann, "Das Mass der Krankheit. Das Pathologische Tierexperiment in der Medizinischen Bakteriologie Robert Kochs," in *Mass und Eigensinn: Studien im Anschluss an Georges Canguilhem*, ed. Cornelius Borck, Volker Hess, and Henning Schmidgen (Munich: Fink, 2005); Robert E. Kohler, *Lords of the Fly: Drosophila Genetics and the Experimental Life* (Chicago: University of Chicago Press, 1994); Ilana Löwy, "From Guinea Pigs to

Man: The Development of Haffkine's Anticholera Vaccine," *Journal of the History of Medicine and Allied Sciences* 47 (1992) and "The Experimental Body"; and Karen Rader, *Making Mice: Standardizing Animals for American Biomedical Research, 1900–1955* (Princeton: Princeton University Press, 2004).

22. Canguilhem, *Knowledge of Life*, p. 11.

23. See Michael Bresalier, "Neutralizing Flu: 'Immunological Devices' and the Making of a Virus Disease."

24. Adele E. Clarke and Joan H. Fujimura, "What Tools? Which Jobs? Why Right?" in *The Right Tools for the Job*, ed. Adele E. Clarke and Joan H. Fujimura (Princeton: Princeton University Press, 1992).

25. William Ian Beardmore Beveridge, *Influenza: The Last Great Plague* (New York: Prodist, 1978), p. 7.

26. Dale, "Patrick Playfair Laidlaw. 1881–1940," p. 435. For a comprehensive account, see Michael Bresalier and Michael Worboys, "'Saving the Lives of Our Dogs': The Development of Canine Distemper Vaccine in Interwar Britain," *British Journal for the History of Science* 47, no. 2 (2013).

27. John Skehel, "Discovery of Human Influenza Virus and Subsequent Influenza Research at the National Institute for Medical Research," in *Microbe Hunters Then and Now*, ed. Hilary Koprowski and Michael B. A. Oldstone (Bloomington: Medi-Ed Press, 1996), p. 205.

28. Dale, "Patrick Playfair Laidlaw. 1881–1940."

29. Skehel, "Discovery of Human Influenza Virus and Subsequent Influenza Research at the National Institute for Medical Research," p. 205.

30. Laidlaw, "Epidemic Influenza," p. 1119. See as well Crosby, *America's Forgotten Pandemic*, p. 288.

31. "The building was a sanctuary of sterility." J. D. Ratcliff, "Cold Comfort," *Collier's Magazine* (1938), p. 13.

32. Greer Williams, *Virus Hunters* (New York: Alfred A. Knopf, 1960), p. 214.

33. Bresalier, "Neutralizing Flu: 'Immunological Devices' and the Making of a Virus Disease," p. 125.

34. Canguilhem, *Idéologie et Rationalité dans l'Histoire des Sciences de la Vie: Nouvelles Études d'Histoire et de Philosophie des Sciences*, p. 64.

35. Laidlaw, "Epidemic Influenza," p. 1119.

36. Ratcliff, "Cold Comfort," p. 13.

37. Dale, "Patrick Playfair Laidlaw. 1881–1940," p. 438. See as well Smith and Stuart-Harris, "Influenza Infection of Man from the Ferret"; Bresalier, "Neutralizing Flu: 'Immunological Devices' and the Making of a Virus Disease."

38. While working with sick animals, Stuart-Harris also infected himself with an influenza virus that had been transmitted serially though 196 ferrets. See Smith and Stuart-Harris, "Influenza Infection of Man from the Ferret."

39. Ratcliff, "Cold Comfort," p. 13.

40. Andrew Cunningham, "Transforming Plague: The Laboratory and the Identity of Infectious Disease," in *The Laboratory Revolution in Medicine*, ed. Andrew

Cunningham and Perry Williams (Cambridge: Cambridge University Press, 2002). For a critical account, see Michael Worboys, "Was There a Bacteriological Revolution in Late Nineteenth-Century Medicine?" *Studies in History and Philosophy of Biology and Biomedical Sciences* 38, no. 1 (2007). Thanks to Michael Bresalier for this reference.

41. Williams, *Virus Hunters*.

42. Olga Amsterdamska, "Medical and Biological Constraints: Early Research on Variation in Bacteriology," *Social Studies of Science* 17 (1987), p. 668.

43. Andrewes, Laidlaw, and Smith, "The Susceptibility of Mice to the Viruses of Human and Swine Influenza." Mice became important animal models once virus workers were able to produce lung lesions in mice with the ferret virus. These lesions were not symptoms but signs of virus infection. Thanks to Michael Bresalier for this clarification.

44. As a recent study has shown, guinea pigs are highly susceptible to infection, but they develop no symptoms at all. Anice C. Lowen et al., "The Guinea Pig as a Transmission Model for Human Influenza Viruses," *PNAS* 103, no. 26 (2006).

45. It was Werner Schäfer, who argued in a 1955 article that fowl plague was caused by an influenza virus. Werner Schäfer, "Vergleichende Sero-Immunologische Untersuchung über die Viren der Influenza und Klassischen Geflügelpest," *Zeitschrift für Naturforschung* 10 (1955). For a historical account, see Lise Wilkinson and A. P. Waterson, "The Development of the Virus Concept as Reflected in Corpora of Studies on Individual Pathogens. 2. The Agent of Fowl Plague—a Model Virus?" *Medical History* 19 (1975).

46. What I mean by causal model is the idea of the virus as the determining factor in the production of disease. Of course, microbiology was not the only discipline promoting causal models. Rather, it redefined causation in terms of the virus as a specific entity responsible for a specific disease.

47. For the "constraints of form," see Marilyn Strathern, *The Gender of the Gift: Problems with Women and Problems with Society in Melanesia* (Berkeley: University of California Press, 1988). These constraints of form were inscribed in Koch's postulates. On Koch's famous postulates, see Carter, "Koch's Postulates in Relation to the Work of Jacob Henle and Edwin Klebs"; Gradmann, "Alles eine Frage der Methode"; and Silvia Berger, *Bakterien in Krieg und Frieden: Eine Geschichte der Medizinischen Bakteriologie in Deutschland, 1870–1933* (Göttingen: Wallstein, 2009).

48. As Ilana Löwy points out, on the basis of his studies of cholera, Robert Koch recognized that it was virtually impossible to find a laboratory animal that reproduced the human disease. Löwy, "From Guinea Pigs to Man," p. 292.

49. Stephanie A. Call et al., "Does This Patient Have Influenza?" *JAMA* 293, no. 8 (2005), p. 987.

50. Latour, *The Pasteurization of France*.

51. Francis, "Transmission of Influenza by a Filterable Virus."

52. John M. Eyler, "De Kruif's Boast: Vaccine Trials and the Construction of a Virus," *Bulletin of the History of Medicine* 80 (2006), p. 409.

53. Report of Dr. Francis (Assisted by Dr. Magill), from Collection RU, Scientific Reports, 1935–1936, Rockefeller Foundation Archives, Rockefeller Archive Center, Sleepy Hollow, New York, p. 167.

54. Agreement Form, from Collection RU, Record Group 210.3, Box Influenza, Rockefeller Foundation Archives, Rockefeller Archive Center, Sleepy Hollow, New York, p. 1.

55. Thomas Francis, "A Consideration of Vaccination against Influenza," *Milbank Memorial Fund Quarterly* 25, no. 1 (1947), p. 5.

56. Michael Bresalier, "Fighting Flu: Military Pathology, Vaccines, and the Conflicted Identity of the 1918–1919 Pandemic in Britain," *Journal of the History of Medicine and Allied Sciences* 68, no. 1 (2013); Eyler, "De Kruif's Boast."

57. J. D. Ratcliff, "They've Got the Flu!," *Collier's Magazine* (1941), p. 18.

58. Eyler, "De Kruif's Boast," p. 425.

59. Francis, "A Consideration of Vaccination against Influenza," p. 14.

60. Philip E. Sartwell and Arthur P. Long, "The Army Experience with Influenza, 1946–1947: Epidemiological Aspects," *American Journal of Epidemiology* 47, no. 2 (1948).

61. A. F. Rasmussen, Julia C. Stokes, and Joseph E. Smadel, "The Army Experience with Influenza, 1946–1947: Laboratory Aspects," *American Journal of Hygiene* 47 (1948).

62. Eyler, "De Kruif's Boast," p. 409.

63. Ibid., p. 436.

64. André Lwoff, "The Concept of Virus: The Third Marjory Stephenson Memorial Lecture," *Journal of General Microbiology* 17, no. 1 (1957), p. 239.

65. Ibid.

66. See Burnet, *Virus as Organism*; Christopher H. Andrewes, "The Place of Viruses in Nature," *Proceedings of the Royal Society B: Biological Sciences* 139, no. 896 (1952); and Patrick P. Laidlaw, *Virus Diseases and Viruses* (Cambridge: Cambridge University Press, 1938). In his second Leeuwenhoek Lecture on the "Place of Viruses in Nature," delivered in December 1951, Christopher Andrewes joined the debate, confessing at the outset of his address that he believed, on the basis of his influenza research, viruses to be "small organisms." Andrewes, "The Place of Viruses in Nature" (p. 313). "The biochemist," Andrewes noted with Wendell Stanley's studies firmly in mind, "sets to work at his bench with relatively pure preparations of a virus" ibid. (p. 314). What he finds is that "viruses all contain nucleo-proteins." The biochemist, Andrewes continued, then compares his findings with other familiar substances, "talks of virus-macromolecules and tends to think of them as chemical entities." The pathologist, by contrast, approaches viruses from a different point of view. What he primarily finds is that "viruses are agents of disease." Because they appear to behave like other small parasites, the pathologist "naturally thinks of them as such." In the course of his lecture, Andrewes proposed six distinctive reasons for regarding viral agents as living organisms. Viruses should be considered living organisms because they 1) multiply, 2) mutate, 3) are chemically complex, 4) are normally antigenic, 5) are of variable size, and 6) behave like a parasite.

67. Lwoff, "The Concept of Virus."

68. Ibid., p. 252.

69. For an excellent account on the crystallization of the tobacco mosaic virus, see Angela N. H. Creager, *The Life of a Virus: Tobacco Mosaic Virus as an Experimental Model, 1930–1965* (Chicago: University of Chicago Press, 2002). Creager also explores the discussion about the nature of viruses in her book.

70. J. Coamp, "The Nature of Viruses," *British Medical Journal* 2, no. 4055 (1938), p. 667.

71. Edwin H. Lennette, "Recent Advances in Viruses: A Brief Survey of Recent Work on Virus Diseases," *Science* 98 (1943), p. 415.

72. Lwoff, "The Concept of Virus."

73. Napier, "Nonself Help," p. 126.

74. Ratcliff, "Cold Comfort," p. 52.

CHAPTER TWO

1. Edwin D. Kilbourne, "Flu to the Starboard! Man the Harpoons! Fill 'em with Vaccine! Get the Captain! Hurry!" *New York Times*, February 13, 1976.

2. Ibid.

3. Sencer was forced out of office amid criticism over the swine flu campaign; later he became the health commissioner of New York City.

4. O'Leary, *Arguing the Apocalypse*.

5. On the concept of "crisis," see Reinhart Koselleck, "The Conceptual History of 'Crisis,'" in *The Practice of Conceptual History: Timing History, Spacing Concepts*, ed. Reinhart Koselleck (Stanford: Stanford University Press, 2002); Janet Roitman, *Anti-Crisis* (Durham, NC: Duke University Press, 2013); and Randolph Starn, "Historians and 'Crisis,'" *Past and Present* 52 (1971). Janet Roitman notes that "crisis narratives are not 'false,' nor are they mere representations, to be compared to a truer narrative or a more solid level underlying mere symbolic terrain. It follows that the aim is not to invalidate 'crisis' or to critique the term as inaccurate or merely symbolic. There is no reason to claim that there are no 'real' crises. Rather, the point is to observe crisis as a blind spot, and hence to apprehend the ways in which it regulates narrative constructions, the ways in which it allows certain questions to be asked while others are foreclosed." Roitman, *Anti-Crisis*, p. 94.

6. Peter Redfield, *Life in Crisis: The Ethical Journey of Doctors without Borders* (Berkeley: University of California Press, 2013), p. 32. For the role of "crisis" as a social imaginary invoked in humanitarian interventions, see as well Didier Fassin, *Humanitarian Reason: A Moral History of the Present* (Berkeley: University of California Press, 2012); Didier Fassin and Mariella Pandolfi, eds., *Contemporary States of Emergency: The Politics of Military and Humanitarian Interventions* (Cambridge: MIT Press, 2010); and Craig Calhoun, "A World of Emergencies: Fear, Intervention, and the Limits of Cosmopolitan Order," *Canadian Review of Sociology and Anthropology* 41 (2004).

7. Redfield, *Life in Crisis*, p. 32.

8. Ibid.

9. For an official review of the program, see Richard E. Neustadt and Harvey V. Fineberg, *The Epidemic That Never Was: Policy-Making and the Swine Flu Scare* (New York: Vintage Books, 1983).

10. Elizabeth W. Etheridge, *Sentinel for Health: A History of the Centers for Disease Control* (Berkeley: University of California Press, 1992).

11. For exhaustive accounts of the events, see Joel C. Gaydos et al., "Swine Influenza A Outbreak, Fort Dix, New Jersey, 1976," *Emerging Infectious Diseases* 12, no. 1 (2006); Arthur M. Silverstein, *Pure Politics and Impure Science. The Swine Flu Affair* (Baltimore: Johns Hopkins University Press, 1981); Richard E. Neustadt and Harvey V. Fineberg, *The Epidemic That Never Was*; Etheridge, *Sentinel for Health*; and David J. Sencer and Donald J. Millar, "Reflections on the 1976 Swine Flu Vaccination Program," *Emerging Infectious Diseases* 12, no. 1 (2006).

12. Sencer and Millar, "Reflections on the 1976 Swine Flu Vaccination Program," p. 30.

13. "Swine Flu: Advice, Dissent and Politics," *Science News* 109 (1976), p. 262.

14. "Swine Flu Dilemma," *Time Magazine*, July 19, 1976, p. 67.

15. A. S. Beare and J. W. Craig, "Virulence for Man of a Human Influenza-A Virus Antigenically Similar to 'Classical' Swine Viruses," *The Lancet* (1976), p. 4.

16. Charles Stuart-Harris, "Swine Influenza in Man: Zoonosis or Human Pandemic?" *The Lancet* (1976), p. 32.

17. "World Flu Experts Meeting to Discuss New Virus," *The Times*, Saturday, March 27, 1976, p. 4.

18. George Dehner, "Who Knows Best? National and International Responses to Pandemic Threats and the 'Lessons' of 1976," *Journal of the History of Medicine and Allied Sciences* 65, no. 4 (2010).

19. For more on the controversy, see Silverstein, *Pure Politics and Impure Science* and Neustadt and Fineberg, *The Epidemic That Never Was*.

20. Etheridge, *Sentinel for Health*, p. 262.

21. Edwin D. Kilbourne, "Influenza Pandemics in Perspective," *JAMA* 237, no. 12 (1977), p. 1225.

22. Cf. Felman, *The Scandal of the Speaking Body*, p. 32.

23. Charles Murray, "What Is Hog 'Flu'?," *Wallaces Farmer* 46, no. 8 (1921), p. 1.

24. Ibid.

25. On the great pandemic of 1918, see among others Barry, *The Great Influenza* and Crosby, *America's Forgotten Pandemic*.

26. Murray, "What Is Hog 'Flu'?"

27. Ibid.

28. W. H. Dreher, "Swine Diseases as We Find Them in the Field," *Journal of the American Veterinary Medical Association* 61 (1922), p. 178.

29. M. Dorset, C. N. McBryde, and W. B. Niles, "Remarks on 'Hog Flu,'" *Journal of the American Veterinary Medical Association* 62 (1923).

30. Quoted in Williams, *Virus Hunters*, pp. 204ff.

31. Dorset, McBryde, and Niles, "Remarks on 'Hog Flu,'" pp. 162ff.

32. "Swine 'Flu,'" *Veterinary Medicine* 18, no. 1 (1923), p. 314.

33. C. N. McBryde, "Some Observations on 'Hog Flu' and Its Seasonal Prevalance in Iowa," *Journal of the American Veterinary Medical Association* 71 (1927), p. 368.

34. Ibid., p. 369.

35. Christopher H. Andrewes, "Richard Edwin Shope 1901–1966," *Biographical Memoirs* 50 (1979), p. 353.

36. Richard E. Shope, "Swine Influenza. I. Experimental Transmission and Pathology," *Journal of Experimental Medicine* 54 (1931). See as well "The Etiology of Swine Influenza," *Science* 73 (1931).

37. Shope, "Swine Influenza. I. Experimental Transmission and Pathology," p. 351.

38. For a more detailed account of the techniques that microbiologists use to compare influenza viruses with one another, see chapter 3.

39. Richard E. Shope, "Serological Evidence for the Occurrence of Infection with Human Influenza Virus in Swine," *Journal of Experimental Medicine* 67 (1938); Richard E. Shope and Thomas Francis, "The Susceptibility of Swine to the Virus of Human Influenza," Journal of Experimental Medicine 64 (1936).

40. Andrewes, "Richard Edwin Shope 1901–1966," p. 355. On the antigenic relationship between swine flu and the human flu viruses, see Richard E. Shope, "The Infection of Mice with Swine Influenza Virus," *Journal of Experimental Medicine* 62 (1935) and "The Incidence of Neutralizing Antibodies for Swine Influenza Virus in the Sera of Human Beings of Different Ages," *Journal of Experimental Medicine* 63 (1936).

41. Laidlaw, "Epidemic Influenza," p. 1123.

42. Shope, "The Incidence of Neutralizing Antibodies for Swine Influenza Virus in the Sera of Human Beings of Different Ages," p. 683.

43. "Flu Epidemic Conquest Seen: Dr. Shope of Rockefeller Staff Makes Discovery," *New York Sun,* 1939. See as well "Flu Origin Quest Leads to Hogs," *Chicago Herald-Times,* 1939.

44. A. V. Hennessy, F. M. Davenport, and Thomas Francis, "Studies of Antibodies to Strains of Influenza Virus in Persons of Different Ages in Sera Collected in a Postepidemic Period," *Journal of Immunology* 75, no. 401–409 (1955), p. 408. See as well F. M. Davenport et al., "Interpretations of Influenza Antibody Patterns of Man," *Bulletin of the World Health Organization* 41 (1969).

45. Ernest T. Takafuji, David E. Johnson, and Herbert E. Segal, "The Swine Antigen in Previous Influenza Vaccines," *New England Journal of Medicine* 295, no. 18 (1976).

46. Nic Masurel and William M. Marine, "Recycling of Asian and Hong Kong Influenza A Virus Hemagglutinins in Man," *American Journal of Epidemiology* 97, no. 1 (1973), p. 48. See as well Nic Masurel, "Swine Influenza Virus and the Recycling of Influenza A Viruses in Man," *The Lancet* (1976) and Edwin D. Kilbourne, "Epidemiology of Influenza," in *The Influenza Viruses and Influenza*, ed. Edwin D. Kilbourne (New York: Academic Press, 1975), p. 517.

47. Masurel and Marine, "Recycling of Asian and Hong Kong Influenza A Virus Hemagglutinins in Man," p. 48.

48. "War against Swine Flu," *Time Magazine*, April 5, 1976, p. 50.

49. Ibid.

50. Ibid., p. 19.

51. Kermode, *The Sense of an Ending*, p. 46.

52. Ibid., p. 190.

53. Ibid., p. 47.

54. Thanks to Jim Faubion for this insight.

55. James Colgrove, *State of Immunity: The Politics of Vaccination in Twentieth-Century America* (Berkeley: University of California Press, 2006), p. 149.

56. Ibid., p. 150.

57. Aidan T. Cockburn, "Eradication of Infectious Diseases," *Science* 133, no. 3458 (1961), p. 1058.

58. Lawrence Galton, "Flu Gets Us All, Eventually," New York Times, March 24, 1974.

59. Edwin D. Kilbourne et al., "Influenza Vaccines. Summary of Influenza Workshop V," *Journal of Infectious Diseases* 129, no. 6 (1974), p. 770.

60. Ibid., p. 771.

61. Masurel and Marine, "Recycling of Asian and Hong Kong Influenza A Virus Hemagglutinins in Man," p. 48.

62. Harold M. Schmeck, "Flu Experts Soon to Rule on Need of New Vaccine," *New York Times*, March 21, 1976, p. 39.

63. Neustadt and Fineberg, *The Epidemic That Never Was*, p. 12.

64. Kilbourne, "Flu to the Starboard!"

65. "Swine Flu: Advice, Dissent and Politics," p. 262.

66. John R. Seal, David T. Sencer, and Harry M. Meyer Jr., "A Status Report on National Immunization against Influenza," *Journal of Infectious Diseases* 133, no. 6 (1976), p. 718.

67. Interview with Edwin D. Kilbourne, June 27, 1989. Unpublished manuscript. Mount Sinai Archives, New York, p. 12.

68. Kilbourne et al., "Influenza Vaccines. Summary of Influenza Workshop V," p. 771.

69. Peter Palese and Jerome L. Schulman, "RNA Pattern of 'Swine' Influenza Virus Isolated from Man Is Similar to Those of Other Swine Influenza Viruses," *Nature* 263 (1976), p. 530.

70. Harold M. Schmeck, "Race for a Swine Flu Vaccine Began in a Manhattan Lab," *New York Times*, May 21, 1976.

71. Peter Palese et al., "Genetic Composition of a High-Yielding Influenza A Virus Recombinant. A Vaccine Strain against 'Swine' Influenza," *Science* 194 (1976). See as well Schmeck, "Race for a Swine Flu Vaccine Began in a Manhattan Lab."

72. Interview with Edwin D. Kilbourne, June 27, 1989, p. 17.

73. Pierre Bourdieu, *Homo Academicus*, trans. Peter Collier (Stanford: Stanford University Press, 1988). See as well *Distinction: A Social Critique of the Judgement of*

Taste (London: Routledge, 1984), p. 246. My thanks to Frédéric Keck for a conversation on Palese's distinction.

74. Walter R. Dowdle, "Influenza Pandemic Periodicity, Virus Recycling, and the Art of Risk Assessment," *Emerging Infectious Diseases* 12, no. 1 (2006).

75. Cooper, "Pre-Empting Emergence," p. 117.

76. IOM, ed. *Emerging Infections: Microbial Threats to Health in the United States* (Washington, DC: National Academies Press, 1992), pp. 167ff.

77. Margaret Chan "World Now at the Start of 2009 Influenza Pandemic." Statement to the Press by WHO Director-General Margaret Chan, June 11, 2009.

78. Ignorance here simply refers to the constitution of a person, thing, or event as unknown.

79. Miyazaki, "The Temporalities of the Market," p. 255.

80. Cooper, "Pre-Empting Emergence."

81. Lakoff, "The Generic Biothreat, or, How We Became Unprepared," p. 401.

82. Ibid., p. 402.

83. Stephen J. Collier, "Enacting Catastrophe: Preparedness, Insurance, Budgetary Rationalization," *Economy and Society* 37, no. 2 (2008).

84. Monica Schoch-Spana, "Bioterrorism: US Public Health and a Secular Apocalypse," *Anthropology Today* 20, no. 5 (2004), p. 12.

CHAPTER THREE

1. "The New Swine Flu," *New York Times*, April 27, 2009.

2. Ibid.

3. Statement of Dr. Wolfgang Wodarg, Council of Europe, January 26, 2010.

4. Ibid.

5. Kezia Barker, "Influenza Preparedness and the Bureaucratic Reflex: Anticipating and Generating the 2009 H1N1 Event," *Health and Place* 18, no. 4 (2012), p. 702.

6. WHO Press Conference with Dr. Keiji Fukuda, Special Advisor to the Director-General on Pandemic Influenza, World Health Organization, January 14, 2010.

7. Jeremy Laurance, "The Swine Flu Backlash," *The Lancet* 375 (2010), p. 367.

8. Ibid.

9. Statement of Dr. Keiji Fukuda on Behalf of WHO at the Council of Europe Hearing on Pandemic (H1N1) 2009, Council of Europe, January 26, 2010.

10. Ibid.

11. Ibid.

12. WHO Press Conference with Dr. Keiji Fukuda, Special Advisor to the Director-General on Pandemic Influenza, World Health Organization, January 14, 2010.

13. Statement of Dr. Keiji Fukuda on Behalf of WHO at the Council of Europe Hearing on Pandemic (H1N1) 2009, Council of Europe, January 26, 2010.

14. Ibid.

15. Beveridge, *Influenza*, p. ix.

16. Anice C. Lowen et al., "Influenza Virus Transmission Is Dependent on Relative Humidity and Temperature," *PLoS Pathogens* 3, no. 10 (2007); "High Temperature (30 Degrees C) Blocks Aerosol but Not Contact Transmission of Influenza Virus," *Journal of Virology* 82, no. 11 (2008); "The Guinea Pig as a Transmission Model for Human Influenza Viruses."

17. Gina Kolata, "Study Shows Why the Flu Likes Winter," *New York Times*, December 5, 2007.

18. Edwin D. Kilbourne, "Afterword. A Personal Summary Presented as a Guide for Discussion," in *Emerging Viruses*, ed. Stephen S. Morse (Oxford: Oxford University Press, 1993), p. 294.

19. Manfred Eigen, "Viral Quasispecies," *Scientific American* 269, no. 1 (1993), p. 42.

20. Ibid.

21. Donna Haraway, "The Biopolitics of Postmodern Bodies: Constructions of Self in Immune System Discourse," in *Simians, Cyborgs, and Women. The Reinvention of Nature* (New York: Routledge, 1991).

22. George K. Hirst, "The Agglutination of Red Cells by Allantoic Fluid of Chick Embryos Infected with Influenza Virus," *Science* 94, no. 2427 (1941), p. 22.

23. According to historian Michael Bresalier, it was the American bacteriologist, George Sternberg, who first used the term "neutralization" in 1892 "to describe how a soluble substance in the serum of immune cows inhibited the pathological effects of vaccinia." See Bresalier, "Neutralizing Flu: 'Immunological Devices' and the Making of a Virus Disease," p. 118.

24. Hirst, "The Agglutination of Red Cells by Allantoic Fluid of Chick Embryos Infected with Influenza Virus" and "Direct Isolation of Human Influenza Virus in Chick Embryos," *Journal of Immunology* 45 (1942).

25. Muriel Lederman and Sue A. Tolin, "Ovatoomb: Other Viruses and the Origins of Molecular Biology," *Journal of the History of Biology* 26, no. 2 (1993), p. 244.

26. George K. Hirst, "Studies of Antigenic Differences among Strains of Influenza A by Means of Red Cell Agglutination," *Journal of Experimental Medicine* 78, no. 5 (1943).

27. Peter Palese, "Why Swine Flu Isn't So Scary," *Wall Street Journal*, May 2, 2009.

28. Ibid.

29. Mapping the distribution of deaths, counting cases of illness, and identifying various modes of transmission, nineteenth-century observers assembled medical records, conducted epidemiological investigations, and began to correlate morbidity and mortality to particular social conditions. As these observers frequently emphasized, outbreaks of influenza varied a great deal from season to season in terms of their overall impact on human populations. According to the detailed tables and charts assembled by these observers, some outbreaks were considerably larger than others, affecting more people in more places. In his 1852 *Annals of*

Influenza or Epidemic Catarrhal Fever in Great Britain from 1510 to 1837, Theophilus Thompson, a physician and fellow of the Royal Society in London, confirmed the general observation of a changing historical pattern of disease. But Thompson did not yet distinguish between epidemic and pandemic forms, a distinction that figured more prominently only a few years later, in 1860, in August Hirsch's influential synthesis of medical geography titled *Handbuch der historisch-geographischen Pathologie*. Hirsch's *Handbook of Historical and Geographical Pathology* was significant because it attempted, for the first time, to describe systematically the global distribution of a large number of pathological conditions. Hirsch's detailed information came from colonial officials working for British, French, German, Spanish, and Russian government agencies and commercial companies. Influenza, Hirsch remarked in his handbook, "always occurs as an epidemic disease, whether within a narrow circle or even confined to particular places, or in general diffusion over wide tracts of a country, over a whole continent, and, indeed, over a great part of the globe as a true pandemic.... [I]t is in this last respect that influenza takes an exceptional place among the acute infective diseases; no other of them has ever shown so pronounced a pandemic character as influenza." The difference between these observed forms of disease was primarily articulated in terms of scale. As a result of Hirsch's geographical perspective, changing patterns of infectious disease became visible. Similar to other contagious diseases, especially cholera and plague, influenza was occasionally able to spread to pandemic proportions, affecting the entire globe. In their accounts, Hirsch, Clemow, and other medical geographers produced detailed reports, documenting the most memorable outbreaks from medieval to modern times; they used charts to visualize the course of the communicable disease along trade and railway routes, and they speculated about the relationship between the two patterns of epidemic and pandemic disease. In their published work, the distinction between epidemics and pandemics thus operated primarily in analytic fashion, identifying two particular patterns of disease, measured in terms of scale. Significantly, the cause of these observed differences in the patterns of disease remained unclear. See Theophilus Thompson, *Annals of Influenza or Epidemic Catarrhal Fever in Great Britain from 1510 to 1837* (London: Sydenham Society, 1852); August Hirsch, *Handbuch der Historisch-Geographischen Pathologie* (Erlangen: Verlag von Ferdinand Enke, 1860); and *Handbook of Geographical and Historical Pathology* (London: Sydenham Society, 1883).

30. David M. Morens, Gregory K. Folkers, and Anthony S. Fauci, "What Is a Pandemic?" *Journal of Infectious Diseases* 200 (2009). See as well Peter Doshi, "The Elusive Definition of Pandemic Influenza," *Bulletin of the World Health Organization* 89, no. 7 (2011).

31. Lederman and Tolin, "Ovatoomb."

32. Amsterdamska, "Achieving Disbelief," p. 485. See as well her "Medical and Biological Constraints: Early Research on Variation in Bacteriology," *Social Studies of Science* 17 (1987).

33. Kilbourne, "Afterword: A Personal Summary Presented as a Guide for Discussion," p. 294.

34. Lowe, "Viral Clouds," p. 627.

35. Stefan Helmreich, "Trees and Seas of Information: Alien Kinship and the Biopolitics of Gene Transfer in Marine Biology and Biotechnology," *American Ethnologist* 30, no. 3 (2003) and *Alien Ocean: Anthropological Voyages in Microbial Seas* (Berkeley: University of California Press, 2009).

36. John Holland, "Replication Error, Quasispecies Populations, and Extreme Evolution Rates of RNA Viruses," in *Emerging Viruses*, ed. Stephen S. Morse (Oxford: Oxford University Press, 1993), p. 207.

37. Jon P. Anderson, Richard Daifuku, and Lawrence A. Loeb, "Viral Error Catastrophe by Mutagenic Nucleosides," *Annual Review of Microbiology* 58 (2004), p. 188. For a critical account see Jesse Summers and Samuel Litwin, "Examining the Theory of Error Catastrophe," *Journal of Virology* 80, no. 1 (2006).

38. Kilbourne, "Afterword: A Personal Summary Presented as a Guide for Discussion," p. 294.

CHAPTER FOUR

1. Taronna R. Maines et al., "Lack of Transmission of H5N1 Avian–Human Reassortant Influenza Viruses in a Ferret Model," *PNAS* 103, no. 32 (2006).

2. Denise Grady, "Making a Ferret Sneeze for Hints to the Transmission of Bird Flu," *New York Times*, March 28, 2006; Jia-Rui Chong, "Bird Flu Findings Cautiously Optimistic," *Chicago Tribune*, August 1, 2006.

3. As we saw in chapter 1, the ferret requires an infrastructure if it is to work as an animal model. As Maines explained to me, "There are only two suppliers of ferrets in the United States, two farms. We always try to communicate closely with them, explaining why it is so important for us to have ferrets without any antibodies to flu at all. One supplier wasn't really into helping us with that and the other one was. And he would actually give his employees a bonus if they didn't have an outbreak in the colony that year, that flu season. And if the employee or the employee's family or anybody was sick they couldn't come in to work. So, you know, he just took drastic measures. And eventually we were able to establish a contract with him where we supplied him with money to retrofit one of his farms, so it's now a HEPA-filtered environment, so ferrets live there in these clean environments. And there's personal protective equipment for people who go in, and we had lengthy meetings about how to set up the facility, how to put the personal protective equipment on, how to make sure that the environment is decontaminated, how you come out, how you bring food in, everything. It was a huge investment, financially. Just to make sure these ferrets were clean. And then whenever the ferrets were transported, sometimes they were flown, every time or practically every time they flew, they seroconverted. At some point during transport they were exposed to viruses. So we were not going to do that anymore. So he started delivering them himself. And he constructed a truck that is climate controlled and has HEPA-filtered crates in it that the animals go in. And then when they are loaded up and when they are unloaded here, the driver

must wear a respirator. And then they go straight into quarantine. And they sit there for two weeks. And then we bleed them and screen them to see if they were exposed at any point. And then they stay there until we use them. And then when we use them, we bleed them again to confirm that they're negative. A ferret's response to infection is going to be completely different if they have preexisting antibodies, even if it is due to a different subtype. There is going to be differences in how the animal responds."

4. Kohler, *Lords of the Fly*; Lorraine Daston, "The Moral Economy of Science," *Osiris* 10 (1995).

5. Ronald M. Atlas and Judith Reppy, "Globalizing Biosecurity," *Biosecurity and Bioterrorism: Biodefense Strategy, Practice, and Science* 3, no. 1 (2005).

6. Gerald L. Epstein, "Bioresponsibility: Engaging the Scientific Community in Reducing the Biological Weapons Threat," *BioScience* 52, no. 5 (2002).

7. Lakoff, "The Generic Biothreat, or, How We Became Unprepared"; Lowe, "Viral Clouds"; Erin Koch, "Disease as Security Threat: Critical Reflections on the Global TB Emergency," in *Biosecurity Interventions: Global Health and Security in Question*, ed. Andrew Lakoff and Stephen Collier (New York: Columbia University Press, 2008); Andrew Lakoff and Stephen Collier, *Biosecurity Interventions: Global Health and Security in Question* (New York: Columbia University Press, 2008); and Kathleen Vogel, "Biodefense: Considering the Sociotechnical Dimension," in *Biosecurity Interventions: Global Health and Security in Question*, ed. Andrew Lakoff and Stephen Collier (New York: Columbia University Press, 2008). For additional examples, see Nick Bingham, Gareth Enticott, and Steve Hinchcliffe, "Biosecurity. Spaces, Practices, and Boundaries," *Environment and Planning A* 40, no. 7 (2008); Stephen J. Collier, Andrew Lakoff, and Paul Rabinow, "Biosecurity: Towards an Anthropology of the Contemporary," *Anthropology Today* 20, no. 5 (2004); Filippa Lentzos and Nikolas Rose, "Governing Insecurity: Contingency Planning, Protection, Resilience," *Economy and Society* 38, no. 2 (2009); and King, "Security, Disease, Commerce."

8. Masco, *The Nuclear Borderlands*; Hugh Gusterson, *Nuclear Rites: A Weapons Laboratory at the End of the Cold War* (Berkeley: University of California Press, 1996); Peter Galison, "Removing Knowledge," *Critical Inquiry* 31 (2004).

9. Eugene Thacker, *The Global Genome: Biotechnology, Politics, and Culture* (Cambridge, MA: MIT Press, 2006); Lily Kay, *Who Wrote the Book of Life? A History of the Genetic Code* (Stanford: Stanford University Press, 2000); Evelyn Fox Keller, *The Century of the Gene* (Cambridge, MA: Harvard University Press, 2000); Hans-Jörg Rheinberger, "Gene Concepts: Fragments from the Perspective of Molecular Biology," in *The Concept of the Gene in Development and Evolution. Historical and Epistemological Studies*, ed. Peter J. Beurton, Raphael Falk, and Hans-Jörg Rheinberger (Cambridge: Cambridge University Press, 2000); and Kaushik Sunder Rajan, *Biocapital: The Constitution of Postgenomic Life* (Durham, NC: Duke University Press, 2006).

10. Sabin Russell, "Deadliest Flu Bug Given New Life in U.S. Laboratory," *San Francisco Chronicle*, October 6, 2005.

11. Terrence M. Tumpey et al., "Existing Antivirals Are Effective against Influenza Virus with Genes from the 1918 Pandemic Virus," *PNAS* 99, no. 21 (2002).

12. An earlier Canadian-European expedition to exhume the bodies of Norwegian miners and recover particles of the 1918 virus from victims of the Spanish flu failed. See Kirsty Duncan, *Hunting the 1918 Flu: A Scientist's Search for a Killer Virus* (Toronto: University of Toronto Press, 2003).

13. Terrence M. Tumpey et al., "Characterization of the Reconstructed 1918 Spanish Influenza Pandemic Virus," *Science* 310 (2005). Before the experiments were conducted, CDC's Institutional Biosafety Committee reviewed the proposed research extensively. All experimental procedures were carried out in a biosafety level 3–enhanced facility, in which there are controlled access, systematic decontamination, primary safety barriers (safety cabinets, isolation chambers, gloves, and gowns), and secondary safety barriers (special facility construction with restricted access and high-efficiency particulate air filtration) to protect the scientists and the public from accidental exposure. The enhanced procedures used for the reconstruction of the 1918 virus included additional respiratory protection, clothing changes, and personal showers before exiting the laboratory. All laboratory workers were also required to take antiviral prophylactics while conducting the experiments. Here, I do not provide a detailed analysis of these precautions, focusing instead on efforts to regulate and modulate the exchange of sensitive scientific information. For more on questions of safety, see chapter 5.

14. Joceyln Kaiser, "Resurrected Influenza Virus Yields Secrets of Deadly 1918 Pandemic," *Science* 310 (October 7, 2005).

15. Lawrence Cohen, "Migrant Supplementarity: Remaking Biological Relatedness in Chinese Military and Indian Five-Star Hospitals," *Body & Society* 17, no. 2–3 (2011).

16. Damien De Blic and Cyril Lemieux, "Le Scandale Comme Épreuve: Éléments de Sociologie Pragmatique," *Politix: Revue des sciences sociales du politique* 18, no. 71 (2005). See as well Luc Boltanski et al., eds., *Affaires, Scandales et Grandes Causes: De Socrate à Pinochet* (Paris Stock, 2007).

17. Wendy Orent, "Playing with Viruses. Replicating This Flu Strain Could Get Us Burned," *Washington Post*, April 17, 2005.

18. Charles Krauthammer, "A Flu Hope, or Horror?" *Washington Post*, October 14, 2005.

19. Ray Kurzweil and Bill Joy, "Recipe for Destruction," *New York Times,* October 17, 2005.

20. Karin Tzamarot, "Letter to the Editor," *New York Times*, October 20, 2005.

21. Katie Collins, "Information Poses Bigger Bioterrorism Threat than Microbes," *Wired*, March 21, 2014.

22. John B. Thompson, *Political Scandal: Power and Visibility in the Media Age* (Cambridge: Polity, 2000), p. 13.

23. William A. Cohen, *Sex Scandal: The Private Parts of Victorian Fiction* (Durham, NC: Duke University Press, 1996), p. 9.

24. Orent, "Playing with Viruses."

25. Charles Krauthammer, "A Flu Hope, or Horror?"

26. Michel Foucault, *Security, Territory, Population: Lectures at the Collège de France, 1977–78*, trans. Graham Burchell (London: Palgrave, 2006). See as well Michel Foucault, *Society Must Be Defended: Lectures at the Collège de France, 1975–1976*, trans. David Macey (New York: Picador, 2003).

27. Foucault, *Security, Territory, Population*.

28. Ibid.

29. Tsing, "The Global Situation."

30. Caitlin Zaloom, *Out of the Pits: Traders and Technology from Chicago to London* (Chicago: University of Chicago Press, 2006).

31. Jean Comaroff, "Beyond Bare Life: AIDS, (Bio)Politics, and the Neoliberal Order," *Public Culture* 19, no. 1 (2007).

32. For others, see the list provided in Gerald R. Fink, *Biotechnology Research in an Age of Terrorism* (Washington, DC: National Academies Press, 2003).

33. "Map of misreading" is Harold Bloom's term. Harold Bloom, *A Map of Misreading* (Oxford: Oxford University Press, 2003).

34. Erika Check, "Biologists Apprehensive over US Moves to Censor Information Flow," *Nature* 415 (2002); James B. Petro and David A. Relman, "Understanding Threats to Scientific Openness," *Science* 302 (2003).

35. For the concept of sensitive but unclassified information, see Genevieve J. Knezo, *"Sensitive but Unclassified" and Other Federal Security Controls on Scientific and Technical Information* (Washington, DC: Congressional Research Service, 2004); Dana A. Shea, *Balancing Scientific Publication and National Security Concerns* (Washington, DC: Congressional Research Service, 2003); Joseph Masco, "'Sensitive but Unclassified': Secrecy and the Counterterrorist State," *Public Culture* 22, no. 3 (2010).

36. See R. M. Atlas et al., "Statement on Scientific Publication and Security," *Science* 299 (2003), p. 1149.

37. NRC, *Biotechnology Research in an Age of Terrorism* (Washington, DC: National Academies Press, 2003).

38. Ronald M. Atlas and Malcom Dando, "The Dual-Use Dilemma for the Life Sciences: Perspectives, Conundrums, and Global Solutions," *Biosecurity and Bioterrorism* 4, no. 3 (2006).

39. Jonathan Culler, "Convention and Meaning: Derrida and Austin," *New Literary History* 13, no. 1 (1981).

40. The recognition of the natural force intrinsic to the sign to break with context and escape the author's control has a long and complex history in modern understandings of language. It has also become an important concern in anthropological debates. Yet my aim here is not to rely on a theory of the sign for the analysis of the empirical material. Rather, I propose to trace a theory of the sign that is already embedded in the empirical material itself. What I suggest, in other words, is to approach the matter of security "sideways." The methodological advantage of approaching security sideways is to avoid taking for granted "the difference between things and forms of explanation or abstraction" as Stefan Helmreich noted in his

work on marine microbiology. I thus treat theories (including theories of the sign) both as "tools for explaining worlds and as phenomena in the world to be examined." Due to the particular theory of the sign embedded in the stuff of security, my object of analysis becomes the very effort to search semiotic materials for a certain type of meaning, which might be realized in the future. Helmreich, *Alien Ocean*.

41. Bloom, *A Map of Misreading*.

42. Jacques Derrida, "Signature Event Context," in *Limited Inc* (Evanston: Northwestern University Press, 1988). See as well Veena Das, "The Signature of the State: The Paradox of Illegibility," in *Anthropology in the Margins of the State*, ed. Veena Das and Deborah Poole, 225–52 (Santa Fe: School of American Research Press, 2004). My thanks to Lawrence Cohen for bringing Veena Das's important essay to my attention and for engaging my work on the matter of security more generally.

43. Bruce Braun, "Biopolitics and the Molecularization of Life," *Cultural Geographies* 14 (2007); Cooper, "Pre-Empting Emergence"; Michael Dillon, "Virtual Security: A Life Science of (Dis)Order," *Millennium* 32, no. 3 (2003).

44. Of equal importance for Foucault's understanding of security was of course the physiocratic thought of the eighteenth century.

45. Nikolas Rose, "The Politics of Life Itself," *Theory, Culture & Society* 18, no. 6 (2001).

46. Michael Dillon and Luis Lobo-Guerrero, "The Biopolitical Imaginary of Species-Being," *Theory, Culture & Society* 26, no. 1 (2009).

47. Melinda Cooper, *Life as Surplus: Biotechnology and Capitalism in the Neoliberal Era* (Seattle: University of Washington Press, 2008).

48. Braun, "Biopolitics and the Molecularization of Life."

49. Lily Kay, *The Molecular Vision of Life: Caltech, the Rockefeller Foundation, and the Rise of the New Biology*, Monographs on the History and Philosophy of Biology (Oxford: Oxford University Press, 1996).

50. Cooper, *Life as Surplus*.

51. Haraway, "The Biopolitics of Postmodern Bodies."

52. Hannah Landecker, "Living Differently in Time: Plasticity, Temporality and Cellular Biotechnologies," *Culture Machine* 7 (2005).

53. N. Katherine Hayles, *How We Became Posthuman: Virtual Bodies in Cybernetics, Literature, and Informatics* (Chicago: University of Chicago Press, 1999); Thacker, *The Global Genome*; Hallam Stevens, "On the Means of Bio-Production: Bioinformatics and How to Make Knowledge in a High-Throughput Genomics Laboratory," *BioSocieties* 6, no. 2 (2011).

54. Of course, viruses kill, not information.

55. Derrida, "Signature Event Context."

56. I am indebted to Hannah Landecker, who suggested these terms to me.

57. This argument presupposes that such vaccines and antiviral drugs are readily available, which might not necessarily be the case.

58. Select agents are pathogenic organisms or toxins that have been declared by U.S. government agencies to have the potential to pose a significant threat to public health.

59. Kurzweil and Joy, "Recipe for Destruction."

60. Hannah Landecker, "Food as Exposure: Nutritional Epigenetics and the New Metabolism," *BioSocieties* 6, no. 2 (2011).

61. The challenges presented by techniques of recombinant DNA were addressed in 1975 at the historic Asilomar conference in Pacific Grove, California, where scientists from around the world gathered to discuss the potential hazards of genetic engineering. These discussions established the foundations of most contemporary safety practices in the biological sciences. The focus at Asilomar was mainly on environmental safety issues and therefore differs considerably from the problematization of the biological sciences in terms of security. On the Asilomar conference, see Richard Hindmarsh and Herbert Gottweis, "Recombinant Regulation: The Asilomar Legacy 30 Years On," *Science as Culture* 14, no. 4 (2005), pp. 299–307; and Sheldon Krimsky, "From Asilomar to Industrial Biotechnology: Risks, Reductionism and Regulation," *Science as Culture* 14, no. 4 (2005), pp. 309–23.

62. NSABB, *Addressing Biosecurity Concerns Related to the Synthesis of Select Agents* (Washington, DC: NSABB, 2006).

63. Ibid.

64. Hans Bügl et al., "DNA Synthesis and Biological Security," *Nature Biotechnology* 25, no. 6 (2007).

65. Evelyn Fox Keller, *A Feeling for the Organism: The Life and Work of Barbara McClintock* (New York: W. H. Freeman, 2001).

66. NSABB, *Addressing Biosecurity Concerns Related to the Synthesis of Select Agents.*

67. Lowe, "Viral Clouds."

68. Maria Boekels Gogarten, Johann Peter Gogarten, and Lorraine C. Olendzenski, eds., *Horizontal Gene Transfer: Genomes in Flux* (New York: Humana Press, 2009).

69. Ibid.

70. Helmreich, "Trees and Seas of Information."

71. Ibid.

72. DHHS, "Screening Framework Guidance for Providers of Synthetic Double-Stranded DNA," (Washington, DC: DHHS, 2010).

73. *ABC News*, February 20, 2012.

74. Martin Enserink, "Controversial Studies Give a Deadly Flu Virus Wings," *Science* 334 (2011), p. 1192.

75. *ABC News*, February 20, 2012.

76. Sander Herfst et al., "Airborne Transmission of Influenza A/H5N1 Virus between Ferrets," *Science* 336 (2012), p. 1535.

77. *ABC News*, February 20, 2012.

78. Masaki Imai et al., "Experimental Adaptation of an Influenza H5 HA Confers Respiratory Droplet Transmission to a Reassortant H5 HA/H1N1 Virus in Ferrets," *Nature* 486, no. 7403 (2012).

79. "An Engineered Doomsday," *New York Times*, January 7, 2012.

80. Enserink, "Controversial Studies Give a Deadly Flu Virus Wings," p. 1192.

81. See http://news.sciencemag.org/scienceinsider/2012/01/prominent-virologists -want-us.html.

82. Bruce Alberts, "Introduction: H5N1," *Science* 336 (2012).

83. Kay, *Who Wrote the Book of Life?*; Fox Keller, *The Century of the Gene.*

84. Rheinberger, "Gene Concepts."

85. Susan Leigh Star and James R. Griesemer, "Institutional Ecology, 'Translations' and Boundary Objects: Amateurs and Professionals in Berkeley's Museum of Vertebrate Zoology, 1907–39," *Social Studies of Science* 19 (1989).

86. Kohler, *Lords of the Fly.*

87. Thanks to Peter Redfield for reminding me here of Kohler's important work.

CHAPTER FIVE

1. Marc Santora, "When a Bug Becomes a Monster," *New York Times*, August 21, 2005.

2. New York City Department of Health and Mental Hygiene, *Pandemic Influenza Preparedness and Response Plan.*

3. Ibid., p. 95.

4. FDA, "Safety Communication: Cautions in Using Rapid Tests for Detecting Influenza A Viruses" (press release).

5. For the concept of trials of strength, see Latour, *The Pasteurization of France.*

6. For an anthropological analysis of the trafficking in sputum samples in Georgia, see Erin Koch, "Beyond Suspicion: Evidence (Un)Certainty, and Tuberculosis in Georgian Prisons," *American Ethnologist* 33, no. 1 (2006). Rayna Rapp has paid attention to the preparation of amniocentesis samples in a classic study; see Rayna Rapp, *Testing Women, Testing the Fetus: The Impact of Aminocentesis in America* (London: Routledge, 2000). Cori Hayden has followed the traffic in plant specimens; see Cori Hayden, *When Nature Goes Public: The Making and Unmaking of Bioprospecting in Mexico* (Princeton: Princeton University Press, 2003). The material infrastructure allowing biological matter to travel near and far is the object of Hannah Landecker's exploration of tissue culture. See Hannah Landecker, *Culturing Life: How Cells Became Technologies* (Cambridge, MA: Harvard University Press, 2007).

7. Edwin D. Kilbourne, "Influenza Pandemics of the 20th Century," *Emerging Infectious Diseases* 12, no. 1 (2006).

8. The proficiency-testing samples produced by Meridian Bioscience were distributed by the College of American Pathologists, the American College of Physicians, the American Academy of Family Physicians, and the American Association of Bioanalysts. Although a number of countries were involved, 98 percent of the labs were located in the United States and Canada.

9. Press Briefing on Distribution of H2N2 Influenza Strain by Julie Gerberding, Centers for Disease Control and Prevention, April 13, 2005.

10. Frances Pouch Downes, "The Flu Pandemic That Didn't Happen—Yet," *Lab-Link* 10, no. 2 (2005), p. 2.

11. See, among many others, Marc Santora, "50s Killer Flu Is Still Here. Why?" *New York Times*, April 17, 2005; Sarah Boseley, Suzanne Goldenberg, and Luke Harding, "Scientists Hunt Thousands of Vials of Deadly Flu Virus Sent across World," *Guardian*, April 14 2005.

12. Santora, "50's Killer Flu Is Still Here."

13. Ibid.

14. "Ahead of the Storm," *South China Morning Post*, August 8, 2012.

15. Press Briefing on Distribution of H2N2 Influenza Strain, April 13, 2005.

16. Prior to the publication of the first edition of the BMBL in 1984, the CDC published a report on the *Classification of Etiologic Agents on the Basis of Hazards* in 1974. In the same year, the NIH published the more limited *National Cancer Institute Safety Standards for Research Involving Oncogenic Viruses,* followed two years later by the important *NIH Guidelines for Research Involving Recombinant DNA Molecules.*

17. *Biosafety in Microbiological and Biomedical Laboratories,* 5th ed. (2007), available at http://www.cdc.gov/OD/ohs/biosfty/bmbl5/bmbl5toc.htm.

18. Ibid.

19. According to Ewald, the principle of precaution "invites one to make the most deceptive malicious demon one's constant companion." François Ewald, "The Return of Descartes' Malicious Demon: An Outline of a Philosophy of Precaution," in *Embracing Risk: The Changing Culture of Insurance and Responsibility,* ed. Tom Baker and Jonathan Simon (Chicago: University of Chicago Press, 2002), p. 289.

20. Marta G. Rivera-Ferre and Miquel Ortega-Cerda, "Recognising Ignorance in Decision-Making," *EMBO Reports* 12, no. 5 (2011), p. 394.

21. Precaution thus implies that conventional political action is always based on certain knowledge. Bruno Latour rightly contests this claim. "[L]'idée que le passage à l'acte provienne d'une connaissance complète de ses causes et conséquences est une aberration. Tout général, tout capitaine, tout caporal sait bien que l'action consiste à sonder, à explorer, à tâtonner pour produire à la fois des informations sur la localisation et sur les intentions de l'ennemi et pour forcer le destin en prenant, quand on le juge nécessaire, des risques jamais exactement calculés qui obligent de ce fait à une vigilance continuelle laquelle, à son tour, permettra de suspendre l'action, de battre en retraite ou, au contraire, de pousser son avantage." (The notion that any decision to take action emerges from complete knowledge of its causes and consequences is an aberration. Generally speaking, every captain, every corporal is aware that taking action is based on scouting, on exploring, on groping one's way, aiming to both produce information about the enemy's localization and the enemy's intentions, and to shape one's destiny by taking risks never calculated before; risks that hence require continuous alertness, which in turn allows one to suspend action, retreat or, on the contrary, to press one's advantage.) Bruno Latour, "Du Principe de Précaution au Principe du Bon Gouvernement: Vers de Nouvelles Règles de la Méthode Expérimentale," *Les Etudes* 3394, no. 339–346 (2000), p. 340.

22. Andy C. Stirling and Ian Scoones, "From Risk Assessment to Knowledge Mapping: Science, Precaution, and Participation in Disease Ecology," *Ecology and Society* 14, no. 2 (2009).

23. Lisa Schnirring, "Debate on H5N1 Death Rate and Missed Cases Continues," CIDRAP, February 24, 2012.

24. I borrow the phrase "anticipation of retrospection" from Miyazaki, "The Temporalities of the Market," p. 259.

25. Osterholm, "Preparing for the Next Pandemic," p. 37.

26. Elizabeth A. Povinelli, *Economies of Abandonment: Social Belonging and Endurance in Late Liberalism* (Durham, NC: Duke University Press, 2011), p. 3.

27. Carol J. Greenhouse, *A Moment's Notice: Time Politics across Cultures* (Ithaca: Cornell University Press, 1996), p. 82.

28. For an account of contemporary states of emergency and the logic of intervention in the field of humanitarianism, see Fassin and Pandolfi, *Contemporary States of Emergency*.

29. François Ewald, Christian Gollier, and Nicolas de Sadeleer, *Le Principe de Précaution* (Paris: Presses Universitaires de France, 2001), p. 47.

30. Interim CDC-NIH Recommendation for Raising the Biosafety Level for Laboratory Work Involving Noncontemporary Human Influenza Viruses (Washington, DC: DHHS, October 2005).

31. Ibid.

32. APHL, *Lessons from a Virus: Public Health Laboratories Respond to the H1N1 Pandemic* (Atlanta: CDC, 2012), p. 9.

33. Ibid., p. 14.

34. Ibid., p. 14.

35. Ibid., p. 13.

36. Ibid., p. 58.

37. Ibid.

38. *The H1N1 Influenza A Virus: A Test Case for a Global Response* (Washington, DC: George Washington University, 2009), p. 2.

39. HHS, *2009 H1N1 Influenza Improvement Plan* (Washington, DC: HHS, 2012).

40. TFAH, *Pandemic Flu Preparedness: Lessons from the Frontlines* (Washington, DC: Trust for America's Health, 2009), p. 1.

41. Ibid.

42. Ibid., p. 17.

43. Ibid.

44. Ibid., p. 2.

45. Ronell, *The Test Drive*, p. 164.

46. Latour, *The Pasteurization of France*, p. 158.

47. APHL, *Lessons from a Virus*, p. 43.

48. Downes, "The Flu Pandemic That Didn't Happen," 2.

49. Lazar, Cagliuso, and Gebbi, "Are We Ready and How Do We Know?" p. 58.

50. Lakoff, "The Generic Biothreat, or, How We Became Unprepared," p. 401.

51. Lazar, Cagliuso, and Gebbie, "Are We Ready and How Do We Know?" p. 58.

52. Fred Guterl, *The Fate of the Species: Why the Human Race May Cause Its Own Extinction and How We Can Stop It* (New York, Bloomsbury, 2012), p. 4.

CHAPTER SIX

1. Warner, *Publics and Counterpublics* (New York, Zone Books, 2005), p. 175.

2. HHS, *HHS Pandemic Influenza Plan* (Washington, DC: HHS, 2005).

3. The ACIP is a prominent advisory body of the U.S. government consisting of fifteen experts in the fields of epidemiology, immunology, and pediatrics, individually selected by the secretary of Health and Human Services. ACIP members regularly convene on the campus of the Centers for Disease Control and Prevention in Atlanta for several days of deliberation and decision making. During the early years of the HIV/AIDS epidemic, meetings of the advisory committee regularly turned into a public site of intensive biopolitical contestation. See Etheridge, *Sentinel for Health*; Steven Epstein, *Impure Science: AIDS, Activism, and the Politics of Knowledge* (Berkeley: University of California Press, 1996).

4. Foucault, *Security, Territory, Population*.

5. Dr. Allos's reference was to the so-called smallpox vaccination program launched by the George W. Bush administration in 2002 just months before the U.S. Army invaded Iraq. On this program, its role in the "war on terror," and its eventual failure, see Dale Rose, "How Did the Smallpox Vaccination Program Come About? Tracing the Emergence of Recent Smallpox Vaccination Thinking," in *Biosecurity Interventions: Global Health and Security in Question*, ed. Andrew Lakoff and Stephen Collier (New York: Columbia University Press, 2008).

6. Robert Roos and Lisa Schnirring, "New Pandemic Vaccine Plan Keeps Focus on Critical Workers," CIDRAP, July 23, 2008.

7. HHS, "HHS and DHS Announce Guidance on Pandemic Vaccination Allocation." August 12, 2008.

8. Jenny Reardon, "Democratic Mis-Haps: The Problem of Democratization in a Time of Biopolitics," *BioSocieties* 2, no. 2 (2007).

9. Lawrence Cohen, "Where It Hurts: Indian Material for an Ethics of Organ Transplantation," *Zygon* 38, no. 3 (2003); Paul Rabinow, *French DNA: Trouble in Purgatory* (Chicago: University of Chicago Press, 1999); Nikolas Rose, *The Politics of Life Itself: Biomedicine, Power, and Subjectivity in the Twenty-First Century* (Princeton: Princeton University Press, 2007); Sarah Franklin, "Ethical Biocapital: New Strategies of Cell Culture," in *Remaking Life and Death: Toward an Anthropology of the Biosciences*, ed. Sarah Franklin and Margaret Lock (Santa Fe: School of American Research Press, 2003); Sperling, *Reasons of Conscience*; and Arthur Kleinman, "Anthropology of Bioethics," in *Writing at the Margin: Discourse between Anthropology and Medicine* (Berkeley: University of California Press, 1995).

10. Cohen, "Where It Hurts"; Warner, *Publics and Counterpublics*.

11. In his lectures on security, Foucault suggests that security is exercised in a territory extending from the population to the public. As he points out, the "population" and the "public" are concepts crucial for the functioning of political power in modernity. In the nineteenth century, the population appeared "as that on which and towards which mechanisms are directed in order to have a particular effect on it." The idea of the population marks the appearance of a scientific understanding of the human species as a group of living beings. "It is a set of elements in which we can note constants and regularities even in accidents, in which we can identify the universal of desire regularly producing the benefit of all, and with regard to which we can identify a number of modifiable variables on which it depends." This notion of the population as a biological species extends to the idea of the public. "The public . . . is the population seen under the aspect of its opinions, ways of doing things, forms of behavior, customs, fears, prejudices, and requirements; it is what one gets a hold on through education, campaigns, and convictions." As a mechanism of power, security seeks to modify ways of thinking, acting, and feeling. Public opinions, behaviors, and affects thus represent essential realities for security because they make the regulation of the population possible. "The population is . . . everything that extends from biological rootedness through the species up to the surface that gives one a hold provided by the public," argues Foucault.

The public engagement meetings that I explored in this chapter show how the public has become not just a means of providing legitimacy to a particular policy but also constitutes the very territory where power is exercised. Today, the mobilization of the "public" is crucial for the regulation of the "population." Foucault underscores that the "population" and the "public" are specific to security, while the "people" are those who resist the experimental governance of bodies and populations. "The people comprises those who conduct themselves in relation to the management of the population, at the level of the population, as if they were not part of the population as a collective subject-object, as if they put themselves outside of it, and consequently the people is those who, refusing to be the population, disrupt the system." And yet, what Foucault describes here as resistance may ultimately represent a form of disruption constitutive for the continuous expansion of security. People who think, act, and feel as if they were not part of the population are security's greatest peril. Foucault, *Security, Territory, Population*, pp. 43–44.

12. On such regimes of pharmaceutical prevention, see João Biehl, "The Activist State: Global Pharmaceuticals, AIDS, and Citizenship in Brazil," *Social Text* 22, no. 3 (2004); Hayden, "A Generic Solution?"; Adriana Petryna, *When Experiments Travel: Clinical Trials and the Global Search for Human Subjects* (Princeton: Princeton University Press, 2009); Andrew Lakoff, *Pharmaceutical Reason: Knowledge and Value in Global Psychiatry* (Cambridge: Cambridge University Press, 2005) and "The Right Patients for the Drug: Managing the Placebo Effect in Antidepressant Trials," *BioSocieties* 2, no. 1 (2007); Adriana Petryna, Andrew Lakoff, and Arthur Kleinman, *Global Pharmaceuticals: Ethics, Markets, Practices* (Durham, NC: Duke University Press, 2006); Sjaak van der Geest and Susan Reynolds Whyte, eds., *The Context of Medicines in Developing Countries. Studies in Pharmaceutical Anthropology*

(Amsterdam: Het Spinhuis, 1991); Sjaak van der Geest, Susan Reynolds Whyte, and Anita Hardon, "The Anthropology of Pharmaceuticals: A Biographical Approach," *Annual Review of Anthropology* 25 (1996); and Joseph Dumit, *Drugs for Life: How Pharmaceutical Companies Define Our Health* (Durham, NC: Duke University Press, 2012).

13. Ragnar E. Lofstedt, *Risk Management in Post-Trust Societies* (Basingstoke: Palgrave Macmillan, 2005); Herbert Gottweis, "Participation and the New Governance of Life," *BioSocieties* 3 (2008).

14. CDC, *Citizen Voices on Pandemic Flu Choices: A Report of the Public Engagement Pilot Project on Pandemic Influenza* (Atlanta: CDC, 2005).

15. Michael Power, *The Risk Management of Everything: Rethinking the Politics of Uncertainty* (London: Demos, 2004); Marilyn Strathern, ed., *Audit Cultures: Anthropological Studies in Accountability, Ethics and the Academy* (London: Routledge, 2000).

16. CDC, *Citizen Voices on Pandemic Flu Choices.*

17. Ibid.

18. Strathern, *The Gender of the Gift: Problems with Women and Problems with Society in Melanesia.*

19. CDC, *Citizen Voices on Pandemic Flu Choices.*

20. Marilyn Strathern, "Robust Knowledge and Fragile Futures," in *Global Assemblages: Technology, Politics, and Ethics as Anthropological Problems*, ed. Aihwa Ong and Stephen Collier (Oxford: Blackwell, 2005).

21. CDC, *Citizen Voices on Pandemic Flu Choices.*

22. Nancy Scheper-Hughes, "Katrina: The Disaster and Its Doubles," *Anthropology Today* 21, no. 6 (2005).

23. Stephen Collier and Andrew Lakoff, "The Vulnerability of Vital Systems: How 'Critical Infrastructure' Became a Security Problem," in *The Changing Logics of Risk and Security*, ed. Myriam Dunn (London: Routledge, 2008); Lakoff, "Preparing for the Next Emergency."

24. NIAC, *The Prioritization of Critical Infrastructure for a Pandemic Outbreak in the United States: Working Group Final Report and Recommendations* (Washington: DHS, 2007).

25. Ibid.

26. Marie Andrée Jacob and Annelise Riles, "The New Bureaucracies of Virtue," *PoLAR: Political and Legal Anthropology Review* 30, no. 2 (2007).

27. Franklin, "Ethical Biocapital."

28. CDC, *Update on Pandemic Flu Preparedness* (Atlanta: CDC, 2007).

29. Ibid.

30. Ibid.

31. Kilbourne, "Influenza Pandemics of the 20th Century."

32. Monica Schoch-Spana, "Post-Katrina, Pre-Pandemic America," *Anthropology News* 47, no. 1 (2006).

33. Testimony before the House Committee On International Relations, December 7, 2005.

34. "CDC Learns from Katrina, Plans for Pandemic," *CDC News*, November 2006.

35. Ibid.

36. Ibid.

37. Ibid.

38. HHS, *Pandemic Planning Update. A Report from Secretary Michael O. Leavitt* (Washington, DC: Department of Health and Human Services, 2006), p. 2.

EPILOGUE

1. Peter Shadbolt, "H7N9 Virus 'One of the Most Lethal So Far,'" CNN, April 26, 2013.

2. Declan Butler, "Novel Bird Flu Kills Two in China. Scientists Are Racing to Assess the Pandemic Potential of H7N9 Flu Virus, *Nature News*, April 2, 2013.

3. Osterholm, "The Next Contagion: Closer than You Think."

4. Ibid.

5. Robert Ross, "CDC Airs H7N9 Worries as Report Profiles Early Victims," CIDRAP News, April 10, 2013.

6. Lisa Schnirring, "China Reports 3 New H7N9 Cases, 64 Total, 14 Deaths," CIDRAP News, April 15, 2013.

7. Robert Ross, "H7N9 Mystery. Why Does Age Profile Tilt Older?" CIDRAP News, April 19, 2013.

8. Braun, "Biopolitics and the Molecularization of Life," p. 21.

9. Ibid., p. 22.

10. Katherine Mason, "Mobile Migrants, Mobile Germs: Migration, Contagion, and Boundary-Building in Shenzhen, China after SARS," *Medical Anthropology* 31, no. 2 (2012), p. 127.

11. Comaroff, "Beyond Bare Life," p. 198.

12. Mary Moran and Daniel Hoffman, "Ebola in Perspective," Cultural Anthropology Online, October 7, 2014, http://www.culanth.org/fieldsights/585-ebola-in-perspective. Accessed January 1, 2015.

13. Vinh-Kim Nguyen, "Ebola: How We Became Unprepared, and What Might Come Next," Cultural Anthropology Online, October 7, 2014, http://www.culanth.org/fieldsights/605-ebola-how-we-became-unprepared-and-what-might-come-next. Accessed January 1, 2015.

14. Kendall Hoyt, "Ebola is Bad, but the Flu is Worse," *Politico Magazine*, October 7, 2014.

15. Michael Specter, "After Ebola," *The New Yorker*, August 1, 2014.

BIBLIOGRAPHY

"Ahead of the Storm." *South China Morning Post*, August 8, 2012.

Alberts, Bruce. "Introduction: H5N1." *Science* 336 (2012): 1521.

Amsterdamska, Olga. "Achieving Disbelief: Thought Styles, Microbial Variation, and American and British Epidemiology, 1900–1940." *Studies in the History and Philosophy of the Biological and Biomedical Sciences* 35 (2004): 483–507.

———. "Medical and Biological Constraints. Early Research on Variation in Bacteriology." *Social Studies of Science* 17 (1987): 657–87.

Anderson, Benedict. *Imagined Communities: Reflections on the Origin and Spread of Nationalism*. London: Verso, 1983.

Anderson, Jon P., Richard Daifuku, and Lawrence A. Loeb. "Viral Error Catastrophe by Mutagenic Nucleosides." *Annual Review of Microbiology* 58 (2004): 183–205.

Andrewes, Christopher H. "The Place of Viruses in Nature." *Proceedings of the Royal Society B: Biological Sciences* 139, no. 896 (1952): 313–26.

———. "Richard Edwin Shope 1901–1966." *Biographical Memoirs* 50 (1979): 353–63.

Andrewes, C. H., P. P. Laidlaw, and Wilson Smith. "The Susceptibility of Mice to the Viruses of Human and Swine Influenza." *The Lancet* (1934): 859–62.

APHL. *Lessons from a Virus: Public Health Laboratories Respond to the H1N1 Pandemic*. Atlanta: CDC, 2012.

Ardner, Edwin. *The Voice of Prophecy and Other Essays*. Oxford: Basil Blackwell, 1989.

Atlas, R. M., P. Campbell, N. R. Cozarelli, G. Curfman, L. Enquist, G. Fink, A. Flanagin, et al. "Statement on Scientific Publication and Security." *Science* 299 (2003): 1149.

Atlas, Ronald M., and Malcom Dando. "The Dual-Use Dilemma for the Life Sciences: Perspectives, Conundrums, and Global Solutions." *Biosecurity and Bioterrorism* 4, no. 3 (2006): 276–86.

Atlas, Ronald M., and Judith Reppy. "Globalizing Biosecurity." *Biosecurity and Bioterrorism: Biodefense Strategy, Practice, and Science* 3, no. 1 (2005): 51–60.

Austin, John L. *How to Do Things with Words*. Cambridge, MA: Harvard University Press, 2001 (1962).

Balfour, Ian. *The Rhetoric of Romantic Prophecy*. Stanford: Stanford University Press, 2002.

Barker, Kezia. "Influenza Preparedness and the Bureaucratic Reflex: Anticipating and Generating the 2009 H1N1 Event." *Health and Place* 18, no. 4 (2012): 701–9.

Barry, John M. *The Great Influenza. The Epic Story of the Deadliest Plague in History*. New York: Penguin Books, 2004.

Beare, A. S., and J. W. Craig. "Virulence for Man of a Human Influenza-A Virus Antigenically Similar to 'Classical' Swine Viruses." *The Lancet* (July 3, 1976): 4–5.

Beck, Ulrich. "Risk Society Revisited: Theory, Politics and Research Programmes." In *Risk Society and Beyond: Critical Issues for Social Theory*, edited by Barbara Adam, Ulrich Beck, and Joost Van Loon, 211–29. London: Sage, 2000.

———. *Risk Society: Towards a New Modernity*. London: Sage, 1992.

———. "World Risk Society as Cosmopolitan Society: Ecological Questions in a Framework of Manufactured Uncertainties." *Theory, Culture & Society* 13, no. 4 (1996): 1–32.

Benjamin, Walter. "Über den Begriff der Geschichte." In *Abhandlungen. Gesammelte Schriften, Band I (2)*, edited by Hermann Schweppenhäuser and Rolf Tiedemann, 691–704. Frankfurt am Main: Suhrkamp Verlag, 1991.

Berger, Silvia. *Bakterien in Krieg und Frieden: Eine Geschichte der Medizinischen Bakteriologie in Deutschland, 1870–1933*. Göttingen: Wallstein, 2009.

Berlant, Lauren. *Cruel Optimism*. Durham, NC: Duke University Press, 2011.

———. "Intuitionists: History and the Affective Event." *American Literary History* 20, no. 4 (2008): 845–60.

———. "Slow Death (Sovereignty, Obesity, Lateral Agency)." *Critical Inquiry* 33, no. 4 (2007): 754–80.

———. "Trauma and Ineloquence." *Cultural Values* 5, no. 1 (2001): 41–58.

Bernard, Claude. *Introduction to the Study of Experimental Medicine*. New York: Dover Publications, 1957.

Beveridge, William Ian Beardmore. *Influenza: The Last Great Plague*. New York: Prodist, 1978.

Biehl, João. "The Activist State: Global Pharmaceuticals, AIDS, and Citizenship in Brazil." *Social Text* 22, no. 3 (2004): 105–32.

Biehl, João, and Adriana Petryna. "Critical Global Health." In *When People Come First: Critical Studies in Global Health*, edited by João Biehl and Adriana Petryna, 1–20. Princeton: Princeton University Press, 2014.

Bingham, Nick, Gareth Enticott, and Steve Hinchcliffe. "Biosecurity. Spaces, Practices, and Boundaries." *Environment and Planning A* 40, no. 7 (2008): 1528–33.

"Bioterror in Context. Interview with William R. Clark." *Pacific Standard*, May 19, 2008. http://www.psmag.com/culture-society/bioterror-in-context-4548. Accessed October 19, 2012.

Blanchot, Maurice. *The Book to Come*. Stanford: Stanford University Press, 2003.

Bloom, Harold. *A Map of Misreading*. Oxford: Oxford University Press, 2003 (1975).

Boltanski, Luc, and Eve Chiapello. *The New Spirit of Capitalism*. London: Verso, 2007.

Boltanski, Luc, Élisabeth Claverie, Nicolas Offenstadt, and Stéphane Van Damme, eds. *Affaires, Scandales et Grandes Causes: De Socrate à Pinochet*. Paris: Stock, 2007.

Boseley, Sarah, Suzanne Goldenberg, and Luke Harding. "Scientists Hunt Thousands of Vials of Deadly Flu Virus Sent across World." *The Guardian*, April 14, 2005.

Bourdieu, Pierre. *Distinction: A Social Critique of the Judgement of Taste*. Translated by Richard Nice. London: Routledge, 1984.

———. *Homo Academicus*. Translated by Peter Collier. Stanford: Stanford University Press, 1988.

Boyer, Paul. *When Time Shall Be No More: Prophecy Belief in Modern American Culture*. Cambridge, MA: Harvard University Press, 1992.

Branigin, William, Mike Allen, and John Mintz. "Tommy Thompson Resigns from HHS. Bush Asks Defense Secretary Rumsfeld to Stay." *Washington Post*, December 3, 2004.

Braun, Bruce. "Biopolitics and the Molecularization of Life." *Cultural Geographies* 14 (2007): 6–28.

Bresalier, Michael. "Fighting Flu: Military Pathology, Vaccines, and the Conflicted Identity of the 1918–1919 Pandemic in Britain." *Journal of the History of Medicine and Allied Sciences* 68, no. 1 (2013): 87–128.

———. "'A Most Protean Disease': Aligning Medical Knowledge of Modern Influenza, 1890–1914." *Medical History* 56, no. 4 (2012): 481–510.

———. "Neutralizing Flu: 'Immunological Devices' and the Making of a Virus Disease." In *Crafting Immunity: Working Histories of Clinical Immunology*, edited by Kenton Kroker, Jennifer Keelan and Pauline M. H. Mazumdar, 107–44. Aldershot: Ashgate, 2008.

———. "Uses of a Pandemic: Forging the Identities of Influenza and Virus Research in Interwar Britain." *Social History of Medicine* 25, no. 2 (2011): 400–24.

Bresalier, Michael, and Michael Worboys. "'Saving the Lives of Our Dogs': The Development of Canine Distemper Vaccine in Interwar Britain." *British Journal for the History of Science* 47, no. 2 (2013): 1–30.

Briggs, Charles L. "Communicating Biosecurity." *Medical Anthropology* 30, no. 1 (2011): 6–29.

Briggs, Charles L., and Mark Nichter. "Biocommunicability and the Biopolitics of Pandemic Threats." *Medical Anthropology* 28, no. 3 (2009): 189–98.

Brock, Thomas Dale. *Robert Koch: A Life in Medicine and Bacteriology*. Madison, WI: Science Tech Publishers, 1988.

Bügl, Hans, John P Danner, Robert J Molinari, John T Mulligan, Han-Oh Park, Bas Reichert, David A Roth, et al. "DNA Synthesis and Biological Security." *Nature Biotechnology* 25, no. 6 (2007): 627–29.

Bulloch, William. *The History of Bacteriology*. London: Oxford University Press, 1960.

Burnet, Frank Macfarlane. *Virus as Organism: Evolutionary and Ecological Aspects of Some Human Virus Diseases*. Cambridge, MA: Harvard University Press, 1946.

Butler, Declan. "Novel Bird Flu Kills Two in China. Scientists Are Racing to Assess the Pandemic Potential of H7N9 Flu Virus." *Nature News*, April 2, 2013.

Butler, Judith. "Performative Agency." *Journal of Cultural Economy* 3, no. 2 (2010): 147–61.

Bynum, W. F. " 'C'est Un Malade': Animal Models and Concepts of Human Disease." *Journal of the History of Medicine and Allied Sciences* 45 (1990): 397–413.

Caduff, Carlo. "On the Verge of Death: Visions of Biological Vulnerability." *Annual Review of Anthropology* 43 (2014): 105–21.

Calhoun, Craig. "A World of Emergencies: Fear, Intervention, and the Limits of Cosmopolitan Order." *Canadian Review of Sociology and Anthropology* 41 (2004): 373–95.

Call, Stephanie A., Mark A. Vollenweider, Carlton A. Hornung, David L. Simel, and W. Paul McKinney. "Does This Patient Have Influenza?" *JAMA* 293, no. 8 (2005): 987–97.

Canguilhem, Georges. "Experimentation in Animal Biology." In *Knowledge of Life*, 3–22. New York: Fordham University Press, 2008.

———. *Idéologie et Rationalité dans l'Histoire des Sciences de la Vie: Nouvelles Études d'Histoire et de Philosophie des Sciences*. Paris: J. Vrin, 2000.

———. *Knowledge of Life*. New York: Fordham University Press, 2008.

———. *The Normal and the Pathological*. New York: Zone Books, 1989.

Carter, K. Codell. "The Development of Pasteur's Concept of Disease Causation and the Emergence of Specific Causes in Nineteenth-Century Medicine." *Bulletin of the History of Medicine* 65, no. 4 (1991): 528–48.

———. "Edwin Klebs' Criteria for Disease Causality." *Medizinhistorisches Journal* 22 (1987): 80–89.

———. "Koch's Postulates in Relation to the Work of Jacob Henle and Edwin Klebs." *Medical History* 29 (1985): 353–74.

———. *The Rise of Causal Concepts of Disease: Case Histories*. Aldershot: Ashgate, 2003.

CDC. *Citizen Voices on Pandemic Flu Choices: A Report of the Public Engagement Pilot Project on Pandemic Influenza*. Atlanta: CDC, 2005.

———. *Update on Pandemic Flu Preparedness*. Atlanta: CDC, 2007.

Check, Erika. "Biologists Apprehensive over US Moves to Censor Information Flow." *Nature* 415 (February 21, 2002): 821.

Chong, Jia-Rui. "Bird Flu Findings Cautiously Optimistic." *Chicago Tribune*, August 1, 2006.

Clarke, Adele E., and Joan H. Fujimura. "What Tools? Which Jobs? Why Right?" In *The Right Tools for the Job*, edited by Adele. E. Clarke and Joan H. Fujimura, 3–44. Princeton: Princeton University Press, 1992.

Coamp, J. "The Nature of Viruses." *British Medical Journal* 2, no. 4055 (1938): 667–68.

Cockburn, Aidan T. "Eradication of Infectious Diseases." *Science* 133, no. 3458 (1961): 1050–58.

Cohen, Lawrence. "Migrant Supplementarity: Remaking Biological Relatedness in Chinese Military and Indian Five-Star Hospitals." *Body & Society* 17, no. 2 & 3 (2011): 31–54.

———. "Where It Hurts: Indian Material for an Ethics of Organ Transplantation." *Zygon* 38, no. 3 (2003): 663–88.

Cohen, William A. *Sex Scandal: The Private Parts of Victorian Fiction.* Durham, NC: Duke University Press, 1996.

Colgrove, James. *State of Immunity: The Politics of Vaccination in Twentieth-Century America.* Berkeley: University of California Press, 2006.

Collier, Stephen J. "Enacting Catastrophe: Preparedness, Insurance, Budgetary Rationalization." *Economy and Society* 37, no. 2 (2008): 224–50.

Collier, Stephen, and Andrew Lakoff. "The Vulnerability of Vital Systems: How 'Critical Infrastructure' Became a Security Problem." In *The Changing Logics of Risk and Security*, edited by Myriam Dunn, 17–39. London: Routledge, 2008.

Collier, Stephen J., Andrew Lakoff, and Paul Rabinow. "Biosecurity: Towards an Anthropology of the Contemporary." *Anthropology Today* 20, no. 5 (2004): 3–7.

Collins, Katie. "Information Poses Bigger Bioterrorism Threat than Microbes." *Wired*, March 21, 2014.

Comaroff, Jean. "Beyond Bare Life: AIDS, (Bio)Politics, and the Neoliberal Order." *Public Culture* 19, no. 1 (2007): 197–219.

Comaroff, Jean, and John L. Comaroff. "Criminal Obsessions, after Foucault: Postcoloniality, Policing, and the Metaphysics of Disorder." *Critical Inquiry* 30, no. 4 (2004): 800–24.

Cooper, Melinda. *Life as Surplus: Biotechnology and Capitalism in the Neoliberal Era.* Seattle: University of Washington Press, 2008.

———. "Pre-Empting Emergence: The Biological Turn in the War on Terror." *Theory, Culture & Society* 23, no. 4 (2006): 113–35.

Coston, Michael. "Avian Flu Diary." http://afludiary.blogspot.ch/2013/04/h5n1-meanwhile-in-vietnam.html. Accessed January 2, 2015.

Creager, Angela N. H. *The Life of a Virus: Tobacco Mosaic Virus as an Experimental Model, 1930–1965.* Chicago: University of Chicago Press, 2002.

Creager, Angela N. H., Elizabeth Lunbeck, and M. Norton Wise, eds. *Science without Laws: Model Systems, Cases, Exemplary Narratives.* Durham, NC: Duke University Press, 2007.

Crosby, Alfred W. *America's Forgotten Pandemic: The Influenza of 1918.* Cambridge: Cambridge University Press, 2003.

———. *Epidemic and Peace.* Westport: Greenwood Press, 1976.

Culler, Jonathan. "Convention and Meaning: Derrida and Austin." *New Literary History* 13, no. 1 (1981): 15–30.

Cunningham, Andrew. "Transforming Plague: The Laboratory and the Identity of Infectious Disease." In *The Laboratory Revolution in Medicine*, edited by Andrew Cunningham and Perry Williams, 209–44. Cambridge: Cambridge University Press, 2002.

Dagognet, François. *Méthodes et Doctrine dans l'Oeuvre de Pasteur.* Paris: PUF, 1967.

———. *Pasteur sans la Légende*. Paris: Synthelabo, 1994.

Dale, Henry Hallett "Patrick Playfair Laidlaw: 1881–1940." *Obituary Notices of Fellows of the Royal Society* 3, no. 9 (1941): 427–47.

Das, Veena. "The Signature of the State: The Paradox of Illegibility." In *Anthropology in the Margins of the State*, edited by Veena Das and Deborah Poole, 225–52. Santa Fe: School of American Research Press, 2004.

Daston, Lorraine. "The Moral Economy of Science." *Osiris* 10 (1995): 2–24.

Davenport, F. M., E. Minuse, A. V. Hennessy, and Thomas Francis. "Interpretations of Influenza Antibody Patterns of Man." *Bulletin of the World Health Organization* 41 (1969): 453–60.

Davies, Pete. *The Devil's Flu*. New York: Henry Holt, 2000.

Davis, David A. "The Forgotten Apocalypse: Katherine Anne Porter's 'Pale Horse, Pale Rider,' Traumatic Memory, and the Influenza Pandemic of 1918." *Southern Literary Journal* 43, no. 2 (2011): 55–74.

Davis, Mike. *The Monster at Our Door: The Global Threat of Avian Flu*. New York: New Press, 2005.

De Blic, Damien, and Cyril Lemieux. "Le Scandale Comme Épreuve: Éléments de Sociologie Pragmatique." *Politix: Revue des sciences sociales du politique* 18, no. 71 (2005): 9–38.

Dehner, George. "Who Knows Best? National and International Responses to Pandemic Threats and the 'Lessons' of 1976." *Journal of the History of Medicine and Allied Sciences* 65, no. 4 (2010): 478–513.

Derrida, Jacques. "Perhaps or Maybe." *PLI—Warwick Journal of Philosophy* 6 (1997): 1–17.

———. "Signature Event Context." In *Limited Inc*, 1–23. Evanston: Northwestern University Press, 1988.

DHHS. "Screening Framework Guidance for Providers of Synthetic Double-Stranded DNA." Washington, DC: DHHS, 2010.

Dillon, Michael. "Virtual Security: A Life Science of (Dis)Order." *Millennium* 32, no. 3 (2003): 531–58.

Dillon, Michael, and Luis Lobo-Guerrero. "The Biopolitical Imaginary of Species-Being." *Theory, Culture & Society* 26, no. 1 (2009): 1–23.

Dorset, M., C. N. McBryde, and W. B. Niles. "Remarks on 'Hog Flu.'" *Journal of the American Veterinary Medical Association* 62 (1923): 162–71.

Doshi, Peter. "The Elusive Definition of Pandemic Influenza." *Bulletin of the World Health Organization* 89, no. 7 (2011): 532–38.

———. "Neuraminidase Inhibitors: The Story behind the Cochrane Review." *British Medical Journal* 339 (2009): 1348–51.

Dowdle, Walter R. "Influenza Pandemic Periodicity, Virus Recycling, and the Art of Risk Assessment." *Emerging Infectious Diseases* 12, no. 1 (2006): 34–39.

Downes, Frances Pouch. "The Flu Pandemic That Didn't Happen—Yet." *LabLink* 10, no. 2 (2005): 1–2.

Dreher, W. H. "Swine Diseases as We Find Them in the Field." *Journal of the American Veterinary Medical Association* 61 (1922): 178–81.

Dumit, Joseph. *Drugs for Life: How Pharmaceutical Companies Define Our Health.* Durham, NC: Duke University Press, 2012.

Duncan, Kirsty. *Hunting the 1918 Flu: A Scientist's Search for a Killer Virus.* Toronto: University of Toronto Press, 2003.

Eigen, Manfred. "Viral Quasispecies." *Scientific American* 269, no. 1 (1993): 42–49.

"An Engineered Doomsday." *New York Times,* January 7, 2012.

Enserink, Martin. "Controversial Studies Give a Deadly Flu Virus Wings."*Science* 334 (2011): 1192–93.

Epstein, Gerald L. "Bioresponsibility: Engaging the Scientific Community in Reducing the Biological Weapons Threat." *BioScience* 52, no. 5 (2002): 398–99.

Epstein, Helen. "Flu Warning: Beware the Drug Companies!" *New York Review of Books* 58, no. 8 (2011).

Epstein, Steven. *Impure Science: AIDS, Activism, and the Politics of Knowledge.* Berkeley: University of California Press, 1996.

Etheridge, Elizabeth W. *Sentinel for Health: A History of the Centers for Disease Control.* Berkeley: University of California Press, 1992.

Evans, D. G. . "Wilson Smith. 1897–1965." *Biographical Memoirs of Fellows of the Royal Society* 12 (1966): 479–87.

Evans-Pritchard, E. E. *Nuer Religion.* Oxford: Clarendon Press, 1956.

———. *Witchcraft, Oracles and Magic among the Azande.* Oxford: Oxford University Press, 1937.

Ewald, François. "The Return of Descartes' Malicious Demon: An Outline of a Philosophy of Precaution." In *Embracing Risk: The Changing Culture of Insurance and Responsibility*, edited by Tom Baker and Jonathan Simon, 273–301. Chicago: University of Chicago Press, 2002.

Ewald, François, Christian Gollier, and Nicolas de Sadeleer. *Le Principe de Précaution.* Paris: Presses Universitaires de France, 2001.

Eyler, John M. "De Kruif's Boast: Vaccine Trials and the Construction of a Virus." *Bulletin of the History of Medicine* 80 (2006): 409–38.

Farmer, Paul. *AIDS and Accusation: Haiti and the Geography of Blame.* Berkeley: University of California Press, 1992.

Fassin, Didier. *Humanitarian Reason: A Moral History of the Present.* Berkeley: University of California Press, 2012.

Fassin, Didier, and Mariella Pandolfi, eds. *Contemporary States of Emergency: The Politics of Military and Humanitarian Interventions.* Cambridge, MA: MIT Press, 2010.

Fassin, Didier, and Richard Rechtman. *The Empire of Trauma: An Inquiry into the Condition of Victimhood.* Princeton: Princeton University Press, 2009.

Faubion, James D. "Comments." *Current Anthropology* 55, no. 3 (2014).

———. *The Shadows and Lights of Waco: Millennialism Today.* Princeton: Princeton University Press, 2001.

Felman, Shoshana. *The Scandal of the Speaking Body: Don Juan with J. L. Austin or Seduction in Two Languages.* Stanford: Stanford University Press, 2002 (1980).

Fink, Gerald R. *Biotechnology Research in an Age of Terrorism*. Washington, DC: National Academies Press, 2003.

"Flu Epidemic Conquest Seen. Dr. Shope of Rockefeller Staff Makes Discovery." *New York Sun*, 1939.

"Flu Origin Quest Leads to Hogs." *Chicago Herald-Times*, 1939.

Foucault, Michel. *The Birth of Biopolitics: Lectures at the College de France, 1978–1979*. New York: Palgrave MacMillan, 2008.

———. *The History of Sexuality: An Introduction*. New York: Vintage Books, 1990 (1976).

———. *Security, Territory, Population: Lectures at the Collège de France, 1977–78*. Translated by Graham Burchell. London: Palgrave, 2006.

———. *"Society Must Be Defended": Lectures at the Collège de France, 1975–1976*. Edited by François Ewald and Alessandro Fontana. Translated by David Macey. New York: Picador, 2003.

Fox Keller, Evelyn. *The Century of the Gene*. Cambridge, MA: Harvard University Press, 2000.

———. *A Feeling for the Organism: The Life and Work of Barbara McClintock*. New York: W. H. Freeman and Company, 2001 (1983).

Francis, Thomas. "A Consideration of Vaccination against Influenza." *Milbank Memorial Fund Quarterly* 25, no. 1 (1947): 5–20.

———. "Transmission of Influenza by a Filterable Virus." *Science* 80, no. 2081 (1934): 457–59.

Franklin, Sarah. "Ethical Biocapital: New Strategies of Cell Culture." In *Remaking Life and Death: Toward an Anthropology of the Biosciences*, edited by Sarah Franklin and Margaret Lock, 97–127. Santa Fe: School of American Research Press, 2003.

Galison, Peter. "Removing Knowledge." *Critical Inquiry* 31 (2004): 229–43.

Galton, Lawrence. "Flu Gets Us All, Eventually." *New York Times*, March 24, 1974.

Gaydos, Joel C., Franklin H. Top, Richard A. Hodder, and Philip K. Russell. "Swine Influenza A Outbreak, Fort Dix, New Jersey, 1976." *Emerging Infectious Diseases* 12, no. 1 (2006): 23–28.

Geison, Gerald L. *The Private Science of Louis Pasteur*. Princeton: Princeton University Press, 1995.

Gihring, Tim. "The Pandemic Prophecy." *Minnesota Monthly* (April 2006).

Gogarten, Maria Boekels, Johann Peter Gogarten, and Lorraine C. Olendzenski, eds. *Horizontal Gene Transfer: Genomes in Flux*. New York: Humana Press, 2009.

Gomel, Elana. "The Plague of Utopias: Pestilence and the Apocalyptic Body." *Twentieth Century Literature* 46, no. 4 (2000).

Gottweis, Herbert. "Participation and the New Governance of Life." *BioSocieties* 3 (2008): 265–86.

Gradmann, Christoph. "Alles eine Frage der Methode. Zur Historizität der Kochschen Postulate 1840–2000." *Medizinhistorisches Journal* 43 (2008): 121–48.

———. "Das Mass der Krankheit. Das Pathologische Tierexperiment in der Medizinischen Bakteriologie Robert Kochs." In *Mass und Eigensinn: Studien im*

Anschluss an Georges Canguilhem, edited by Cornelius Borck, Volker Hess, and Henning Schmidgen, 71–90. Munich: Fink, 2005.

————. *Krankheit im Labor: Robert Koch und die Medizinische Bakteriologie*. Göttingen: Wallstein Verlag, 2005.

Grady, Denise. "Making a Ferret Sneeze for Hints to the Transmission of Bird Flu." *New York Times*, March 28, 2006.

Greenhouse, Carol J. *A Moment's Notice: Time Politics across Cultures*. Ithaca: Cornell University Press, 1996.

Gusterson, Hugh. *Nuclear Rites: A Weapons Laboratory at the End of the Cold War*. Berkeley: University of California Press, 1996.

Guterl, Fred. *The Fate of the Species: Why the Human Race May Cause Its Own Extinction and How We Can Stop It*. New York: Bloomsbury, 2012.

Guyer, Jane I. "Prophecy and the Near Future: Thoughts on Macroeconomic, Evangelical, and Punctuated Time." *American Ethnologist* 34, no. 3 (2007): 409–21.

The H1N1 Influenza A Virus: A Test Case for a Global Response. Washington, DC: George Washington University, 2009.

Haraway, Donna. "The Biopolitics of Postmodern Bodies: Constructions of Self in Immune System Discourse." In *Simians, Cyborgs, and Women: The Reinvention of Nature*, 203–30. New York: Routledge, 1991.

Harding, Susan Friend. *The Book of Jerry Falwell: Fundamentalist Language and Politics*. Princeton: Princeton University Press, 2000.

Hayden, Cori. "A Generic Solution? Pharmaceuticals and the Politics of the Similar in Mexico." *Current Anthropology* 48, no. 4 (2007): 475–89.

————. "Rethinking Reductionism, or, the Transformative Work of Making the Same." *Anthropological Forum: A Journal of Social Anthropology and Comparative Sociology* 22, no. 3 (2012): 271–83.

————. *When Nature Goes Public: The Making and Unmaking of Bioprospecting in Mexico*. Princeton: Princeton University Press, 2003.

Hayles, N. Katherine. *How We Became Posthuman: Virtual Bodies in Cybernetics, Literature, and Informatics*. Chicago: University of Chicago Press, 1999.

Helmreich, Stefan. *Alien Ocean: Anthropological Voyages in Microbial Seas*. Berkeley: University of California Press, 2009.

————. "Trees and Seas of Information: Alien Kinship and the Biopolitics of Gene Transfer in Marine Biology and Biotechnology." *American Ethnologist* 30, no. 3 (2003): 340–58.

Helvoort, Ton van. "A Bacteriological Paradigm in Influenza Research in the First Half of the Twentieth Century." *History and Philosophy of the Life Sciences* 15 (1993): 3–21.

Hennessy, A. V., F. M. Davenport, and Thomas Francis. "Studies of Antibodies to Strains of Influenza Virus in Persons of Different Ages in Sera Collected in a Postepidemic Period." *Journal of Immunology* 75, no. 5 (1995): 401–9.

Herfst, Sander, Eefje J. A. Schrauwen, Martin Linster, Salin Chutinimitkul, Emmie de Wit, Vincent J. Munster, Erin M. Sorrell, et al. "Airborne Transmission of Influenza A/H5N1 Virus between Ferrets." *Science* 336 (2012): 1534–41.

HHS. *2009 H1N1 Influenza Improvement Plan*. Washington, DC: HHS, 2012.
———. "HHS and DHS Announce Guidance on Pandemic Vaccination Alloca-
tion." Washington, DC: HHS, 2008.
———. *HHS Pandemic Influenza Plan*. Washington, DC: HHS, 2005.
———. *Pandemic Planning Update: A Report from Secretary Michael O. Leavitt*.
Washington, DC: HHS, 2006.
Hindmarsh, Richard, and Herbert Gottweis. "Recombinant Regulation: The Asi-
lomar Legacy 30 Years On." *Science as Culture* 14, no. 4 (2005): 299–307.
Hirsch, August. *Handbook of Geographical and Historical Pathology*. London: Syden-
ham Society, 1883.
———. *Handbuch der Historisch-Geographischen Pathologie*. Erlangen: Verlag von
Ferdinand Enke, 1860.
Hirst, George K. "The Agglutination of Red Cells by Allantoic Fluid of Chick
Embryos Infected with Influenza Virus." *Science* 94, no. 2427 (1941): 22–23.
———. "Direct Isolation of Human Influenza Virus in Chick Embryos." *Journal of
Immunology* 45 (1942): 293–302.
———. "Studies of Antigenic Differences among Strains of Influenza A by Means of
Red Cell Agglutination." *Journal of Experimental Medicine* 78, no. 5 (1943):
407–23.
Holland, John. "Replication Error, Quasispecies Populations, and Extreme Evolu-
tion Rates of RNA Viruses." In *Emerging Viruses*, edited by Stephen S. Morse,
203–18. Oxford: Oxford University Press, 1993.
Hoyt, Kendall. "Ebola is Bad, but the Flu is Worse." *Politico Magazine*, October 7, 2014.
IOM, ed. *Emerging Infections: Microbial Threats to Health in the United States*. Wash-
ington, DC: National Academies Press, 1992.
Jacob, Marie Andrée, and Annelise Riles. "The New Bureaucracies of Virtue."
PoLAR: Political and Legal Anthropology Review 30, no. 2 (2007): 181–91.
Kaiser, Joceyln. "Resurrected Influenza Virus Yields Secrets of Deadly 1918 Pan-
demic." *Science* 310 (October 7, 2005): 28–29.
Kay, Lily. *The Molecular Vision of Life: Caltech, the Rockefeller Foundation, and the
Rise of the New Biology*. Monographs on the History and Philosophy of Biology.
Oxford: Oxford University Press, 1996.
———. *Who Wrote the Book of Life? A History of the Genetic Code*. Stanford: Stan-
ford University Press.
Keck, Frédéric. *Un Monde Grippé*. Paris: Flammarion, 2010.
Kermode, Frank. *The Sense of an Ending: Studies in the Theory of Fiction*. Oxford:
Oxford University Press, 2000.
Kilbourne, Edwin D. "Afterword: A Personal Summary Presented as a Guide for Dis-
cussion." In *Emerging Viruses*, edited by Stephen S. Morse, 290–95. Oxford:
Oxford University Press, 1993.
———. "Epidemiology of Influenza." In *The Influenza Viruses and Influenza*, ed-
ited by Edwin D. Kilbourne, 483–538. New York: Academic Press, 1975.
———. "Flu to the Starboard! Man the Harpoons! Fill 'em with Vaccine! Get the
Captain! Hurry!" *New York Times*, February 13, 1976, 32.

———. "Influenza Pandemics in Perspective." *JAMA* 237, no. 12 (1977): 1225–28.

———. "Influenza Pandemics of the 20th Century." *Emerging Infectious Diseases* 12, no. 1 (2006): 9–14.

Kilbourne, Edwin D., R. M. Chanock, P. W. Choppin, F. M. Davenport, J. P. Fox, M. B. Gregg, G. G. Jackson, and P. D. Parkman. "Influenza Vaccines: Summary of Influenza Workshop V." *Journal of Infectious Diseases* 129, no. 6 (1974): 750–71.

King, Nicholas B. "The Influence of Anxiety: September 11, Bioterrorism and American Public Health." *Journal of the History of Medicine and Allied Sciences* 58 (2003): 433–41.

———. "The Scale Politics of Emerging Diseases." *Osiris* 19 (2004): 62–76.

———. "Security, Disease, Commerce: Ideologies of Postcolonial Global Health." *Social Studies of Science* 32, no. 5–6 (2002): 763–89.

Kleinman, Arthur. "Anthropology of Bioethics." In *Writing at the Margin: Discourse between Anthropology and Medicine*, 41–67. Berkeley: University of California Press, 1995.

Kleinman, Arthur M., Barry R. Bloom, Anthony Saich, Katherine A. Mason, and Felicity Aulino. "Asian Flus in Ethnographic and Political Context: A Biosocial Approach." *Anthropology & Medicine* 15, no. 1 (2008): 1–5.

———. "Avian and Pandemic Influenza: A Biosocial Approach." *Journal of Infectious Diseases* 197 (2008): S1–S3.

Knezo, Genevieve J. *"Sensitive but Unclassified" and Other Federal Security Controls on Scientific and Technical Information.* Washington, DC: Congressional Research Service, 2004.

Knobler, Stacey L., Alison Mack, Adel Mahmoud, and Stanley Lemon. *The Threat of Pandemic Influenza: Are We Ready?* Washington, DC: National Academies Press, 2005.

Koch, Erin. "Beyond Suspicion: Evidence (Un)Certainty, and Tuberculosis in Georgian Prisons." *American Ethnologist* 33, no. 1 (2006): 50–62.

———. "Disease as Security Threat: Critical Reflections on the Global TB Emergency." In *Biosecurity Interventions: Global Health and Security in Question*, edited by Andrew Lakoff and Stephen Collier, 121–46. New York: Columbia University Press, 2008.

Kohler, Robert E. *Lords of the Fly: Drosophila Genetics and the Experimental Life.* Chicago: University of Chicago Press, 1994.

Kolata, Gina. *Flu: The Story of the Great Influenza Pandemic of 1918 and the Search for the Virus That Caused It.* New York: Simon & Schuster, 2005.

———. "Study Shows Why the Flu Likes Winter." *New York Times*, December 5, 2007.

Koselleck, Reinhart. "The Conceptual History of 'Crisis.'" In *The Practice of Conceptual History: Timing History, Spacing Concepts*, 236–47. Stanford: Stanford University Press, 2002.

———. *Futures Past. On the Semantics of Historical Time.* Translated by Keith Tribe. Cambridge, MA: MIT Press.

Krauthammer, Charles. "A Flu Hope, or Horror?" *Washington Post*, October 14, 2005.

Krimsky, Sheldon. "From Asilomar to Industrial Biotechnology: Risks, Reductionism and Regulation." *Science as Culture* 14, no. 4 (2005): 309–23.

Kurzweil, Ray, and Bill Joy. "Recipe for Destruction." *New York Times*, October 17, 2005.

Laidlaw, Patrick P. "Epidemic Influenza: A Virus Disease." *The Lancet* (1935): 1118–24.

———. *Virus Diseases and Viruses*. Cambridge: Cambridge University Press, 1938.

Lakoff, Andrew. "The Generic Biothreat, or, How We Became Unprepared." *Cultural Anthropology* 23, no. 3 (2008): 399–428.

———. *Pharmaceutical Reason. Knowledge and Value in Global Psychiatry*. Cambridge: Cambridge University Press, 2005.

———. "Preparing for the Next Emergency." *Public Culture* 19, no. 2: 247–71.

———. "The Right Patients for the Drug: Managing the Placebo Effect in Antidepressant Trials." *BioSocieties* 2, no. 1 (2007): 57–71.

Lakoff, Andrew, and Stephen Collier. *Biosecurity Interventions: Global Health and Security in Question*. New York: Columbia University Press, 2008.

Landecker, Hannah. *Culturing Life: How Cells Became Technologies*. Cambridge, MA: Harvard University Press, 2007.

———. "Food as Exposure: Nutritional Epigenetics and the New Metabolism." *BioSocieties* 6, no. 2 (2011): 167–94.

———. "Living Differently in Time: Plasticity, Temporality and Cellular Biotechnologies." *Culture Machine* 7 (2005). http://www.culturemachine.net/index.php /cm/article/view/26/33. Accessed May 2, 2014.

Latour, Bruno. "Du Principe de Précaution au Principe du Bon Gouvernement: Vers de Nouvelles Règles de la Méthode Expérimentale." *Les Etudes* 3394 (2000): 339–46.

———. *The Pasteurization of France*. Translated by Alan Sheridan and John Law. Cambridge, MA: Harvard University Press, 1988 (1984).

Laurance, Jeremy. "The Swine Flu Backlash." *The Lancet* 375 (January 30, 2010): 367.

Lazar, Eliot J., Nicholas Cagliuso, and Kristine M. Gebbie. "Are We Ready and How Do We Know? The Urgent Need for Performance Metrics in Hospital Emergency Management." *Disaster Medicine* 3, no. 1 (2009): 57–60.

Lea, Andrew. "Balancing Panic and Threat. What 'Contagion' Tells Us about Pandemics Today." *Harvard College Global Health Review*, October 20, 2011.

Lederman, Muriel, and Sue A. Tolin. "Ovatoomb: Other Viruses and the Origins of Molecular Biology." *Journal of the History of Biology* 26, no. 2 (1993): 239–54.

Lennette, Edwin H. "Recent Advances in Viruses: A Brief Survey of Recent Work on Virus Diseases." *Science* 98 (1943): 415–23.

Lentzos, Filippa, and Nikolas Rose. "Governing Insecurity: Contingency Planning, Protection, Resilience." *Economy and Society* 38, no. 2 (2009): 230–54.

Lofstedt, Ragnar E. *Risk Management in Post-Trust Societies*. Basingstoke: Palgrave Macmillan, 2005.

Lowe, Celia. "Viral Clouds: Becoming H5N1 in Indonesia." *Cultural Anthropology* 25, no. 4 (2010): 625–49.

Lowen, Anice C., Samira Mubareka, John Steel, and Peter Palese. "High Temperature (30 Degrees C) Blocks Aerosol but Not Contact Transmission of Influenza Virus." *Journal of Virology* 82, no. 11 (2008): 5650–52.

———. "Influenza Virus Transmission Is Dependent on Relative Humidity and Temperature." *PLoS Pathogens* 3, no. 10 (2007): 1470–76.

Lowen, Anice C., Samira Mubareka, Terrence M. Tumpey, Garcia-Sastre-Adolfo, and Peter Palese. "The Guinea Pig as a Transmission Model for Human Influenza Viruses." *PNAS* 103, no. 26 (2006): 9988–92.

Löwy, Ilana. "The Experimental Body." In *Medicine in the Twentieth Century,* edited by Roger Cooter and John Pickstone, 435–49. Amsterdam: Harwood Academic Publishers, 2000.

———. "From Guinea Pigs to Man: The Development of Haffkine's Anticholera Vaccine." *Journal of the History of Medicine and Allied Sciences* 47 (1992): 270–309.

Luhmann, Niklas. *Observations on Modernity.* Translated by William Whobrey. Stanford: Stanford University Press, 1998.

Lwoff, André. "The Concept of Virus: The Third Marjory Stephenson Memorial Lecture." *Journal of General Microbiology* 17, no. 1 (1957): 239–53.

MacPhail, Theresa. *The Viral Network: A Pathography of the H1N1 Influenza Pandemic.* Ithaca: Cornell University Press, 2014.

Maines, Taronna R., Li-Mei Chen, Yumiko Matsuoka, Hualan Chen, Thomas Rowe, Juan Ortin, Ana Falco, et al. "Lack of Transmission of H5N1 Avian–Human Reassortant Influenza Viruses in a Ferret Model." *PNAS* 103, no. 32 (August 8, 2006): 12121–26.

Mandavilla, Apoorva. "Profile of Robert Webster." *Nature Medicine* 9, no. 12 (2003).

Martin, Emily. "Toward an Anthropology of Immunology: The Body as Nation State." *Medical Anthropology Quarterly* 4, no. 4 (1990): 410–26.

Masaki, Imai, Tokiko Watanabe, Masato Hatta, Subash C. Das, Makoto Ozawa, et al. "Experimental Adaptation of an Influenza H5 HA Confers Respiratory Droplet Transmission to a Reassortant H5 HA/H1N1 Virus in Ferrets." *Nature* 486, no. 7403 (2012): 420–28.

Masco, Joseph. "Atomic Health, or How the Bomb Altered American Notions of Death." In *Against Health: How Health Became the New Morality,* edited by Jonathan M. Metzl and Anna Kirkland, 133–53. New York: New York University Press, 2010.

———. *The Nuclear Borderlands: The Manhattan Project in Post-Cold War New Mexico.* Princeton: Princeton University Press, 2006.

———. "'Sensitive but Unclassified': Secrecy and the Counterterrorist State." *Public Culture* 22, no. 3 (2010): 433–63.

———. "'Survival Is Your Business': Engineering Ruins and Affect in Nuclear America." *Cultural Anthropology* 23, no. 2 (2008): 361–98.

———. *The Theater of Operations: National Security Affect from the Cold War to the War on Terror.* Durham, NC: Duke University Press, 2014.

Mason, Katherine. "Mobile Migrants, Mobile Germs. Migration, Contagion, and Boundary-Building in Shenzhen, China after SARS." *Medical Anthropology* 31, no. 2 (2012): 113–31.

Masurel, Nic. "Swine Influenza Virus and the Recycling of Influenza A Viruses in Man." *The Lancet* (1976): 244–47.

Masurel, Nic, and William M. Marine. "Recycling of Asian and Hong Kong Influenza A Virus Hemagglutinins in Man." *American Journal of Epidemiology* 97, no. 1 (1973): 44–49.

McBryde, C. N. "Some Observations on 'Hog Flu' and Its Seasonal Prevalance in Iowa." *Journal of the American Veterinary Medical Association* 71 (1927): 368–77.

Mendelsohn, Andrew J. *Cultures of Bacteriology: Formation and Transformation of a Science in France and Germany, 1870–1914.* Unpublished dissertation. Princeton: Princeton University, 1996.

Miyazaki, Hirokazu. "Arbitraging Faith and Reason." *American Ethnologist* 34, no. 3 (2007): 430–32.

———. "The Temporalities of the Market." *American Anthropologist* 105, no. 2 (2003): 255–65.

Moran, Mary and Daniel Hoffman. "Ebola in Perspective." Cultural Anthropology Online, October 7, 2014. http://www.culanth.org/fieldsights/585-ebola-in-perspective. Accessed January 1, 2015.

Morens, David M., Gregory K. Folkers, and Anthony S. Fauci. "What Is a Pandemic?" *Journal of Infectious Diseases* 200 (2009): 1018–21.

Murray, Charles. "What Is Hog 'Flu?'" *Wallaces' Farmer* 46, no. 8 (1921): 1.

Napier, A. David. 2013. "Disaster Play." *Social Anthropology* 21, no. 1 (2013): 57–61.

———. "Nonself Help: How Immunology Might Reframe the Enlightenment." *Cultural Anthropology* 27, no. 1 (2012): 122–37.

Neher, André. *The Prophetic Existence.* London: Thomas Yoseloff, 1969.

Neustadt, Richard E., and Harvey V. Fineberg. *The Epidemic That Never Was: Policy-Making and the Swine Flu Scare.* New York: Vintage Books, 1983.

"The New Swine Flu." *New York Times*, April 27, 2009.

New York City Department of Health and Mental Hygiene. *Pandemic Influenza Preparedness and Response Plan.* New York: New York City Department of Health and Mental Hygiene, 2006.

———. *A Plan to Stabilize and Strengthen New York's Health Care System: Final Report of the Commission on Health Care Facilities in the 21st Century.* New York: New York City Department of Health and Mental Hygiene, 2006.

NIAC. *The Prioritization of Critical Infrastructure for a Pandemic Outbreak in the United States Working Group: Final Report and Recommendations.* Washington, DC: DHS, 2007.

NRC. *Biotechnology Research in an Age of Terrorism.* Washington, DC: National Academies Press, 2003.

NSABB. *Addressing Biosecurity Concerns Related to the Synthesis of Select Agents.* Washington, DC: NSABB, 2006.

O'Leary, Stephen D. *Arguing the Apocalypse: A Theory of Millennial Rhetoric.* Oxford: Oxford University Press, 1994.

Orent, Wendy. "Playing with Viruses: Replicating This Flu Strain Could Get Us Burned." *Washington Post,* April 17, 2005.

Orr, Jackie. *Panic Diaries: A Genealogy of Panic Disorder.* Durham, NC: Duke University Press.

Osterholm, Michael T. "The Next Contagion: Closer than You Think." *New York Times,* May 9, 2013.

———. "Preparing for the Next Pandemic." *Foreign Affairs* 84, no. 4 (2005): 24–37.

———. "Unprepared for a Pandemic." *Foreign Affairs* 86, no. 2 (2007): 47–57.

Osterholm, Michael T., and John Schwartz. *Living Terrors: What America Needs to Know to Survive the Coming Bioterrorist Catastrophe.* New York: Dell Publishing, 2000.

Palese, Peter. "Why Swine Flu Isn't So Scary." *Wall Street Journal,* May 2, 2009.

Palese, Peter, Mary B. Ritchey, Jerome L. Schulman, and Edwin D. Kilbourne. "Genetic Composition of a High-Yielding Influenza A Virus Recombinant: A Vaccine Strain against 'Swine' Influenza." *Science* 194 (1976): 334–35.

Palese, Peter, and Jerome L. Schulman. "RNA Pattern of 'Swine' Influenza Virus Isolated from Man Is Similar to Those of Other Swine Influenza Viruses." *Nature* 263 (1976): 528–30.

Petro, James B., and David A. Relman. "Understanding Threats to Scientific Openness." *Science* 302 (December 12, 2003): 1898.

Petryna, Adriana. *When Experiments Travel: Clinical Trials and the Global Search for Human Subjects.* Princeton: Princeton University Press, 2009.

Petryna, Adriana, Andrew Lakoff, and Arthur Kleinman. *Global Pharmaceuticals: Ethics, Markets, Practices.* Durham, NC: Duke University Press, 2006.

"Plan for Pandemic but Avoid Panic." *Financial Times,* April 27, 2009.

Povinelli, Elizabeth A. *Economies of Abandonment: Social Belonging and Endurance in Late Liberalism.* Durham, NC: Duke University Press, 2011.

Power, Michael. *The Risk Management of Everything: Rethinking the Politics of Uncertainty.* London: Demos, 2004.

Preston, Richard. *The Hot Zone.* New York: Random House, 1994.

Rabinow, Paul. *French DNA: Trouble in Purgatory.* Chicago: University of Chicago Press, 1999.

———. *Marking Time: On the Anthropology of the Contemporary.* Princeton: Princeton University Press, 2008.

Rader, Karen. *Making Mice: Standardizing Animals for American Biomedical Research, 1900–1955.* Princeton: Princeton University Press, 2004.

Rapp, Rayna. *Testing Women, Testing the Fetus: The Impact of Aminocentesis in America.* London: Routledge, 2000.

Rasmussen, A. F., Julia C. Stokes, and Joseph E. Smadel. "The Army Experience with Influenza, 1946–1947: Laboratory Aspects." *American Journal of Hygiene* 47 (1948): 142–49.

Ratcliff, J. D. "Cold Comfort." *Collier's Magazine*, February 26, 1938, 13/52.

———. "They've Got the Flu!" *Collier's Magazine*, January 18, 1941, 18/48.

Rawles, James Wesley. *How to Survive the End of the World as We Know It*. London: Penguin Books, 2009.

Reardon, Jenny. "Democratic Mis-Haps: The Problem of Democratization in a Time of Biopolitics." *BioSocieties* 2, no. 2 (2007): 239–56.

Redfield, Peter. *Life in Crisis: The Ethical Journey of Doctors without Borders*. Berkeley: University of California Press, 2013.

Redlener, Irwin. *Americans at Risk: Why We Are Not Prepared for Megadisasters and What We Can Do*. New York: Random House, 2006.

Rheinberger, Hans-Jörg. "Gene Concepts: Fragments from the Perspective of Molecular Biology." In *The Concept of the Gene in Development and Evolution: Historical and Epistemological Studies*, edited by Peter J. Beurton, Raphael Falk and Hans-Jörg Rheinberger, 219–39. Cambridge: Cambridge University Press, 2000.

Ricoeur, Paul. *Freud and Philosophy: An Essay on Interpretation*. New Haven: Yale University Press, 1970.

Rivera-Ferre, Marta G., and Miquel Ortega-Cerda. "Recognising Ignorance in Decision-Making." *EMBO Reports* 12, no. 5 (2011): 393–97.

Rivers, Thomas M. "Viruses." *Science* 75, no. 1956 (1932): 654–56.

Roitman, Janet. *Anti-Crisis*. Durham, NC: Duke University Press, 2013.

Ronell, Avital. *Finitude's Score: Essays for the End of the Millennium*. Lincoln: University of Nebraska Press, 1994.

———. *The Test Drive*. Urbana: University of Illinois Press, 2005.

Roos, Robert, and Lisa Schnirring. "New Pandemic Vaccine Plan Keeps Focus on Critical Workers." CIDRAP, July 23, 2008.

Rose, Dale. "How Did the Smallpox Vaccination Program Come About? Tracing the Emergence of Recent Smallpox Vaccination Thinking." In *Biosecurity Interventions: Global Health and Security in Question*, edited by Andrew Lakoff and Stephen Collier, 89–119. New York: Columbia University Press, 2008.

Rose, Nikolas. "The Politics of Life Itself." *Theory, Culture & Society* 18, no. 6 (2001): 1–30.

———. *The Politics of Life Itself: Biomedicine, Power, and Subjectivity in the Twenty-First Century*. Princeton: Princeton University Press, 2007.

Rosner, David, and Gerald Markowitz. *Are We Ready? Public Health since 9/11*. Berkeley: University of California Press, 2006.

Russell, Sabin. "Deadliest Flu Bug Given New Life in U.S. Laboratory." *San Francisco Chronicle*, October 6, 2005.

Samimian-Darash, Limor. "Governing Future Potential Biothreats: Toward an Anthropology of Uncertainty." *Current Anthropology* 54, no. 1 (2013): 1–22.

———. "Governing through Time: Preparing for Future Threats to Health and Security." *Sociology of Health and Illness* 33, no. 6 (2011): 930–45.

———. "A Pre-Event Configuration for Biological Threats: Preparedness and the Constitution of Biosecurity Events." *American Ethnologist* 36, no. 3 (2009): 478–91.

Santora, Marc. "50's Killer Flu Is Still Here. Why?" *New York Times*, April 17, 2005.

———. "When a Bug Becomes a Monster." *New York Times*, August 21, 2005.

Sartwell, Philip E., and Arthur P. Long. "The Army Experience with Influenza, 1946–1947: Epidemiological Aspects." *American Journal of Epidemiology* 47, no. 2 (1948): 135–41.

Schäfer, Werner. "Vergleichende Sero-Immunologische Untersuchung über die Viren der Influenza und Klassischen Geflügelpest." *Zeitschrift für Naturforschung* 10 (1955): 81–91.

Scheper-Hughes, Nancy. "Katrina: The Disaster and Its Doubles." *Anthropology Today* 21, no. 6 (2005): 2–4.

Schmeck, Harold M. "Flu Experts Soon to Rule on Need of New Vaccine." *New York Times*, March 21, 1976, 39.

———. "Race for a Swine Flu Vaccine Began in a Manhattan Lab." *New York Times*, May 21, 1976, 55.

Schnirring, Lisa. "Debate on H5N1 Death Rate and Missed Cases Continues." CIDRAP, February 24, 2012.

Schoch-Spana, Monica. "Bioterrorism: US Public Health and a Secular Apocalypse." *Anthropology Today* 20, no. 5 (2004): 8–13.

———. "Post-Katrina, Pre-Pandemic America." *Anthropology News* 47, no. 1 (2006): 32–36.

Seal, John R., David T. Sencer, and Harry M. Meyer Jr. "A Status Report on National Immunization against Influenza." *Journal of Infectious Diseases* 133, no. 6 (1976): 715–20.

Sencer, David J., and Donald J. Millar. "Reflections on the 1976 Swine Flu Vaccination Program." *Emerging Infectious Diseases* 12, no. 1 (2006): 29–33.

Shea, Dana A. *Balancing Scientific Publication and National Security Concerns.* Washington, DC: Congressional Research Service, 2003.

Shope, Richard E. "The Etiology of Swine Influenza." *Science* 73 (1931): 214–15.

———. "The Incidence of Neutralizing Antibodies for Swine Influenza Virus in the Sera of Human Beings of Different Ages." *Journal of Experimental Medicine* 63 (1936): 669–84.

———. "The Infection of Mice with Swine Influenza Virus." *Journal of Experimental Medicine* 62 (1935): 561–72.

———. "Seriological Evidence for the Occurrence of Infection with Human Influenza Virus in Swine." *Journal of Experimental Medicine* 67 (1938): 739–48.

———. "Swine Influenza. I. Experimental Transmission and Pathology." *Journal of Experimental Medicine* 54 (1931): 349–62.

Shope, Richard E., and Thomas Francis. "The Susceptibility of Swine to the Virus of Human Influenza." *Journal of Experimental Medicine* 64 (1936): 791–805.

Silverstein, Arthur M. *Pure Politics and Impure Science: The Swine Flu Affair.* Baltimore: Johns Hopkins University Press, 1981.

Sipress, Alan. *The Fatal Strain: On the Trail of Avian Flu and the Coming Pandemic.* New York: Penguin Books, 2009.

Skehel, John. "Discovery of Human Influenza Virus and Subsequent Influenza Research at the National Institute for Medical Research." In *Microbe Hunters Then and Now*, edited by Hilary Koprowski and Michael B. A. Oldstone, 205–9. Bloomington, IN: Medi-Ed Press, 1996.

Smith, Wilson, C. H. Andrewes, and P. P. Laidlaw. "A Virus Obtained from Influenza Patients." *The Lancet* (1933): 66–68.

Smith, Wilson, and C. H. Stuart-Harris. "Influenza Infection of Man from the Ferret." *The Lancet* (1936): 121–23.

Specter, Michael. "After Ebola." *The New Yorker*, August 1, 2014.

———. "Nature's Bioterrorist: Is There Any Way to Prevent a Deadly Avian-Flu Pandemic?" *The New Yorker*, February 28, 2005, 50–61.

Spencer, Paul. *Time, Space, and the Unknown: Massai Configurations of Power and Providence*. London: Routledge, 2003.

Sperling, Stefan. *Reasons of Conscience: The Bioethics Debate in Germany*. Chicago: University of Chicago Press, 2013.

Star, Susan Leigh, and James R. Griesemer. "Institutional Ecology, 'Translations' and Boundary Objects. Amateurs and Professionals in Berkeley's Museum of Vertebrate Zoology, 1907–39." *Social Studies of Science* 19 (1989): 387–420.

Starn, Randolph. "Historians and 'Crisis.'" *Past and Present* 52 (1971): 3–22.

Stevens, Hallam. "On the Means of Bio-Production: Bioinformatics and How to Make Knowledge in a High-Throughput Genomics Laboratory." *BioSocieties* 6, no. 2 (2011): 217–42.

Stewart, Kathleen, and Susan Friend Harding. "Bad Endings: American Apocalypsis." *Annual Review of Anthropology* 28 (1999): 285–310.

Stirling, Andy C., and Ian Scoones. "From Risk Assessment to Knowledge Mapping: Science, Precaution, and Participation in Disease Ecology." *Ecology and Society* 14, no. 2 (2009).

Strathern, Marilyn, ed. *Audit Cultures: Anthropological Studies in Accountability, Ethics and the Academy*. London: Routledge, 2000.

———. *The Gender of the Gift: Problems with Women and Problems with Society in Melanesia*. Berkeley: University of California Press, 1988.

———. "Robust Knowledge and Fragile Futures." In *Global Assemblages: Technology, Politics, and Ethics as Anthropological Problems*, edited by Aihwa Ong and Stephen Collier, 464–81. Oxford: Blackwell, 2005.

Stuart-Harris, Charles. "Swine Influenza in Man: Zoonosis or Human Pandemic?" *The Lancet* (July 3 1976): 31–32.

Summers, Jesse, and Samuel Litwin. "Examining the Theory of Error Catastrophe." *Journal of Virology* 80, no. 1 (2006): 20–26.

Sunder Rajan, Kaushik. *Biocapital: The Constitution of Postgenomic Life*. Durham, NC: Duke University Press, 2006.

Sundkler, Bengt G. M. *Bantu Prophets in South Africa*. London: Lutterworth Press, 1948.

"Swine 'Flu.'" *Veterinary Medicine* 18, no. 1 (1923): 314–15.

"Swine Flu: Advice, Dissent and Politics." *Science News* 109 (1976): 261–62.

"Swine Flu Dilemma." *Time Magazine*, July 19, 1976, 67.

Takafuji, Ernest T., David E. Johnson, and Herbert E. Segal. "The Swine Antigen in Previous Influenza Vaccines." *New England Journal of Medicine* 295, no. 18 (1976): 1018.

TFAH. *Pandemic Flu Preparedness. Lessons from the Frontlines.* Washington, DC: Trust for America's Health, 2009.

Thacker, Eugene. *The Global Genome: Biotechnology, Politics, and Culture.* Cambridge, MA: MIT Press, 2006.

Thompson, John B. *Political Scandal: Power and Visibility in the Media Age.* Cambridge: Polity, 2000.

Thompson, Theophilus. *Annals of Influenza or Epidemic Catarrhal Fever in Great Britain from 1510 to 1837.* London: Sydenham Society, 1852.

Tsing, Anna. "The Global Situation." *Cultural Anthropology* 15, no. 3 (2000): 327–60.

Tumpey, Terrence M., Christopher F. Basler, Patricia V. Aguilar, Hui Zeng, Alicia Solorzano, David E. Swayne, Nancy J. Cox, et al. "Characterization of the Reconstructed 1918 Spanish Influenza Pandemic Virus." *Science* 310 (2005): 77–80.

Tumpey, Terrence M., Adolfo Garcia-Sastre, Andrea Mikulasova, Jeffery K. Taubenberger, Swayne David E., Peter Palese, and Christopher F. Basler. "Existing Antivirals Are Effective against Influenza Virus with Genes from the 1918 Pandemic Virus." *PNAS* 99, no. 21 (2002): 13849–54.

Tyrrell, D. A. J. "Christopher Howard Andrewes. 7 June 1896–31 December 1987." *Biographical Memoirs of Fellows of the Royal Society* 37 (1991): 34–54.

Tzamarot, Karin. "Letter to the Editor." *New York Times*, October 20, 2005.

van der Geest, Sjaak, and Susan Reynolds Whyte, eds. *The Context of Medicines in Developing Countries: Studies in Pharmaceutical Anthropology.* Amsterdam: Het Spinhuis, 1991.

van der Geest, Sjaak, Susan Reynolds Whyte, and Anita Hardon. "The Anthropology of Pharmaceuticals: A Biographical Approach." *Annual Review of Anthropology* 25 (1996): 153–78.

Vogel, Kathleen. "Biodefense: Considering the Sociotechnical Dimension." In *Biosecurity Interventions: Global Health and Security in Question*, edited by Andrew Lakoff and Stephen Collier, 227–55. New York: Columbia University Press, 2008.

Wagar, Warren W. *Terminal Visions: The Literature of Last Things.* Bloomington: Indiana University Press, 1982.

"War against Swine Flu." *Time Magazine*, April 5, 1976, 50.

Warner, Michael. *Publics and Counterpublics.* New York: Zone Books, 2005.

Webby, Richard J., and Robert G. Webster. "Are We Ready for Pandemic Influenza." *Science* 302 (2003): 1519–22.

Westermann, Claus. *Basic Forms of Prophetic Speech.* Cambridge: Lutterworth Press, 1991.

Wilkinson, Lise, and A. P. Waterson. "The Development of the Virus Concept as Reflected in Corpora of Studies on Individual Pathogens. 2. The Agent of Fowl Plague—a Model Virus?" *Medical History* 19 (1975): 52–72.

Williams, Greer. *Virus Hunters*. New York: Alfred A. Knopf, 1960.

Wolfe, Nathan. *The Viral Storm: The Dawn of a New Pandemic Age*. New York: Henry Holt, 2011.

Worboys, Michael. *Spreading Germs: Disease Theories and Medical Practice in Britain*. Cambridge: Cambridge University Press, 2000.

———. "Was There a Bacteriological Revolution in Late Nineteenth-Century Medicine?" *Studies in History and Philosophy of Biology and Biomedical Sciences* 38, no. 1 (2007): 20–42.

"World Flu Experts Meeting to Discuss New Virus." *The Times*, Saturday, March 27, 1976, 4.

Young, Allan. *The Harmony of Illusions: Inventing Post-Traumatic Stress Disorder*. Princeton: Princeton University Press.

Yurchak, Alexei. *Everything Was Forever, until It Was No More: The Last Soviet Generation*. Princeton: Princeton University Press, 2006.

Zaloom, Caitlin. *Out of the Pits: Traders and Technology from Chicago to London*. Chicago: University of Chicago Press, 2006.

Zinsser, Hans. "The Etiology and Epidemiology of Influenza." *Medicine* 1, no. 2 (1922): 213–304.

INDEX

ABC News report on mutated bird flu virus, 123–24

accidental infections of researchers, 69, 137, 140–41, 143

ACIP. *See* Advisory Committee on Immunization Practices

acute respiratory disease epidemic, 32, 63

Advisory Committee on Immunization Practices (ACIP, U.S.), 64, 159–60, 164, 173, 218n3

Africa: Ebola virus outbreak, 182–83; Smallpox Eradication and Measles Control Program, 162; spread of H5N1 virus, 104

Allos, Ban Mishu, 160–61, 218n5

American Society of Microbiology, 125

American Type Culture Collection, 146–47

America's forgotten pandemic. *See* H1N1 (swine flu) influenza virus, 1918 pandemic

Andrewes, Christopher Howard: "Can We Beat Influenza?," 41*fig.*; comparison of viruses, 69; ferret research, 31, 41–50, 47*fig.*, 91, 94; initial isolation of human influenza virus, 40–41; mice research, 41, 50, 200n43; "Place of Viruses in Nature" lecture, 201n66; reason for success of, 44

animal models in experimental research, 43, 45–46, 50, 105, 198–99n21. *See also* ferret research; fertilized chicken eggs research; mice research

Annals of Influenza or Epidemic Catarrhal Fever in Great Britain from 1510–1837 (Thompson), 207–8n29

anthrax, 18–19, 113, 117, 172

antiviral drugs, 1, 3, 12, 18, 78, 117–18, 160

apocalyptic thinking. *See* pandemic prophecy

Armed Forces Institute of Pathology (Maryland), 108

Asia. *See* H2N2 influenza subtype (Asian pandemic); H7N9 influenza subtype (China)

Association of Public Health Laboratories report (2012), 148

Atlas, Ronald, 106

Austin, John, 22–23

avian influenza. *See* H5N1 avian influenza virus

Balfour, Ian, 35

Berlant, Lauren, 192n56

Bernard, Claude, 42–43

Bernier, Roger: launch of experimental influenza project, 164; on public engagement meetings, 168; testimony on thimerosal in vaccines, 162–63

Biochemic Division (Bureau of Animal Industry), 68

biological terrorism, concerns about, 136

biology, contextualization of, 116–19

biopolitics: Foucault on, 188–89n23; Helmreich on, 122; of postmodern bodies, 115; of security, 114–16, 122

France: lectures of Foucault, 107, 114, 188–89n23; scientific research in, 43; understanding of causality in, 188–89n10

Francis, Thomas, Jr., 52–53, 54

Franklin, Sarah, 162, 173

Fukuda, Keiji, 83–84, 98, 102, 179

Gao, Qinshan, 89, 91–93, 94*fig.*, 95. *See also* fertilized chicken eggs research

Garrett, Laurie, 124

genetic sequence guidelines (U.S., 2000), 122

Gerberding, Julie, 134, 136, 145, 174, 176

Germany: scientific research in, 43; understanding of causality in, 188–89n10

germ theory of disease, 30–31, 36, 97

Giulianni, Rudolph, 191–92n55

"Good Farming, Clear Thinking, Right Living" (Murray, *Wallaces Farmer*), 67

Great Britain: ferret research, 31, 40–50, 94; Francis's confirmation of work in, 52; human swine flu experiment, 65; mapping of deaths, 19th century, 207–8n29

Greater New York Hospital Association, 16

Great Pandemic. *See* H1N1 (swine flu) influenza virus, 1918 pandemic

Greenhouse, Carol, 146

Ground Zero (World Trade Center attack site), 12–13

Gruber, Max von, 91

Guillain-Barré syndrome, 65

Guyer, Jane, 188n17

H1N1 influenza virus (swine flu): as "0.5 pandemic virus" (Palese), 97; as foreshadow of coming plague, 70–71; identification challenges, 87–95; immunization campaign, 65, 66, 75, 77*fig.*; Koen and, 67–68; *The Lancet*, 1976 article, 65; as member of H1 group of viruses, 98; in Mexico, 82; microbe farmer's research, 66, 69, 70; *New York Sun* article, 70; *New York Times* article, 82; public hearing, Council of Europe, 82–83; Stuart-Harris's self-infection

with, 199n38; suspended U.S. vaccine program, 65–66; *Veterinary Medicine* editorial, 68; *Wall Street Journal* article, 95–96. *See also* H1N1 influenza virus, 1918 pandemic; H1N1 influenza virus, 1976 outbreak; H1N1 influenza virus, 2009 pandemic

H1N1 influenza virus (swine flu), 1918 pandemic: anti-influenza treatment method, 116; concerns of U.S. Army, 53–54, 64; framing as "America's forgotten pandemic," 8; Gerberding's comment on, 174; historical accounts of, 189–90n27; McBryde, Shope, Laidlaw, on origins of, 69–70; methods of spreading of virus, 54; mortality rate, 7, 71, 174; prediction of return, 71; professional journal articles, 67, 70; speed of person-to-person movement, 174; three waves of, 176; Tumpey's role in research, 108; vaccine experiments, 116–17. *See also* reconstruction of 1918 H1N1 virus; *Science* journal, article on Spanish flu reconstruction

H1N1 influenza virus (swine flu), 1976 outbreak, 62; immunization campaign, 65, 66, 75, 77*fig.*; Kilbourne's comments on, 73–74; *New York Times* article, 70, 71; projections of deaths, 71; WHO pandemic declaration, 65

H1N1 influenza virus (swine flu), 2009 pandemic: Cagliuso's comments on, 151–55; Chan's announcement, 79; consideration as "low risk," 134; death data, 83; development of immunity from, 95–96, 117; Ebright's comments on, 117–18; "false pandemic" label, 81; limited severity of, 102; Lipsitch's comments on, 126; Mexico's response, 82; Palese's comments on, 94, 117; real-world test response to, 147–49; susceptibility to anti-viral drugs, 117, 118; WHO pandemic declaration, 79, 82–84, 149

H2N2 influenza subtype (Asian pandemic), 11, 79, 133–35, 137, 138–39, 143, 144, 147

H3N2 influenza subtype (Hong Kong pandemic), 2, 11, 133, 134, 138

Laidlaw, Patrick Playfair: "Can We Beat Influenza?," 41*fig.*; comparison of viruses, 69; ferret research, 31, 41–50, 47*fig.*, 91, 94; initial isolation of human influenza virus, 40–41; leadership of National Institute for Medical Research, 45; mice research, 41, 50, 200n43; reason for success of, 44; on swine flu origination, 69

Lakoff, Andrew, 20, 80

The Lancet, swine flu article (1976), 65

Landecker, Hannah, 115

Latour, Bruno, 150, 216n21

Leavitt, Michael O., 12, 14, 161, 176–77

Lebanon, 136

Lederberg, Joshua, 100–101

Lederman, Muriel, 94

Lewis, Paul, 69

Lipsitch, Marc, 126

Lords of the Fly (Kohler), 128

Lowe, Celia, 99

Lowen, Anice, 87–88

Löwy, Ilana, 43, 200n48

Luhmann, Niklas, 20–21

Lwoff, André, 56–58

Maines, Taronna: concerns for research security, 106; evaluation of H5N1 pandemic potential, 104–5, 123; ferret research, 105, 209n3

Marcuse, Edgar, 164

Markel, Howard, 136

Masco, Joseph, 5

mass vaccination program, U.S., 64–65; changing view of microbe farmers, 78; Palese's doubts about, 74–75, 76

McBryde, C. N., 68–69

measles, 72, 73, 162

media: ABC News report on mutated bird flu virus, 123–24; apocalyptic stories of 1918 pandemic, 110; coverage of research scandals, 123–26; culture of danger promoted by, 5–6; on global distribution of hazardous samples, 32–33; "killer flu virus" frenzy, 136; *New York Sun* article, 70; role in informing the public, 12, 14, 118; warnings on reconstruction of Spanish flu virus, 109–11; on Webster

as "pope of influenza," 2; on worst-case pandemic disaster scenarios, 2, 3. *See also Nature* magazine; *New York Times* articles; *Science* journal

Medical Reserve Corps, 15, 30

Meet the Press TV news show, 110

Melanesian society study (Strathern), 166

Meridian Bioscience, H1N1, H3N2 influenza samples, 134, 139, 215n8

mice research, of Andrewes, Laidlaw, Smith, 41, 50, 200n43

microbe farming (and microbe farmers): accidental contamination occurrences, 140–43; accidental infections of researchers, 69, 137, 140–41, 143, 199n38; challenges of, 31, 37–40, 79–80, 88–89; comparative studies, 86; confidence in success of, 64; containment concerns and strategies, 46, 104, 119, 136–39; contamination concerns, incidents, 133, 134–35, 139–43; debates inspired by, 122–23; efforts at achieving recognition, 76; epidemic *vs.* pandemic distinction, 86–89; at Erasmus Medical Center, 123; evaluation of H7N9 influenza, 179; ferret research, 31, 41–50, 51, 91, 94; fertilized chicken eggs research, 89–95, 90*fig.*, 108, 138–39, 143, 158; fowl plague virus, 138; Francis on, 53; H2N2 isolation and storage, 133; importance of, 32; infrastructure requirements, 58; Kilbourne's swine flu vaccine research, 75–76; Koch's postulates criteria for, 40; Lwoff's comment on, 57; mice research, 41, 50; mutant strains, cosmology of, 78–81; National Institute for Medical Research success, 31–32, 40; ontological understanding of infectious diseases, 97; relation of microbiology's authority to, 52; sample storage, laboratory freezers, 140*fig.*; skepticism of, 75; swine flu identification, concerns, 66, 69, 70; on value of publishing research results, 127–28; viral plasticity concerns, 55–56, 59

Microbe Hunters (De Kruif), 52–53

microbial revolution, 196–97n10

microbiologists: awareness of changing nature of disease, 99; challenges in investigating viruses, 36–40, 55, 58–59; differentiation of the normal and pathological, 36–37, 50; on how pandemics occur, 32–33; identification of true *vs.* false pandemics, 87; Napier's comment on, 58; reasons for investigating specific animal bodies, 43; role in containing spread and control of a disease, 2–3, 30–31; role in protecting information, 127. *See also* microbe farming (and microbe farmers); individual microbiologists

Miyazaki, Hirokazu, 21

modernity: Foucault on, 219n11; Luhmann on, 20; nightmares of, 181

molecular biology, scientific impact of, 115

The Monster at our Door: The Global Threat of Avian Flu (Davis), 25*fig.*

Mount Sinai School of Medicine (NYC), Microbiology Department: Palese's leadership of, 26, 27, 74–75; research projects of Palese's research team, 30; reverse genetics technology development, 105; role in swine flu vaccine development, 75; Spanish flu virus reconstruction, 107–8, 118

Mubareka, Samira, 87–88, 141

Muckenfuss, Ralph, 53

Murray, Charles, 67

mutant strains, cosmology of, 78–81

Napier, David, 58, 127, 187n9

nasal mucus, 37, 40–41, 48

National Academy of Science, 164

National Immunization Program, 162

National Influenza Immunization Program, 64

National Infrastructure Advisory Council (NIAC), 172–73

National Institute for Medical Research (England), 31–32, 40

National Institutes of Health (NIH): biological safety responsibility of, 18, 136, 137; 1976 conference attendance, 63; revised handling recommendations, 147

National Microbiology Laboratory (Canada), 133

National Pandemic Preparedness and Response Plan (Mexico), 64, 82

National Preparedness Month (U.S.), 15

National Research Council of the National Academies, 113

National Science Advisory Board for Biosecurity (NSABB): concerns for reconstruction of 1918 virus, 119; genomic research taxonomic challenges, 119–23; *Nature* and *Science* articles, withdrawal recommendation, 125; opinion of *Nature* and *Science* articles, 125; review of *Science* article on Spanish flu reconstruction, 108–9; risk assessment of synthetic biological agents, 119; U.S. government charges against, 119

National Strategy for Pandemic Influenza, Homeland Security Council (2005), 17*fig.*

National Vaccine Advisory Committee (NVAC, U.S.), 159

National Vaccine Program Office (NVPO, U.S.), 160

Nature magazine, 110; article of Palese and Schulman, 74–75; article on avian viruses, 123; editorial statement on "prospect of bioterrorism," 113; NSABB recommended withdrawal of Spanish flu article, 109; recommendation for publishing Spanish flu article, 125

Neher, André, 178

neuraminidase subtypes (N1–N9), 98

New Jersey: acute respiratory disease epidemic, 32, 63; Fort Dix swine flu epidemic, 63–64, 71; Fort Monmouth respiratory illness epidemic, 54–55

New Jersey Health Department, 63

Newsweek article (2005), 14–15

"new" viruses/strains of viruses, 55, 63, 64, 79, 82, 84, 86–88, 96–101, 105, 133, 159, 178–80

New York Academy of Medicine, 157

New York Academy of Sciences, 27–28

New York City Department of Health and Mental Hygiene, 30, 129

New York City health care system, 16

New York City Office of Emergency Management, 191–92n55

New York-Presbyterian Healthcare System, 151

New York Sun article (1939), 70

New York Times articles, 40; comment by Shreeve, 119; on danger of deadly pathogens in the public domain, 136; "doomsday virus" editorial, 124; Kilbourne's scientifically inspired prophetic editorial, 60–63; on Lowen and Mubareka's research, 87–88; Osterholm on the next contagion, 179–80; race for the flu vaccine, 75; responses to Kurzweil and Joy, 110; on swine flu in Mexico, 82; warning on *Science* publishing Spanish flu reconstruction article, 109–10

NIH. *See* National Institutes of Health

Niles, W. B., 68

1918 pandemic. *See* H1N1 (swine flu) influenza virus, 1918 pandemic

1976 swine flu outbreak. *See* H1N1 (swine flu) influenza virus, 1976 outbreak

NSAAB. *See* National Science Advisory Board for Biosecurity

Obama, Barack, 15, 183

Observations on Modernity (Luhmann), 20

Ompad, Danielle, 157

Orent, Wendy, 109

Osterholm, Michael T.: agreement with Markel, 136; appearance on Oprah, 15; commission creation recommendation, 145; debate with Palese, 27–28; *Foreign Affairs*, 2005 editorial, 1–2, 10, 11–12; on importance of drafting a plan, 14; influenza pandemic prediction, 1–2, 11–12, 18; *New York Times*, 2013 article, 179–80; post-Hurricane Katrina testimony, 176; prediction of next contagion, 179–80; testimony on Capitol Hill, 176

Palese, Peter: as "biologist of context," 118; comment on Fukuda's WHO announcement, 98; comments on H5N1 virus, 26–27, 29; comments on *Science* journal article, 74–75, 116; *Daily News* interview with, 76; development of

reverse genetics technology, 105; distress over Fouchier and Kawaoka's paper, 123; distress over media coverage of research scandals, 123–26; doubts about mass vaccination program, 74–75; Ebright's questioning research of, 117; on pandemic as "global epidemic," 96–97; professional credentials of, 26, 27, 29; on protection against Spanish flu with H1N1 vaccine, 117; recommendation to NSABB about Spanish flu article, 125; reverse genetics pioneering work, 27, 105, 108; on Spanish flu *Science* article, 116–17, 123; on swine flu virus as "0.5 pandemic virus," 97; *Wall Street Journal* swine flu article, 95–96. *See also* Mount Sinai School of Medicine (NYC), Microbiology Department

Pandemic Influenza Plan (HHS), 159, 160

Pandemic Influenza Preparedness and Response Plan (NYC Department of Health and Mental Hygiene), 129

pandemic preparedness, 10; Cagliuso's comments on effectiveness of, 14, 151–55; CDC's concerns about fading interest in, 180; Center for Domestic Preparedness program, 19–20; Cold War era emergency drills, simulations, 80–81; exercises and drills for health care providers, 155; faith and reason components, 20–24, 26, 126; false alarms, 34, 135, 147; FEMA TV commercial, 149, 150*fig*.; globalization, modernity, and, 181; HHS poster, 12, 13*fig*.; Homeland Security Policy Institute report, 148; Homeland Security terrorism advisory system, 17, 19; by hospitals, 130; Hurricane Katrina's contribution to discussion, 169–72, 174–77; Lederberg's comment on, 101; Mexico's plan, 64, 82; *Newsweek* article on individual responsibility, 14–15; Nguyen on ebola epidemic and, 182–83; Obama's call for National Preparedness Month, 15; Ompad's comment on, 157; planning and testing, 130–31, 145–47; preparedness testing by hospitals, 130; resource allocation for,

Weber, Max, 60
Webster, Robert: comments on the H5N1
 virus, 2, 19, 147; evaluation of H5N1
 virus, 2–3, 139; on nature as "the real
 bioterrorist," 19
Wellcome Laboratories (London),
 influenza outbreak, 44–45
Winfrey, Oprah, 15
Wodarg, Wolfgang, 82–83
World Health Organization (WHO), 30;
 concerns for H7N9 influenza in China,
178–79; confirmation of Canadian
H2N2 virus, 133; Fukuda's swine flu
announcement defense, 83, 84, 98, 102;
H1N1, 1976 declaration, 65; H1N1,
2009 pandemic declaration, 79, 82–84,
149; pandemic declaration, 65, 82–83,
84, 86, 100, 102; pandemic phase
reporting system, 17–18; 2009 pandemic
declaration, 82–83

Zinsser, Hans, 37